Controversies in Cognitive Neuroscience

CW00551678

Controversies in Cognitive Neuroscience

Scott Slotnick

First published 2013 by
PALGRAVE MACMILLAN

Palgrave Macmillan in the UK is an imprint of Macmillan Publishers Limited,
registered in England, company number 785998, of Houndmills, Basingstoke,
Hampshire RG21 6XS.

Palgrave Macmillan in the US is a division of St Martin's Press LLC,
175 Fifth Avenue, New York, NY 10010.

Palgrave Macmillan is the global academic imprint of the above companies
and has companies and representatives throughout the world.

Palgrave® and Macmillan® are registered trademarks in the United States,
the United Kingdom, Europe and other countries.

ISBN 978–0–230–30110–8 hardback
ISBN 978–0–230–30111–5 paperback

This book is printed on paper suitable for recycling and made from fully
managed and sustained forest sources. Logging, pulping and manufacturing
processes are expected to conform to the environmental regulations of the
country of origin.

A catalogue record for this book is available from the British Library.

A catalog record for this book is available from the Library of Congress.

10   9   8   7   6   5   4   3   2   1
22 21 20 19 18 17 16 15 14 13

Printed and bound in China

This book is dedicated to my awesome daughter Sonya, who will always hold my heart. At the age of six, she already thrives on healthy intellectual controversy and, with no effort, can out-debate her father.

Contents

Figures

Tables

Preface

The field of cognitive neuroscience has been fueled by active debate since its inception in the early 1990s. However, students are almost exclusively exposed to the majority view of each controversy that is most widely believed, rather than being presented with evidence and arguments from both sides of a given debate. This largely imbalanced approach to education in cognitive neuroscience misses out on the excitement and passion that drives research forward.

This book has its roots in a lesson from my thesis advisor, Stan Klein, who stressed that when reading a scientific article it takes little thought to accept what investigators have done right, but a primary role of a scientist is to uncover what has been done wrong. This led me to critically examine every article I consumed, to question whether the evidence and arguments supporting a particular view were sound (regardless of how good the story sounded), and to come up with alternative hypotheses. With this mindset, it became clear over the years that each actively investigated topic in cognitive neuroscience has a majority view and a minority view, and that an accurate portrayal of any issue requires weighing the evidence and arguments that support each of these opposing views. Moreover, the majority view is not necessarily correct – in this book it is concluded that the majority view is incorrect half of the time.

To better educate my students, I developed an advanced undergraduate/graduate seminar that covers many of the major controversies in cognitive neuroscience, and this serves as a model for this book. In this course, half of the students are assigned to be on the majority view side of a given controversy and the other half of the students are assigned to be on the minority view side. In the first class on each controversy, I give an overview of the debate, after which the students discuss four assigned articles in seminar format (two supporting each view, the *suggested readings* at the end of each chapter in this book). In the second class on each controversy, a pair of students on each side of the debate is charged with finding two additional articles to support their position. These articles are disseminated to the entire class a few days before the class meets, and then an active debate is held based on the evidence in all eight articles. This book was written, in part, to serve as a complete introduction to each of the controversies covered in such an advanced undergraduate/graduate seminar. It was also written to serve as a supplement in an intermediate undergraduate course on cognitive neuroscience, to aid instructors who aim to provide a more complete education for their students.

When reading this book, students are advised to continually evaluate the evidence and arguments as the information unfolds. Weaknesses can almost always be found if you scrutinize the material presented, rather than simply believe what sounds plausible. Students should keep an eye out for inconsistencies in the results or poor arguments that may be pointed out later in each chapter, and they may identify inconsistencies that are never pointed out (I shall be glad to know if I have missed something). It is not unusual for some of the strongest evidence against the majority view to be found in the results that are purported to support this view. From the other perspective, in half of the debates, proponents of the minority view support the *null hypothesis*, where the findings of the majority view are not observed. Although such null findings are taken as evidence against that majority view, this actually reflects a lack of evidence that is always questionable (a point that will be emphasized repeatedly throughout this book).

I am keenly aware that this book will anger some cognitive neuroscientists, particularly if someone's work was not included, deemed weak, completely discounted, or taken to support their opposition. This book was intentionally written in a controversial style to provide students with insight into the nature of actual scientific inquiry. It was a difficult balancing act to accurately convey both sides of each controversy without potentially injuring egos. I apologize in advance to those who will be offended.

While every effort was made to include only sound evidence and arguments in this book, my opinion will often shine through (or be blatantly obvious). However, it should be underscored that I have absolutely no concern about which side of a given cognitive neuroscience debate *wins*. Even when I have published on a specific topic and taken a stance, I am always more than happy to be proven wrong. When conducting my own research, I regularly think about how to disprove my favoured hypotheses, as this is a very effective way to uncover the truth.

I would like to thank my students, particularly Britt Jeye, Sam Robinson, and Halle Zucker, who provided invaluable comments on chapter drafts. I will also be forever grateful to Raich White whose unparalleled thoughts run throughout this book. Finally, I would like to thank Paul Stevens and Jenny Hindley (at Palgrave Macmillan), Jamie Joseph (now at HarperCollins), and Elizabeth Stone (at Bourchier), who could not have been more supportive during this wonderful endeavour.

Scott Slotnick

1

Cognitive Neuroscience: The Bare Bones

The field of cognitive neuroscience lies at the intersection between the field of cognitive psychology (the study of the mind) and the field of neuroscience (the study of the brain; Figure 1.1). Cognitive neuroscientists investigate the neural basis of human mental function including perception, attention, long-term memory, working memory, language, imagery, and social processing.

Research in cognitive neuroscience, like any field of science, has been driven by intense debate between scientists who hold the majority view that is most widely believed and scientists who hold the minority view. Introductory textbooks generally have to ignore such debates and focus on the majority view to avoid unnecessarily complicating the material. However, considering both sides of a debate in full detail, from both empirical and theoretical perspectives, is necessary to truly understand an issue. The present book considers both the majority view and the minority view in eight debates within cognitive neuroscience. Before turning to these debates, the relevant functional neuroanatomy, the cognitive neuroscience methods, and the chapter organization of this book will be briefly covered.

FUNCTIONAL NEUROANATOMY

Humans are inherently visual animals, so it is not surprising that cognitive neuroscience has focused on the neural basis of visual processing. The debates covered in this book can be considered within a visual processing framework. When viewing an object, light is reflected from that object into our eyes. This information

Figure 1.1 *Relationships between the fields of cognitive psychology, cognitive neuroscience, and neuroscience.*

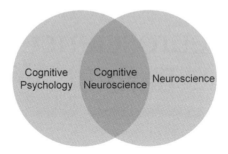

is transmitted through the optic nerves to a sub-cortical structure called the thalamus, and then the signal arrives at V1 (which is also referred to as primary visual cortex or striate cortex), the first visual cortical processing region in the occipital lobe of the brain. The *what pathway* extends from V1 into extrastriate cortex and then into the ventral occipital-temporal cortex (including the fusiform gyrus) and mediates object identification, while the *where pathway* extends from V1 into extrastriate cortex and then into the dorsal occipital-parietal cortex and mediates object spatial localization (Figure 1.2).

The debates on attention (Chapter 3) and imagery (Chapter 7) focus on whether these cognitive processes can modulate activity in V1 or only modulate activity in higher-level regions such as extrastriate cortex. The debates on perception (Chapter 2) and language (Chapter 6) assess whether these processes selectively activate the right hemisphere fusiform gyrus and the left hemisphere fusiform gyrus, respectively. Chapter 6 also considers word processing activity in the posterior superior temporal gyrus and the posterior inferior frontal gyrus that have been associated with word comprehension and word production, respectively. The long-term memory debate (Chapter 4) deals with the nature of processing in the hippocampus. The working memory debate (Chapter 5) questions whether the what-where pathways extend anteriorly into the middle frontal gyrus and the inferior frontal sulcus/gyrus within the ventral prefrontal cortex and the superior frontal sulcus within the dorsal prefrontal cortex, respectively. The social debate (Chapter 8) focuses on whether processing animate others is mediated by a network of regions including the medial prefrontal cortex, the cingulate cortex, the amygdala, the superior temporal sulcus,

Figure 1.2 *Functional-anatomic depiction of the debates covered in this book. Top, cortical surface of the right hemisphere (lateral view, occipital pole at the left; gyri and sulci are shown in light and dark gray, respectively). The lobes of the brain, the central sulcus (CS), and anatomic regions-of-interest are labeled including V1, ventral extrastriate cortex (ES), the fusiform gyrus (FG), the superior temporal sulcus (STS), the superior temporal gyrus (STG), the posterior inferior frontal gyrus (PIFG), the middle frontal gyrus (MFG), the inferior frontal sulcus (IFS), the inferior frontal gyrus (IFG), and the superior frontal sulcus (SFS). The what pathway and the where pathway extend from V1 into the inferior temporal cortex and the parietal cortex, respectively (illustrated by white arrows). Middle, medial view of the same hemisphere (occipital pole at the right). Regions-of-interest are labeled including the medial prefrontal cortex (mPFC), the cingulate cortex (CC), the amygdala (amyg.), and the hippocampus (HC). Bottom, cognitive processes (and corresponding chapters) associated with the regions-of-interest above that are demarcated by ovals with the same pattern.*

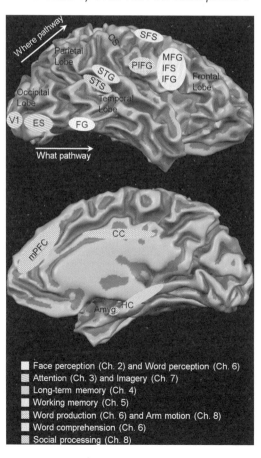

4

Figure 1.3 *Regions associated with visual processing in monkeys. Between-region connections are illustrated by lines. Occipital regions include V1 and V2 (magnocellular, M, parvo-blob, P-B, and parvo-interblob, P-I, cells), V3, ventral posterior (VP), V3A, V4, ventral occipitotemporal (VOT), V4 transitional (V4t), and middle temporal (MT). Temporal regions include floor of superior temporal (FST), dorsal and ventral posterior inferotemporal (PITd, PITv), dorsal and ventral central inferotemporal (CITd, CITv), dorsal and ventral anterior inferotemporal (AITd, AITv), posterior and anterior superior temporal polysensory (STPp, STPa), parahippocampal areas TF and TH, Brodmann area 36*

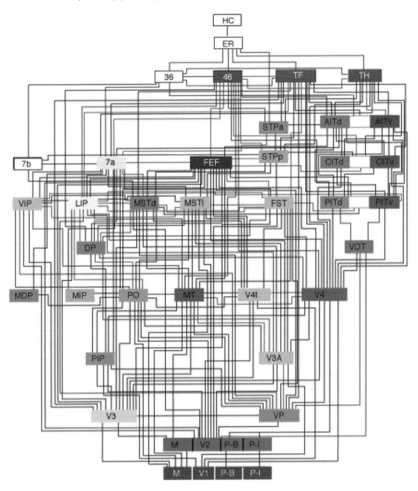

(Felleman and Van Essen, Distributed hierarchical processing in the primate cerebral cortex, Cerebral Cortex, 1991, 1, 1, 1–47, by permission of Oxford University Press.)

Figure 1.3   *(Continued) (Brodmann areas are discussed below),*
entorhinal cortex (ER), and the hippocampus (HC). Parietal regions include
dorsal and lateral medial superior temporal (MSTd, MSTI),
parieto-occipital (PO), posterior intraparietal (PIP), lateral intraparietal
(LIP), ventral intraparietal (VIP), medial intraparietal (MIP), medial dorsal
parietal (MDP), dorsal prelunate (DP), Brodmann area 7a, and
Brodmann area 7b. Frontal regions include the frontal eye field (FEF)
and Brodmann area 46.

and the fusiform gyrus, or is rather mediated by motor processing regions including a region of motor cortex within the posterior
inferior frontal gyrus that is associated with arm motion (which
may reflect mirroring the movements of others). Note that some
of the preceding cognitive processes have been preferentially associated with a particular hemisphere, such as language processing in
the left hemisphere, which will be discussed when relevant. Functional neuranatomy is considered in more detail within each of the
subsequent debate chapters.

When considering any cognitive neuroscience evidence, it is useful to keep in mind that brain function is inherently complex.
Felleman & Van Essen (1991) showed that visual processing in
monkeys, and thus in humans, involves over 30 regions that are
hierarchically organized from V1 to the hippocampus (Figure 1.3).
The level of each region in the hierarchy was based on the pattern of between-region connections. This hierarchical organization
implies that visual processing begins in lower regions (such as line
orientation processing in V1), becomes more abstract in higher
regions (such as object processing in ventral temporal cortex), and
ultimately reaches the hippocampus (where visual information is
encoded into memory). There is also massive between-region con-
nectivity, with approximately 40 percent of all possible pairs of
regions directly connected, and the large majority of linked regions
are connected in both directions. This high between-region connec-
tivity indicates that cortical regions do not operate in isolation, but
rather interact with many other regions during a given cognitive
process.

Despite the fact that the neural architecture of the brain is
highly interconnected, cognitive neuroscientists generally assume
that a single brain region can selectively mediate a single cognitive

function. This process-to-region mapping is partly due to our over reliance on functional magnetic resonance imaging (fMRI), the most widely used method in the field. The final debate in this book evaluates whether fMRI is adequate to study the neural basis of cognitive processing (Chapter 9), and is followed by the ramifications for the future of cognitive neuroscience if the field continues to primarily rely on this method (Chapter 10). The evidence considered will show that a given cognitive process is mediated by many different regions that interact rapidly over time. To track the neural basis of cognitive processing in both space and time, cognitive neuroscientists employ a number of methodologies.

METHODS

Cognitive neuroscience methods are complicated, with each technique typically requiring years of training to master all aspects of data acquisition, analysis, and interpretation. It should be underscored that a given method either has high spatial resolution or high temporal resolution – there is currently no noninvasive method that used in isolation has both high spatial resolution and high temporal resolution. Each technique will be briefly described to highlight its fundamental mechanisms, strengths, and weaknesses.

High spatial resolution methods

fMRI is considered the gold standard in cognitive neuroscience (Chapter 9), as this method alone has excellent spatial resolution, is widely accessible, and is noninvasive. During fMRI, a participant lies on a scanner bed and their position is adjusted such that their head is moved inside the scanner bore (Figure 1.4).

Current is passed through a huge coil of superconducting wire surrounding the scanner bore that induces a strong magnetic field (typically 3 Tesla) directed along the axis of the bore. Although the protons (hydrogen ions) within the brain are usually oriented in random directions, they act like tiny magnets and align with the magnetic field in the scanner bore. Then, while a participant is engaged in a cognitive task, a stimulating coil applies a smaller magnetic field that essentially knocks over the protons in the brain

Figure 1.4 *MRI scanner (3 Tesla) with protruding bed and bore shown at the centre in white.*

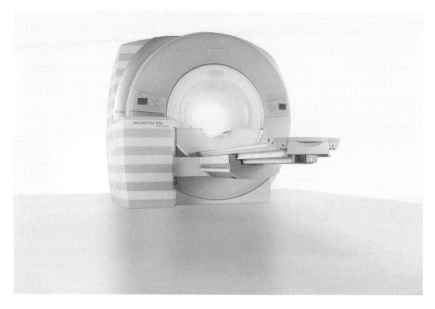

(Siemens, 2011, reprinted with permission.)

such that they are perpendicular (orthogonal) to their original orientation. Of direct relevance, if a brain region is active this leads to an increase in oxygenated blood delivered to that region that in turn stabilizes the orthogonal precessing (spinning) protons in that region (this proton stabilization actually reflects a decrease in the relative amount of deoxygenated hemoglobin in the blood, which is paramagnetic and thus destabilizes the precessing protons). Other magnetic fields are also applied such that the protons precess at unique frequencies depending on their spatial location in the brain, and these signals are picked up by a receiving coil. Of importance, the magnetic fields applied during fMRI are in the safe low-energy radio frequency range. The frequency components of the fMRI signal are used to identify the location of neural activity to within a few millimetres. The excellent spatial resolution of fMRI is completely sufficient to answer the large majority of questions that are currently of interest in cognitive neuroscience. However, it takes a couple of seconds to measure activity from the entire brain and, as discussed below, fMRI activity is temporally delayed and extended as compared to the underlying neural activity (and the temporal characteristics of fMRI activity can vary across different brain regions). Therefore, fMRI cannot be used to investigate the temporal dynamics of cognitive processing. For instance, the poor temporal resolution of fMRI could not track the rapid neural processing that mediates object identification, which takes less than a second. fMRI could not even measure the temporal dynamics of relatively slow cognitive processes such as conscious retrieval from long-term memory, which takes approximately two seconds. This method essentially takes a single snapshot of all the brain regions that were active during an entire cognitive process.

There are many ways in which fMRI results can be displayed. The results can be projected onto a three-dimensional cortical surface and displayed in a lateral view (Figure 1.2, top, and Figure 1.5, top left), a medial view (Figure 1.2, bottom), a top view (Figure 1.5, bottom left), a bottom view, a posterior view, or an anterior view (the latter three views are not shown). fMRI results have been more often projected onto a two-dimensional image and displayed in a coronal view (Figure 1.5, top right), an axial view (Figure 1.5, middle), or a sagittal view (Figure 1.5, bottom right).

fMRI activity is nearly always localized to a specific gyrus or sulcus, but is sometimes also localized to a specific *Brodmann area* according to a brain map (Figure 1.6) created over a century ago by Korbinian Brodmann (1909). This map was based on anatomic characteristics that were used to differentiate regions such as cell shape, density, and layering. Such anatomic differences give rise to functional differences, thus it is reasonable to assume that a specific Brodmann region could be preferentially associated with a particular cognitive process (or a set of related cognitive processes).

Positron emission tomography (PET) is another technique that also depends on the increase in blood flow to an active region of the brain. A low level of radioactive material is injected into the bloodstream of the participant. During a cognitive task, a relatively greater amount of blood flows to more active regions, which in turn produces a higher degree of radioactive emissions that are detected and localized. It takes approximately half a minute to measure brain activity using PET. Compared with fMRI, PET has lower spatial resolution, lower temporal resolution, and can be harmful to participants due to the use of radioactive material. Thus, although PET has produced very important findings in the past, this method is now rarely used to conduct research in cognitive neuroscience.

Figure 1.5   *Views to display fMRI results. Top left, lateral view of a cortical surface (occipital pole at the left, crossed arrows to the left illustrate the superior, S, inferior, I, posterior, P, and anterior, A, directions). Top right, coronal view corresponding to the location of the vertical dashed arrow to the left. Unless otherwise specified, coronal views are oriented according to the crossed arrows to the right (which illustrate the superior, inferior, left, L, and right, R, directions). Middle, axial view corresponding to the location of the horizontal dashed arrow above (occipital pole at the left, crossed arrows to the left show the corresponding directions). Bottom left, top view of a cortical surface (occipital pole at the bottom, crossed arrows to the left illustrate the corresponding directions). Bottom right, sagittal view corresponding to the location of the vertical dashed arrow to the left (occipital pole at the left, crossed arrows to the right illustrate the corresponding directions).*

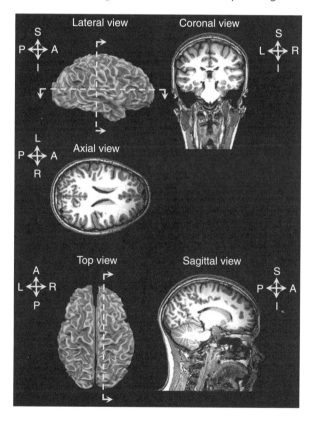

High temporal resolution methods

While fMRI and PET offer relatively high spatial resolution, event-related potential (ERP) recording is the primary method used

Figure 1.6 *Brodmann areas. Lateral view (top) and medial view (bottom) illustrating Brodmann (1909) areas (the occipital pole is at the right in both views).*

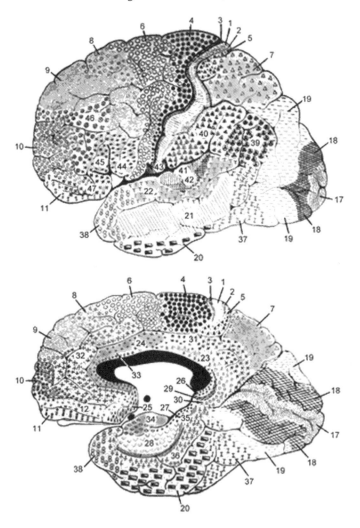

to track neural activity in real-time. During ERP recording, the participant sits in a comfortable chair while electrodes are placed on the scalp (Figure 1.7). While performing a cognitive task, brain activity generates an electromagnetic field that induces a voltage (also referred to as *potential*) that is measured at each electrode. The analysis is conducted separately for each electrode, where the voltage response for all trials of a given event type are averaged to produce the ERP.

Figure 1.7   *ERP cap (128-channel) on a glass display head (lateral view).*

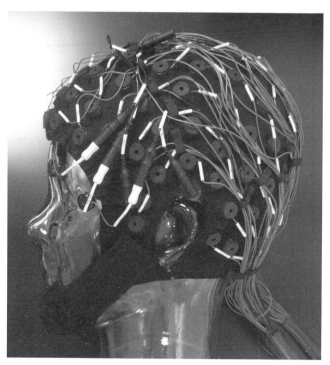

Magnetoencephalograhy (MEG) recording is also based on the electromagnetic field produced by brain activity, but superconducting coils are used as measurement devices. Because ERP and MEG recording are based directly on neural activity, these techniques can track neural activity in milliseconds, which is sufficient to measure the temporal dynamics of any cognitive process. However, both of these techniques measure brain activity near the scalp such that relatively distant brain activity is blurred or can even be undetectable thus limiting the spatial resolution to centimetres. Although it is generally thought that MEG recording has better spatial resolution than ERP recording, due to less distortion from the brain, cerebral spinal fluid, skull, and scalp, these methods actually have similar spatial resolutions (Cohen & Cuffin, 1991; Baumgartner, 2004). This is not surprising as the electric field (that produces ERP activity) and the corresponding magnetic field (that produce MEG activity) are mathematically linked (Maxwell, 1865; Einstein, 1905). However, an MEG system requires the maintenance of a superconducting environment, which is much more costly than a comparable ERP system. This cost disparity is a major reason why ERP recording is more widely used than MEG recording.

Considering the techniques thus far, fMRI and PET have excellent or good spatial resolution and poor temporal resolution, while ERP recording and MEG recording have excellent temporal resolution and poor spatial resolution. Single-cell recording, another technique related to ERP/MEG recording, involves recording from an electrode inserted directly into a specific brain region. This technique is very invasive such that it is almost completely restricted to experiments conducted with animals during tasks that can be assumed to engage similar cognitive and neural processes as in humans, such as visual perception or visual attention. Under rare circumstances, single-cell recording or recording from electrodes placed on the surface of the brain has been used in humans, typically with epilepsy patients who have electrodes placed for clinical purposes. As long it poses no additional risk, these patients can elect to participate in cognitive tasks while electrode activity is recorded.

Figure 1.8 *Monkey V1 single-cell and fMRI results. Left, image illustrating an electrode tip extending from the bottom left into V1 in addition to fMRI activity (in white) within the same region (partial axial view, occipital pole at the bottom). Right, a checkerboard stimulus (stim) was presented for 12 seconds, illustrated by the boxcar function at the bottom (key to the right). This produced electrode activity (raw, in analog to digital converter, ADC, units) and blood oxygen level dependent (BOLD) fMRI activity (percent modulation) in V1.*

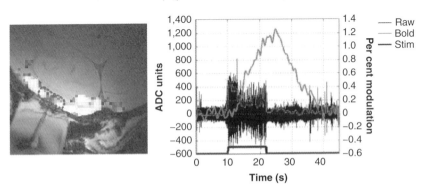

(Reprinted by permission from Macmillan Publishers Ltd: *Nature, 412*, Logothetis et al., copyright 2001.)

Logothetis, Pauls, Augath, Trinath, and Oeltermann (2001) pre-sented a monkey with a visual checkerboard stimulus while simul-taneously measuring activity in V1 using single-cell recording and fMRI (Figure 1.8, left). While single-cell activity tracked the 12-second stimulus onset and duration, fMRI activity had an approximately two-second delayed onset followed by a duration that was approximately twice as long as the stimulation period (Figure 1.8, right). These results illustrate the high temporal res-olution of single-cell recording and by extension ERP and MEG recording, as these methods are all based on modulations of the electromagnetic field associated with neural activity, and also illus-trate the poor temporal resolution of fMRI.

Lesion methods

All the previously described methods track neural activity during a particular cognitive process, and it is reasonable to assume that such activity reflects the neural mechanisms mediating that cogni-tive process. However, activity in a region might only be correlated with a process, such as if that region was co-activated through a con-nection with another region that actually mediated that process. Transcranial magnetic stimulation (TMS) can temporarily disrupt neural activity in a targeted neural region to assess whether that region is necessary for a given cognitive process. During TMS, par-ticipants are seated in a chair while a stimulation coil is held, either manually or with a mechanical arm, very close to the scalp over the target region (Figure 1.9). Current is passed through the coil inducing an electromagnetic field that disrupts neural processing in the cortex immediately below the centre of the coil. The TMS target location can be based on anatomic landmarks on the head, such as a specific distance from the inion (a skull protrusion on the back of the head), or can be guided by fMRI activity to focus on a very specific brain region.

Even if a precise method of targeting is employed, the electromag-netic field generated by the TMS coil is not a perfectly cylindrical beam and thus stimulates cortex surrounding the target location to some degree. As such, this method has a spatial resolution in centimetres. Moreover, only cortical regions near the surface of the scalp can be stimulated. A standard TMS protocol stimulates at one pulse per second (Hertz) for ten minutes, which temporarily dis-rupts processing in the targeted region for approximately five to ten minutes after the stimulation period. During this period of cortical

Figure 1.9   *TMS system with a figure eight stimulation coil at the upper left.*

disruption, participants perform a task and investigators evaluate whether behavioural performance is impaired. If so, this implies the disrupted cortical region is required for the associated cognitive process. Although TMS has poor spatial resolution and poor temporal resolution (when the standard 1 Hertz stimulation protocol is employed), this is the only noninvasive method that can be used to assess whether a specific region is necessary for a cognitive process.

Patients with cortical lesions typically caused by a stroke have also been evaluated to assess whether a region is necessary for a given cognitive process. However, patient lesions are typically widespread and have unclear boundaries such that the spatial resolution is usually extremely poor. Still, more isolated patient lesions have been used to provide evidence that a region is necessary for a particular process, and can be particularly compelling if the findings complement those provided by fMRI.

Head-to-head method comparisons

Cognitive neuroscientists clearly have many tools with which to investigate the neural basis of cognition. These techniques can be

Figure 1.10 *Spatial resolution and temporal resolution associated with the methods used in cognitive neuroscience.*

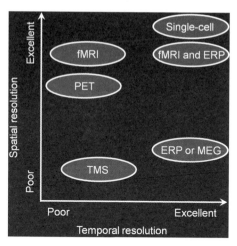

directly compared based on their spatial resolution and temporal resolution to assess the relative advantages and disadvantages on these dimensions (Figure 1.10). Single-cell recording has both excellent spatial resolution and excellent temporal resolution, but is largely restricted to research with animals thus limiting the cognitive processes that can be investigated to those that are convincingly shared with humans. The methods that have been commonly used in cognitive neuroscience have either high spatial resolution (fMRI and PET) or high temporal resolution (ERP and MEG recording). TMS has poor spatial resolution and poor temporal resolution but can test whether a region is necessary for a cognitive process. These comparisons highlight that none of the techniques employed in isolation can safely track the spatial-temporal dynamics of brain activity.

To overcome the limitations of individual techniques, some cognitive neuroscientists have combined methods, such as fMRI and ERPs, with the aim of studying the actual neural mechanisms that mediate a given cognitive process (Chapter 9).

Subtractive logic

The methods in cognitive neuroscience allow for the measurement of neural activity during cognitive tasks. To isolate the brain regions associated with a specific cognitive process, the magnitude of activity produced by a baseline task that does not involve the cognitive process of interest is compared with (subtracted from) the magnitude of activity produced by a primary task that does involve the cognitive process of interest. Such subtractive logic has been used for well over a century to measure the speed of nerve conduction (Helmholtz, 1850) and mental processing (Donders, 1868), and rests on the assumption that the pair of measurements only differ with regard to the process of interest (it is also assumed that this process can be added without influencing other processes, which could be but is rarely tested; Sternberg, 1969). Thus, although subtractive logic is ubiquitous in cognitive neuroscience, it only produces interpretable results (i.e., that cannot be attributed to confounding factors) if the primary task and the baseline task differ by the single cognitive process of interest. When considering cognitive neuroscience results, it is important to keep in mind that the cognitive processes that mediate a given task are largely determined through introspection, which is fallible.

CHAPTER ORGANIZATION

Each of the subsequent chapters, except the last, covers a debate from the core areas of cognitive neuroscience (perception, attention, long-term memory, working memory, language, imagery, and social processing) in addition to a methodology debate. Each debate chapter includes a brief introduction, provides evidence and arguments supporting the majority view, provides evidence and arguments supporting the minority view, discusses additional counterpoints, and then offers a conclusion. The majority view is presented from the perspective of a *believer*, meaning that sometimes evidence or arguments supporting the minority view will be ignored. While proponents of the minority view also sometimes ignore evidence supporting the majority view, this occurs much less often since the majority view is more widely accepted and pervasive in the field. Counterpoints include responses from both sides of the debate to the evidence and arguments provided by the opposing view, in addition to other relevant considerations. It should be highlighted that the aim of each chapter is not to make a case that a particular side of a debate is more likely to be correct, but is rather to provide evidence and arguments on both sides of each debate so that the issues can be more fully understood.

It is hoped that a detailed consideration of these controversies will shed light on the major weaknesses that have steered cognitive neuroscience toward a rapidly approaching cliff, such that we might correct our course and continue to thrive as field of scientific inquiry (Chapter 10).

REFERENCES

Baumgartner, C. (2004). Controversies in clinical neurophysiology. MEG is superior to EEG in the localization of interictal epileptiform activity: Con. *Clinical Neurophysiology, 115, 5*, 1010–1020.

Brodmann, K. (1909). *Vergleichende Lokalisationslehre der Grosshirnrinde in ihren Prinzipien dargestellt auf Grund des Zellenbaues.* Leipzig: Johann Ambrosius Barth Verlag.

Cohen, D., & Cuffin, B. N. (1991). EEG versus MEG localization accuracy: Theory and experiment. *Brain Topography, 4, 2*, 95–103.

Donders, F. C. (1868). Over de snelheid van psychische processen. *Onderzoekingen gedaan in het Physiologisch Laboratorium der Utrechtsche Hoogeschool, 1868–1869, Tweede reeks, II*, 92–120.

Einstein, A. (1905). Zur Elektrodynamik bewegter Körper. *Annalen der Physik, 322*, 891–921.

Felleman, D. J., & Van Essen, D. C. (1991). Distributed hierarchical processing in the primate cerebral cortex. *Cerebral Cortex, 1*, 1–47.

Helmholtz, H. von (1850). Vorläufiger Bericht über die Fortpflanzungsgeschwindigkeit der Nervenreizung. *Archiv für Anatomie, Physiologie und wissenschaftliche Medicin*, 71–73.

Logothetis, N. K., Pauls, J., Augath, M., Trinath, T., & Oeltermann, A. (2001). Neurophysiological investigation of the basis of the fMRI signal. *Nature, 412*, 150–157.

Maxwell, J. C. (1865). A dynamical theory of the electromagnetic field. *Philosophical Transactions of the Royal Society of London, 155*, 459–512.

Sternberg, S. (1969). The discovery of processing stages: Extensions of Donders' method. *Acta Psychologica, 30*, 276–315.

2   The Fusiform Face Area

Does the human brain consist of individual regions that are each specialized for a single cognitive process? The present chapter addresses this general question by considering a specific debate on the neural basis of face perception. Over a decade ago, it was reported that a region of the right fusiform cortex, within the ventral occipital-temporal visual processing stream, was specialized for processing faces and labeled the *fusiform face area* (the *FFA*; Kanwisher, McDermott, & Chun, 1997). The existence of a specialized brain processing region was and still is intuitively appealing, so it is not surprising that belief in the FFA has grown rapidly and is now widespread in the field of cognitive neuroscience. To illustrate, Figure 2.1 shows that the number of articles with the term *fusiform face area* in the title or abstract between 1998 and 2010 has grown exponentially (articles were identified using PubMed). The articles supporting the existence of the FFA have been published at a relatively constant rate (about one publication per year), so the rapid growth of studies employing the FFA illustrates an ever increasing number of cognitive neuroscientists who assume this area exists. Proponents of the minority view do not believe that the FFA is specialized for face processing and have, rather, proposed that face processing is mediated by numerous regions of the brain.

MAJORITY VIEW

FFA activation evidence

The existence of the FFA has been based largely on fMRI evidence, where activity in the fusiform gyrus has been produced by comparing face perception with non-face object perception. Nancy Kanwisher has been the major proponent of the FFA since its discovery.

Figure 2.1 *Number of articles with the term* fusiform face area *in the title or abstract published between 1998 and 2010.*

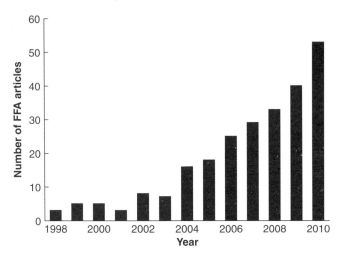

Kanwisher et al. (1997) first identified the FFA using fMRI by presenting participants with many stimulus classes including photographs of faces, two-tone faces created by luminance thresholding the photographs, faces in ski hats that were angled (viewed from the side), common objects (Figure 2.2, upper left), hands, houses, and scrambled two-tone faces that were constructed by rearranging the internal segments of each face rendering it unrecognizable (Figure 2.2, bottom left). Participants either passively viewed items or identified whether each item matched the previous item to foster detailed stimulus processing, referred to as a *1-back* task. The results did not differ as a function of task in this study or in almost any of the following studies, and thus will only be considered when relevant. In the first experiment, the contrast between photographs of faces and photographs of common objects produced consistent activity in only one region, the FFA (Figure 2.2, top). In the second experiment, the FFA from the previous experiment served as a region of interest to further investigate the selectivity of this region. FFA activity associated with faces was greater than both objects and houses, and activity associated with two-tone faces was greater than scrambled two-tone faces (Figure 2.2, bottom). The latter comparison shows that the FFA was not driven by low-level visual features, which were matched across these stimulus classes. In a third experiment, the FFA from Experiment 1 again served as a region of interest. Faces in ski hats that were angled

Figure 2.2   *First FFA evidence. Top, contrasting faces and objects (left)*
produced consistent activity in the right hemisphere fusiform face area
(FFA, centre, outlined in black; axial view, occipital pole at the bottom,
right hemisphere on the left). This is illustrated (right) by a greater
magnitude of FFA activity (percent signal change) during face
(F) stimulation periods than during object (O) stimulation periods.
Bottom, intact (I) faces also produced a greater FFA response than
scrambled (S) faces.

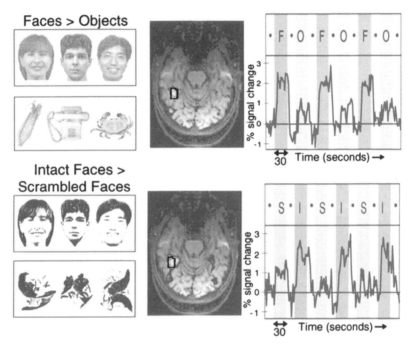

(Kanwisher, et al., 1997; The journal of neuroscience: the official
journal of the Society for Neuroscience by SOCIETY FOR
NEUROSCIENCE Copyright 1997. Reproduced with permission.)

produced a greater response in the FFA than hands. Across experiments in this study, the FFA was responsive to faces (front-view,
two-toned, and angled) to a greater degree than non-face stimuli (objects, hands, houses, and scrambled two-tone faces). The
same year as the Kanwisher et al. study was published, McCarthy
, Puce, Gore, & Allison (1997) also reported consistently greater
fMRI activity in the right fusiform gyrus during face than object
processing.

Subsequent fMRI studies provided additional evidence that the FFA selectively processes faces. In all of these studies the FFA and other regions of interest were first identified by contrasting faces and objects, and then the degree of face selectivity was evaluated by comparing the magnitude of activation in this region during face perception and during non-face object perception. Note that only studies that compared face to non-face object processing were considered to allow for the evaluation of the specific degree of face selectivity in the FFA. To assess whether the FFA was associated with face processing rather than low-level visual features present in faces, Kanwisher, Tong, & Nakayama (1998) employed two-tone *Mooney faces* (Mooney, 1957) that were only recognizable as faces when upright (Figure 2.3). These faces activated the FFA to a greater degree when they were upright than when they were inverted.

It was also reported that greyscale photographs of both upright and inverted faces produced a more similar magnitude of response in the FFA, as compared with Mooney upright and inverted faces. These findings suggested that FFA is activated whenever a face is recognizable. Kanwisher, Stanley, & Harris (1999) showed that the FFA responded to greyscale photographs of both human faces and animal faces, showing that this region responded to faces more generally. The FFA also responded to a greater degree to whole humans (i.e., the head/face and body) than whole animals, which argues

Figure 2.3   *Upright and inverted Mooney face.*

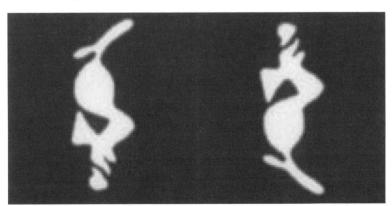

(Reprinted from Cognition, 68/1, Kanwisher et al., The effect of face inversion on the human fusiform face area, B1–B11, Copyright 1998, with permission from Elsevier.)

Figure 2.4 *Stimuli used to produce FFA activation.*

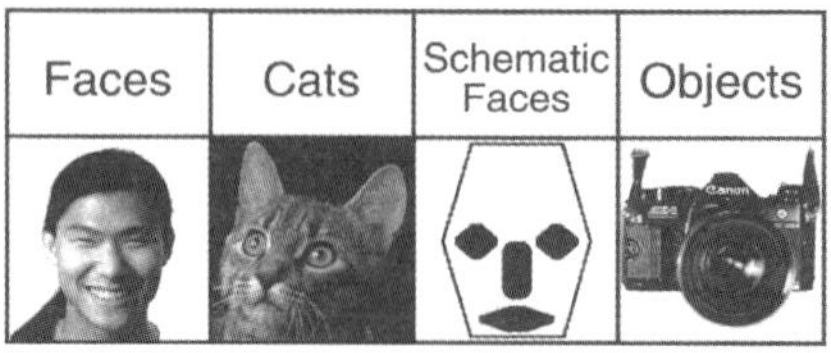

Faces	Cats	Schematic Faces	Objects

(Response properties of the human fusiform face area, Tong et al., Cognitive Neuropsychology, 2000, reprinted by permission of Taylor & Francis Ltd, http://www.tandf.co.uk/journals.)

against the possibility that the FFA is specialized for all animate objects. Tong, Nakayama, Moscovitch, Weinrib, & Kanwisher (2000) used additional stimulus classes (Figure 2.4) to further probe the FFA and found this region was activated by human faces, cat faces, and cartoon faces (including inverted cartoon faces) to a greater degree than objects. However, the FFA was not very responsive to face schematics, suggesting that activation of this region requires detailed facial features.

Grill-Spector, Knouf, & Kanwisher (2004) presented greyscale photographs of faces, birds, flowers, houses, cars, guitars, or textures for 33 to 50 milliseconds (the duration was adjusted in an effort to equate difficulty across participants), so brief that they were often difficult to perceive. Stimuli from only one category were shown in a given sequence, and participants classified each stimulus according to whether it matched a previously learned target object (e.g., Harrison Ford for the male face category or a pigeon for the bird category), whether it was another object, or whether it was not an object (i.e., it was a texture).

The right hemisphere FFA, corresponding to the face processing region in the previous studies, and the left hemisphere FFA were activated during correct identification of target faces to a greater degree than correct detection of faces, and correct detection of faces produced greater FFA activity than faces that were not detected. The same pattern of activity was observed for birds, which is not surprising given that birds have faces. This pattern of activity during face processing was not observed in the FFA for flowers, houses, guitars, or as strongly with cars, which indicated that activity in the FFA is not driven by identification of specific items within generic object categories (Jiang, Dricot, Weber, Righi, Tarr, Goebel, & Rossion,

2011, also reported a greater magnitude of activity in the right hemisphere FFA during face detection than car detection).

To produce a detailed response profile of the right hemisphere FFA and other categorical processing regions, Downing, Chan, Peelen, Dodds, & Kanwisher (2006) employed stimuli from 20 different object categories and found that the FFA response was highest for faces, was second highest for bodies, and was lower for other object categories (Figure 2.5). The second most effective category is of particular relevance as it can be used to estimate the maximum FFA response to non-face objects, thus serving as a baseline measure of activity to quantify the degree of face selectivity in this region.

Table 2.1 illustrates the magnitude of FFA activity (percent signal change) in response to faces in addition to the magnitude of activity in response to the second most effective non-face/baseline stimulus category in six studies that employed objects, inverted Mooney faces, bodies, objects, cars, and bodies, respectively. The average face-to-baseline activity ratio was 2.3, which shows that the FFA produces approximately twice the response to faces as compared with non-face objects and suggests this region is specialized for processing faces.

Figure 2.5 *Activity in the right hemisphere FFA associated with each of twenty stimulus categories. Beta is an estimate of activation magnitude.*

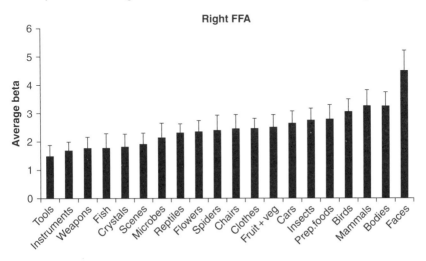

(Downing et al., Domain specificity in visual cortex. *Cerebral Cortex, 2006, 16, 10*, 1453–1461, by permission of Oxford University Press.)

Table 2.1   *FFA activity (fMRI percent signal change) associated with faces, the second most effective stimulus category (baseline), and the face-to-baseline activity ratio*

Study	Faces	Baseline	Ratio
Kanwisher et al. (1997)	3.3	1.2	2.8
Kanwisher et al. (1998)	2.3	1.3	1.8
Kanwisher et al. (1999)	2.0	1.0	2.0
Tong et al. (2000)	1.7	0.7	2.4
Grill-Spector et al. (2004)	2.1	0.9	2.4
Tsao et al. (2008)	2.7	1.1	2.5
Average activity	2.4	1.0	2.3

FFA lesion evidence

Patients with prosopagnosia, a deficit in face recognition, have provided convergent evidence that the FFA is specialized for processing faces. It should be noted that the lesions in the large majority of patient studies have uncertain locations, precluding definitive localization to the FFA, and thus were not considered (this includes brain lesions that occurred during development, where the functional organization of intact cortex is unknown due to the possibility of cortical reorganization). Barton, Press, Keenan, & O'Connor (2002) reported-four patients with lesions to the right hemisphere FFA (Figure 2.6) that had impaired perception of the spatial configuration of face parts in a task that involved identifying spatial shifts in eye and mouth positions in altered photographs.

By comparison, a patient who also had prosopagnosia with more anterior left and right temporal lobe lesions that did not include the FFA (patient 1, the lesion is not shown) was not markedly impaired at discriminating face configuration. Wada & Yamamoto (2001) also reported a patient with a relatively restricted lesion that included the right fusiform cortex who had impaired face recognition. These lesion results complement the fMRI results and further suggest that the FFA is necessary for face processing.

Additional face processing regions

The face–object contrast employed in the Grill-Spector et al. (2004) study described above, which is the standard method of identifying the right hemisphere FFA and the left hemisphere FFA, also revealed

Figure 2.6   *FFA lesion evidence. Lesion locations of four patients (key to the bottom right). Images progress from the frontal cortex at the upper left to the occipital cortex at the bottom right (coronal views, right hemisphere on the left). The overlapping lesion location (in black) included the FFA and is indicated by the arrow.*

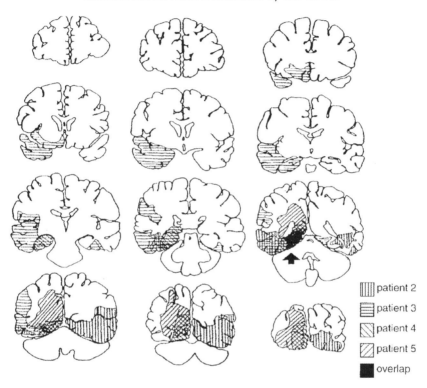

(Barton et al., 2002, Lesions of the fusiform face area impair perception of facial configuration in prosopagnosia, Neurology, 58, 1, 71–78, reprinted with permission from Wolters Kluwer Health.)

face activity in the left and right occipital cortex (the *occipital face area, OFA*), and this region had the same pattern of face activity as the FFA. In addition, face selective activity was observed in the left and right *face selective superior temporal sulcus* (the *fSTS*). These three face selective regions, the FFA, OFA, and fSTS, have been consistently observed in subsequent studies, and additional face selective regions have also been reported. For instance, two face selective regions have been reported anterior to FFA and labeled the *anterior face patch 1* (*AFP1*) and the *anterior face patch 2* (*AFP2*; Tsao, Moeller, & Freiwald, 2008; a face selective region anterior to the

FFA has also been observed that appears to correspond to AFP1; Rajimehr, Young, & Tootell, 2009), and an additional face selective region has been observed in the right inferior frontal cortex (Chan & Downing, 2011; Jiang et al., 2011).

To better characterize the functions of the FFA, OFA, and fSTS, Liu, Harris, & Kanwisher (2010) used photographs of faces with the parts (eyes, nose, and mouth) either intact or replaced by black ovals (similar to the schematic face shown in Figure 2.4), and these parts could be in the correct or incorrect spatial locations. OFA and fSTS responded to face parts to a greater degree than black ovals regardless of spatial configuration. By comparison, the FFA was sensitive to both face parts and spatial configuration, which suggests that this region may be uniquely sensitive to the holistic processing of faces.

MINORITY VIEW

There is also evidence that the FFA processes categories of objects other than faces, which questions the degree to which the FFA is selective for processing faces. Moreover, there is evidence that face processing is distributed across numerous brain regions, which challenges the notion that the FFA is localized to a single region. If the FFA is neither selective for faces nor localized to a specific area, it would be difficult to convincingly argue for the existence of a face processing region in the brain.

The activation evidence described above, which was taken to support the majority view, also indicates that the FFA does not selectively process faces. Table 2.1 shows that FFA activity in six studies was consistently greater for faces than non-face objects, and this difference was taken to support face specificity. However, although the magnitude of activity associated with faces was about twice that of non-face objects, the magnitude of FFA activity associated with non-face objects was also greater than the baseline level of activity, as shown by the consistently positive magnitude of non-face object activity. This indicates that the FFA responds to non-face objects, which is at odds with the view that the FFA selectively processes faces. This analysis was based on the absolute magnitude of activity associated with a single task (i.e., the magnitude of non-face object processing activity was compared with 0). By comparison, cognitive neuroscience analyses typically only consider the relative magnitudes of activity associated with two tasks (based on subtractive logic; Chapter 1). Desimone (1991) made the following point that is directly relevant to the interpretation of these findings when referring to the possibility that face selective cells exist in the monkey:

> In some studies, a few cells classified as face selective responded only twice as well to faces as to nonface stimuli … Yet, the greater the response to nonface stimuli, the more likely it is that a cell is actually tuned to some more general object feature, such as shape or texture.
>
> (p. 3)

Following this reasoning, a region that is truly face selective should respond only to faces and produce no response to non-face objects, and if there is a non-face object response this suggests the region likely processes a feature that is shared by faces and objects (such visual features are discussed below). While this could be considered a strong definition of selectivity, relaxing the requirement – such as requiring a region to produce twice the response to faces as compared with non-face objects – weakens the term *selective* such that it has little validity. For instance, under conditions of weak selectivity, it could be said that the criterion for labeling a region as selective is arbitrary, and those who aim to find a selective region need only choose the degree of selectivity that is observed in their results. Such an arbitrary procedure is clearly not good scientific practice. To make a strong case for selectivity, it would be much more compelling if a region responded to a single stimulus class and produced no response to other object classes.

Grill-Spector et al. (2004), a study discussed in the majority view section, provided further evidence that the FFA does not selectively respond to faces. Figure 2.7 shows the right hemisphere FFA and the left hemisphere FFA, identified by contrasting faces and objects (outlined in black), and the activity (in white) associated with identification versus detection of objects from six categories. Face processing activated 93 percent of the FFA; however, processing of all other object categories also produced activity within the FFA. Specifically, excluding birds, which have faces, the other non-face categories activated 26 percent of the FFA on average. Although the authors argued that the face greater than non-face

Figure 2.7 *FFA and activity associated with identification of objects from six categories. FFA in the right hemisphere and the left hemisphere (outlined in black) and activity (in white) associated with object identification in the specified categories (inferior view, occipital pole at the bottom; the arrow head at the bottom right demarcates the fusiform gyrus, fus; keys at the bottom).*

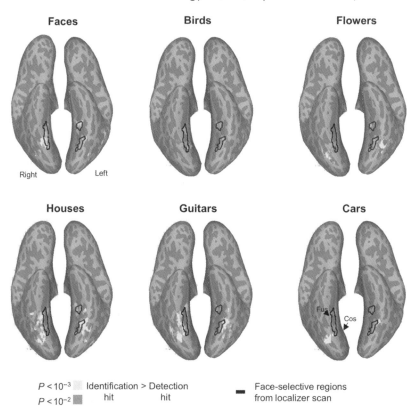

(Reprinted by permission from Macmillan Publishers Ltd: *Nature Neuroscience*, 7, Grill-Spector et al., copyright 2004.)

object response supported face selectivity, these results also show an object response in the FFA, which undermines the notion that this region is selective for faces. It is also worth noting that activity associated with face identification versus detection (Figure 2.7, upper left) was not restricted to the FFA. Approximately half of the face activity was outside of this region and distributed across the ventral occipital-temporal cortex, similar to the distributed pattern of activity associated with all other object categories.

Ishai, Ungerleider, Martin, Schouten, & Haxby (1999) fore-shadowed the previous findings when they reported that the FFA responded maximally to faces but also showed that this region produced robust responses to houses and chairs. Consistent with these results, Joseph & Gathers (2002) reported that objects activated the FFA, and Ewbank, Schluppeck, & Andrews (2005) found that the FFA responded less strongly to repeated objects than novel objects. The latter adaptation response, referred to as *repetition priming*, indicates that the FFA is involved in non-face object processing (Chao, Weisberg, & Martin, 2002, reported a similar finding). In addition to casting doubt on the selectivity of the FFA, Ishai et al. (1999) reported that regions maximally responsive to houses and chairs were activated by faces in the ventral temporal cortex, indicating that face processing is mediated, to some degree, outside of the FFA. Ishai, Ungerleider, Martin, & Haxby (2000) also reported a distributed pattern of activity in ventral temporal cortex associated with these object classes (faces, houses, and chairs) that extended into ventral occipital cortex.

Lesion evidence has further suggested that the FFA does not selectively process faces. As discussed previously, Barton et al. (2002) reported four patients with lesions that included the FFA and had impaired face perception (Figure 2.6). However, non-face objects were not tested in that study, leaving open the possibility that the deficit was not restricted to face processing. In a follow-up study, Barton, Cherkasova, Press, Intriligator, & O'Connor (2004) tested the same four participants with both face and non-face objects and found that all of the patients were impaired at face recognition, replicating the previous finding, but these patients were additionally impaired at fruit and vegetable recognition. These results suggest that the FFA mediates both face processing and non-face object processing. In the separate case study considered previously, Wada & Yamamoto (2001) reported a patient with impaired face perception following a lesion that included the right fusiform cortex. However, a very limited set of non-face objects were tested (e.g., fruit and vegetable recognition was not evaluated), such that the degree of selectivity in this patient should be treated with caution. These results indicate that a strong argument for face selectivity is not supported by the current lesion evidence.

The preceding results indicate that the FFA is not particularly selective for faces, given that this region has also been shown to process non-face objects. A related line of evidence, touched on above, has indicated that face processing is not primarily localized to the FFA but is rather distributed across ventral temporal cortex. Haxby, Gobbini, Furey, Ishai, Shouten, & Pietrini (2001) investigated the pattern of fMRI activity in ventral temporal cortex produced by many different object categories including faces, houses, chairs, and shoes. Figure 2.8 shows the regions of ventral temporal cortex that were activated (in darker grey/black) or deactivated (in lighter grey/white) by each object category. The analysis was conducted separately for even runs and odd runs, in part to test whether the pattern of activation associated with each category was consistently produced across runs. The high within category correlations across even and odd runs show that these patterns of activation were robust (Figure 2.8; an r value of 1 indicates maximum correlation, an r value of 0 indicates no correlation, and an r value of -1 indicates maximum anti-correlation). In direct opposition to the view that face processing is localized to the fusiform gyrus, face activity was not restricted to this region but was rather distributed across ventral temporal cortex, like the other object categories. The overall pattern of activity associated with each object was distinct, as indicated by the negative between category correlations (shown adjacent to slanted arrow heads in Figure 2.8). An analysis was also conducted whereby each stimulus in half of the entire stimulus set was identified based on comparing the pattern of ventral temporal activity produced by that stimulus with the pattern of ventral temporal activity produced by each of the separate stimulus categories generated from the other half of the stimulus set. The category of each stimulus was taken to be the category with the highest correlation with that stimulus. This analysis procedure identified the category of individual stimuli with a remarkably high accuracy of 96 percent. The same analysis was conducted after excluding the activity that responded maximally to faces, which included the FFA, and this had no effect on the perfect face identification accuracy. These results indicate that the FFA does not have a privileged role in face processing and that face processing is distributed across the ventral temporal cortex. Furthermore, based on the findings of Ishai et al. (2000), face processing is distributed across the ventral occipital cortex as well.

The evidence that face processing is distributed across ventral temporal cortex may at first seem at odds with the evidence

Figure 2.8 *Face, house, chair, and shoe patterns of ventral temporal activity (axial views, occipital pole at the bottom of each image). Darker grey/black and lighter grey/white illustrate progressively greater positive and negative activation magnitudes, respectively. Within and between-category correlations (r values) are shown adjacent to the vertical and diagonal arrows, respectively.*

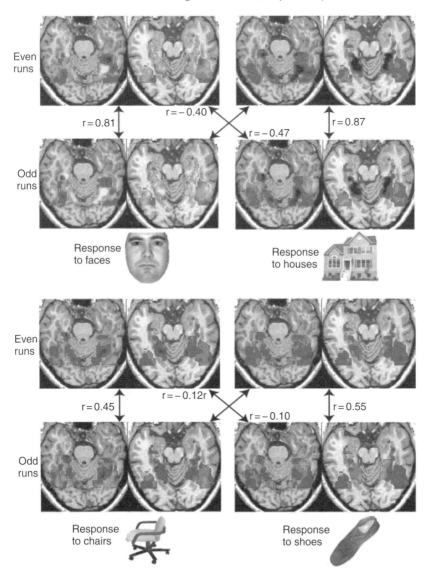

(From Haxby et al., 2001, Distributed and overlapping representations of faces and objects in ventral temporal cortex, Science, 293, 2425–2430. Reprinted with permission from AAAS.)

supporting the majority view that the FFA is specialized for face processing, but the findings taken to support both views are actually consistent. As described above, while Kanwisher et al. (1997) originally defined the FFA as being localized to a single region within the right hemisphere, subsequent studies by proponents of the FFA have reported increasing numbers of face processing regions including left and right FFA, OFA, and fSTS (Grill-Spector et al., 2004; Liu et al., 2010), left and right AFP1 and AFP2 (Tsao et al., 2008; Rajimehr et al., 2009), and the right inferior frontal cortex (Chan & Downing, 2011; Jiang et al., 2011). This puts the current face processing region tally from FFA proponents at a minimum of six (and up to 12 if counted separately in each hemisphere), and new face processing regions appear to be discovered on a regular basis (e.g., Jiang et al., 2011, reported face selective activity in left and right amygdala, and Ku, Tolias, Logothetis, & Goense, 2011, observed many other face selective regions using fMRI in monkeys). This substantial number of face processing regions is inconsistent with the notion of a single or even a few localized face processing regions, and rather supports the distributed model of face processing. Related to this, ERP evidence was not considered in this chapter because face processing has been associated with many regions, making the localization of the underlying neural sources inherently uncertain.

The evidence that face processing is distributed across ventral occipital-temporal cortex leads to the question of what type of processing is occurring in each of these islands of activation (Figure 2.8). What is the neural code? The answer is currently unknown, but Tanaka's (1993) study of visual object processing in monkey inferior temporal cortex has provided important clues. Tanaka found that the inferior temporal cortex is organized in columns of cells that respond to complex visual features (Figure 2.9), much more complex than the simple features such as line orientation or colour that are coded in earlier visual regions of the occipital cortex.

These results suggest that the distributed pattern of activity in ventral temporal cortex associated with a particular object, such as a face or a house, reflects processing in regions that code the complex visual features that comprise the object. Again, exactly which complex visual feature is coded by each specific region of ventral

Figure 2.9   *Monkey inferior temporal cortical columns respond to complex visual features. Left, illustration of the procedure used to isolate the complex visual features that activated individual cells in the monkey inferior temporal cortex. In this example, a cell was similarly activated by a tiger head at the object level of processing (the top stimulus), stimuli at intermediate levels of processing (the next three stimuli), and two black rectangles overlapping a white square (the second stimulus from the bottom), the complex features that can be assumed to have produced the object response as further decomposition (the bottom stimulus) produced a weaker response. Right, schematic of cell columns in the monkey inferior temporal cortex that respond to complex visual features.*

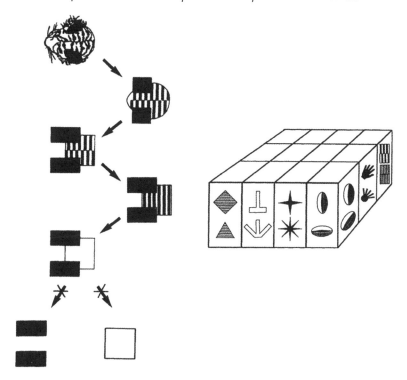

(From Tanaka, 1993, Neuronal mechanisms of object recognition, Science, 262, 685–688. Reprinted with permission from AAAS.)

temporal cortex has yet to be delineated. To make headway toward understanding the neural basis of object processing, future research will need to focus on deciphering the visual feature processing code in the ventral occipital-temporal cortex.

COUNTERPOINTS

Rather than the FFA being selective for face processing, it has been proposed that this region processes objects of expertise given that we are all face experts. Gauthier, Tarr, Anderson, Skudlarski, & Gore (1999) trained participants for approximately seven hours on novel object stimuli they named greebles (Figure 2.10), and found that greeble processing produced a larger FFA response for greeble experts than greeble novices (as expected, faces produced an FFA response for both greeble experts and novices).

In a related study, Gauthier, Skudlarski, Gore, & Anderson (2000) reported that pictures of birds produced greater activity in the right FFA of bird experts but not car experts (i.e., there was a bird expertise effect in the right FFA); however, a standard analysis did not reveal a corresponding car expertise effect. Using a similar paradigm, Xu (2005) reported the opposite pattern of findings, a car expertise effect in the right FFA but little if any bird expertise effect. Employing a different class of stimuli, Harley, Pope, Villablanca, Mumford, Suh, Mazziotta, Enzmann, & Engel (2009) presented lung radiographs to radiology experts or novices. A standard analysis did

Figure 2.10   *Novel objects (greebles) used to test whether the FFA responds to stimuli of expertise.*

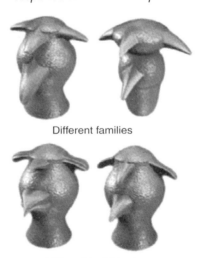

Different families

Different individuals

(Reprinted by permission of Macmillan Publishers Ltd: *Nature Neuroscience*, *2*, Gauthier et al., copyright 1999.)

not produce any activation difference in the right FFA for experts versus novices; however, an expertise effect was revealed by correlating FFA activity as a function of each individual participant's level of expertise. The expertise explanation of FFA activation is widely considered viable; however, this view has many serious limitations. First, it assumes the FFA exists, which may be incorrect. Second, an expertise explanation of FFA activation is not a hypothesis about how information is processed in the brain – which is of primary interest in cognitive neuroscience – but is simply a potential confound associated with faces. By comparison, the distributed processing view is a viable alternative to the existence of an FFA. Third, almost all of the stimuli that have been used to study expertise have face-like properties, including greebles (Figure 2.10), birds, and even the front of cars can be mapped onto a face (e.g., the windshield could be processed like eyes as in the movie Cars). As such, experts of a given object class may be allocating greater attention to the face-like properties of their objects of expertise. That is, *expertise effects* might actually reflect *attention effects* as it is known that attention to faces can increase activity in the FFA (Serences, Schwarzbach, Courtney, Golay, & Yantis, 2004). For instance, if a car expert processes a car and attends to its face-like features, it follows that the magnitude of FFA activity will increase due to attentional amplification of neural activity in this region (Chapter 3), as opposed to activity reflecting expertise processing. Fourth, expertise effects are inherently weak, sometimes they occur in the FFA, but just as often they are not observed. By comparison, face responses in the FFA are extremely robust, therefore it is highly unlikely that weak expertise effects are driving the strong face responses observed in the FFA. McKone, Kanwisher, & Duchaine (2006) pointed out the two latter limitations, but also incorrectly claimed that faces and objects of expertise should produce the same pattern of results. This could be considered a straw man – a misrepresentation of an opponent's position – as face processing effects would actually be expected to produce more robust effects given that this object class is arguably of greater potential relevance to everyone (i.e., face processing can be considered particularly important for survival). The previous limitations show that there is little, if any, compelling evidence to support the expertise explanation of FFA activation. Future work in this area might benefit from the use of untapped stimulus classes that have absolutely no face-like properties. Moreover, proponents of this view must explain how weak and inconsistent expertise effects might explain the robust and consistent face processing effects. Perhaps expertise effects could be strengthened by employing a stimulus class associated with a level of expertise that rivals faces, possibly through extensive training. However, such stimulus classes have long been sought out and no compelling results have been revealed; therefore, it is anticipated that the expertise explanation of FFA activity will eventually dissipate.

In response to the evidence that face processing is distributed across the ventral occipital-temporal cortex, Kanwisher & Yovel (2006) have articulated multiple arguments. It was first claimed that the FFA does not contain information that can be used to discriminate between non-face objects, based on evidence from Spiridon & Kanwisher (2002). This empirical study specifically tested whether FFA activity could be used to identify non-face stimuli, using a correlation analysis like Haxby et al. (2001) that was described previously. It was found that FFA activity could discriminate between faces versus objects with very high accuracy (98 percent) and could discriminate between houses versus objects with intermediate accuracy (66 percent). Based on these results, it was argued that the FFA was not part of a homogenous distributed pattern across ventral temporal cortex, and rather that this region was selective for faces. It is notable that the FFA was most highly associated with faces; however, activity in this region was also associated with non-face objects, which is consistent with all the findings detailed in this chapter. As stated previously, the point is not whether the FFA responds more to faces, but is whether or not the FFA responds only to faces. When non-face object responses are observed in the FFA, such results show that this region is not particularly selective for faces. Moreover, the argument that the FFA should show a similar magnitude of activity to all object classes is a straw man, similar to that proposed above when arguing that face and non-face expertise effects should be equivalent. This strategy of suggesting an opponent's theory predicts equivalence, when it does not, and then discounting that prediction could be interpreted as intentionally misleading. In reality, proponents of the distributed object processing view would predict exactly the pattern of results observed by Spiridon & Kanwisher. Specifically, the number of face-like features shared by faces and non-face objects should produce a relatively greater response to faces in the FFA because faces have more of these features, while features of faces and non-face objects that are processed in other regions of the ventral occipital-temporal cortex should produce activation outside of the FFA. A second argument against the distributed face processing view is that face activations outside of the FFA might not be used in perceptual performance (Cohen & Tong, 2001, made the same argument). The problem with this argument is that FFA proponents are choosing the region believed to be responsible for face perception, the FFA, and ignoring all other activations. Such selection bias – choosing results that support a favoured hypothesis and ignoring results that don't fit that hypothesis – is poor scientific practice, and cannot be considered as a valid basis for an argument. The third argument against the distributed processing view is that FFA responses to non-face objects is due to spatial blurring of activity from neighbouring regions that process non-face objects into the FFA, which can happen with fMRI because of the limited spatial resolution of this technique. For instance, Schwarzlose, Baker, & Kanwisher (2005) reported that headless bodies activated a region adjacent to the FFA, and spatial blurring of such activity could produce a body response in the FFA even though bodies might not actually be processed in this region. This is the first sound argument, and makes the testable prediction that non-face objects processed in regions spatially adjacent to the FFA (such as bodies) will produce the greatest magnitude of FFA response. However, the evidence contradicts this prediction. Table 2.1 shows that objects, rather than bodies, produced the greatest magnitude of activation in the FFA. This finding indicates that the FFA response to non-face objects is not simply due to spatial blurring, and such responses can rather be attributed to non-face object processing within the FFA. Thus, the preceding arguments against the distributed face processing view by Kanwisher & Yovel (2006) can all be discounted. However, because the existence of the FFA is the majority view, even an ill founded challenge appears to be sufficient for the widespread belief in the FFA to continue.

Assessment of whether or not the FFA exists should be based on evidence. To date, the evidence supports the distributed processing view and is inconsistent with the existence of the FFA. To reiterate, the FFA consistently responds to non-face objects, and face processing is not restricted to a spatially circumscribed area. Therefore, there is little if any empirical basis that the term *face* or the term *area* should be used to label a *fusiform face area*. A more accurate description of this region is that it responds maximally to faces, but also responds to non-face objects, and that face processing is shared across numerous other regions in the ventral occipital-temporal cortex and beyond. This description fits other object classes as well, indicating that faces are processed in ventral occipital-temporal cortex in the same way as all other objects. It is important to highlight that distributed object processing proponents can explain the FFA results – the region of activity with the maximal response to faces – but FFA proponents cannot explain the numerous face processing activations that support the distributed processing view.

It is almost certain that the present arguments will not dissuade FFA proponents, even though some of the most compelling evidence against their position comes from their own work. Still, it is useful to consider what type of findings could provide support for the existence of an FFA. First, a face processing region should be extremely selective for faces, otherwise there is a question of whether the region is processing a feature that is shared with other objects (Desimone, 1991). As mentioned previously, the FFA produces approximately twice the response to faces than non-face objects, which is far from being selective, unless the definition of selective is relaxed to fit the results.

For argument's sake, assume that the FFA was completely face selective (i.e., produced no response to non-face objects). Such selectivity has been reported in single-cell responses within the medial temporal lobe (Kreiman, Koch, & Fried, 2000). For instance, an entorhinal cortex neuron responded to animals but did not respond to stimuli from eight other categories. Thus, following the logic of naming object selective regions based on their response category, this could be labeled the *entorhinal animal cell* (the *EAC*). However, the same group of investigators conducted an analysis of the response properties of 1425 medial temporal lobe neurons and concluded that each neuron responded to 50 to 150 distinct object representations (Waydo, Kraskov, Quian Quiroga, Fried, & Koch, 2006). While these results may seem at odds, the apparent object selectivity in the first study can be attributed to the limited number of stimulus categories employed (similar to the results of Barton et al., 2002, that suggested face selectivity in the FFA, until Barton et al., 2004, employed a larger number of stimulus classes and showed this region did not selectively process faces). These results might imply that FFA investigators should use numerous object categories to assess whether the FFA is selective for faces.

However, Downing et al. (2006) already conducted this experiment and face selectivity was weak, with faces producing less than twice the magnitude of response as the next most responsive category (Figure 2.5). Moreover, as reviewed above, all the evidence has shown that face processing occurs in numerous brain regions. A strategy that might prove fruitful for proponents of the majority view is to attempt to identify a particular type of computation that is specific to the FFA that does not occur in the other face processing regions. If this could be convincingly shown, some form of face processing specialization might be attributed to the FFA.

CONCLUSION

The evidence reviewed in this chapter indicates that the FFA is not selective for faces, nor is face processing localized to the fusiform gyrus. Thus, there is no compelling evidence supporting the majority view that the FFA is a specialized region for processing faces. By comparison, all the results are compatible with the minority view that faces and non-face objects are processed in distributed regions of the ventral occipital-temporal cortex. The primary limitation of the minority view is the absence of a neural code that details how the individual activations reflect the processing of specific visual features that comprise an object. It is hoped that the present considerations will promote research in this direction. Despite the large body of evidence to the contrary, there is currently widespread belief that the FFA exists (for reasons further discussed in Chapter 9), and this unfounded belief will in all likelihood continue for the foreseeable future.

SUGGESTED READINGS

Majority view

Kanwisher, N., McDermott, J., & Chun, M. M. (1997). The fusiform face area: A module in human extrastriate cortex specialized for face perception. *The Journal of Neuroscience, 17*, 4302–4311. Open access.

Grill-Spector, K., Knouf, N., & Kanwisher, N. (2004). The fusiform face area subserves face perception, not generic within-category identification. *Nature Neuroscience*, *7*, 555–562.

Minority view

Haxby, J. V., Gobbini, M. I., Furey, M. L., Ishai, A., Schouten, J. L., & Pietrini, P. (2001). Distributed and overlapping representations of faces and objects in ventral temporal cortex. *Science*, *293*, 2425–2430. Open access.

Tanaka, K. (1993). Neuronal mechanisms of object recognition. *Science*, *262*, 685–688.

REFERENCES

Barton, J. J., Cherkasova, M. V., Press, D. Z., Intriligator, J. M., & O'Connor, M. (2004). Perceptual functions in prosopagnosia. *Perception*, *33*, 939–956.

Barton, J. J., Press, D. Z., Keenan, J. P., & O'Connor, M. (2002). Lesions of the fusiform face area impair perception of facial configuration in prosopagnosia. *Neurology*, *58*, 71–78.

Chan, A. W., & Downing, P. E. (2011). Faces and eyes in human lateral prefrontal cortex. *Frontiers in Human Neuroscience*, *5*, 1–10.

Chao, L. L., Weisberg, J., & Martin, A. (2002). Experience-dependent modulation of category-related cortical activity. *Cerebral Cortex*, *12*, 545–551.

Cohen, J. D., & Tong, F. (2001). Neuroscience: The face of controversy. *Science*, *293*, 2405–2407.

Desimone, R. (1991). Face-selective cells in the temporal cortex of monkeys. *Journal of Cognitive Neuroscience*, *3*, 1–8.

Downing, P. E., Chan, A. W., Peelen, M. V., Dodds, C. M., & Kanwisher, N. (2006). Domain specificity in visual cortex. *Cerebral Cortex*, *16*, 1453–1461.

Ewbank, M. P., Schluppeck, D., & Andrews, T. J. (2005). fMR-adaptation reveals a distributed representation of inanimate objects and places in human visual cortex. *NeuroImage*, *28*, 268–279.

Gauthier, I., Skudlarski, P., Gore, J. C., & Anderson, A. W. (2000). Expertise for cars and birds recruits brain areas involved in face recognition. *Nature Neuroscience*, *3*, 191–197.

Gauthier, I., Tarr, M. J., Anderson, A. W., Skudlarski, P., & Gore, J. C. (1999). Activation of the middle fusiform 'face area' increases with expertise in recognizing novel objects. *Nature Neuroscience, 2*, 568–573.

Grill-Spector, K., Knouf, N., & Kanwisher, N. (2004). The fusiform face area subserves face perception, not generic within-category identification. *Nature Neuroscience, 7*, 555–562.

Harley, E. M., Pope, W. B., Villablanca, J. P., Mumford, J., Suh, R., Mazziotta, J. C., Enzmann, D., & Engel, S. A. (2009). Engagement of fusiform cortex and disengagement of lateral occipital cortex in the acquisition of radiological expertise. *Cerebral Cortex, 19*, 2746–2754.

Haxby, J. V., Gobbini, M. I., Furey, M. L., Ishai, A., Schouten, J. L., & Pietrini, P. (2001). Distributed and overlapping representations of faces and objects in ventral temporal cortex. *Science, 293*, 2425–2430.

Ishai, A., Ungerleider, L. G., Martin, A., & Haxby, J. V. (2000). The representation of objects in the human occipital and temporal cortex. *Journal of Cognitive Neuroscience, 12, Supplement 2*, 35–51.

Ishai, A., Ungerleider, L. G., Martin, A., Schouten, J. L., & Haxby, J. V. (1999). Distributed representation of objects in the human ventral visual pathway. *Proceedings of the National Academy of Sciences of the United States of America, 96*, 9379–9384.

Jiang, F., Dricot, L., Weber, J., Righi, G., Tarr, M. J., Goebel, R., & Rossion, B. (2011). Face categorization in visual scenes may start in a higher order area of the right fusiform gyrus: Evidence from dynamic visual stimulation in neuroimaging. *Journal of Neurophysiology, 106*, 2720–2736.

Joseph, J. E., & Gathers, A. D. (2002). Natural and manufactured objects activate the fusiform face area. *NeuroReport, 13*, 935–938.

Kanwisher, N., & Yovel, G. (2006). The fusiform face area: A cortical region specialized for the perception of faces. *Philosophical Transactions of the Royal Society B: Biological Sciences, 361*, 2109–2128.

Kanwisher, N., McDermott, J., & Chun, M. M. (1997). The fusiform face area: A module in human extrastriate cortex specialized for face perception. *The Journal of Neuroscience, 17*, 4302–4311.

Kanwisher, N., Stanley, D., & Harris, A. (1999). The fusiform face area is selective for faces not animals. *NeuroReport, 10*, 183–187.

Kanwisher, N., Tong, F., & Nakayama, K. (1998). The effect of face inversion on the human fusiform face area. *Cognition, 68,* B1–B11.

Kreiman, G., Koch, C., & Fried, I. (2000). Category-specific visual responses of single neurons in the human medial temporal lobe. *Nature Neuroscience, 3,* 946–953.

Ku, S. P., Tolias, A. S., Logothetis, N. K., & Goense, J. (2011). fMRI of the face-processing network in the ventral temporal lobe of awake and anesthetized macaques. *Neuron, 70,* 352–362.

Liu, J., Harris, A., & Kanwisher, N. (2010). Perception of face parts and face configurations: An fMRI study. *Journal of Cognitive Neuroscience, 22,* 203–211.

McCarthy, G., Puce, A., Gore, J. C., & Allison, T. (1997). Face-specific processing in the human fusiform gyrus. *Journal of Cognitive Neuroscience, 9,* 605–610.

McKone, E., Kanwisher, N., & Duchaine, B. C. (2007). Can generic expertise explain special processing for faces? *Trends in Cognitive Sciences, 11,* 8–15.

Mooney, C. M. (1957). Age in the development of closure ability in children. *Canadian Journal of Psychology, 11,* 219–226.

Rajimehr, R., Young, J. C., & Tootell, R. B. (2009). An anterior temporal face patch in human cortex, predicted by macaque maps. *Proceedings of the National Academy of Sciences of the United States of America, 106,* 1995–2000.

Schwarzlose, R. F., Baker, C. I., & Kanwisher, N. (2005). Separate face and body selectivity on the fusiform gyrus. *The Journal of Neuroscience, 25,* 11055–11059.

Serences, J. T., Schwarzbach, J., Courtney, S. M., Golay, X., & Yantis, S. (2004). Control of object-based attention in human cortex. *Cerebral Cortex, 14,* 1346–1357.

Spiridon, M., & Kanwisher, N. (2002). How distributed is visual category information in human occipito-temporal cortex? An fMRI study. *Neuron, 35,* 1157–1165.

Tanaka, K. (1993). Neuronal mechanisms of object recognition. *Science, 262,* 685–688.

Tong, F., Nakayama, K, Moscovitch, M., Weinrib, O., & Kanwisher, N. (2000). Response properties of the human fusiform face area. *Cognitive Neuropsychology, 17,* 257–280.

Tsao, D. Y., Moeller, S., & Freiwald, W. A. (2008). Comparing face patch systems in macaques and humans. *Proceedings of the*

National Academy of Sciences of the United States of America, 105, 19514–19519.

Wada, Y., & Yamamoto, T. (2001). Selective impairment of facial recognition due to a haematoma restricted to the right fusiform and lateral occipital region. *Journal of Neurology, Neurosurgery & Psychiatry, 71,* 254–257.

Waydo, S., Kraskov, A., Quian Quiroga, R., Fried, I., & Koch, C. (2006). Sparse representation in the human medial temporal lobe. *The Journal of Neuroscience, 26,* 10232–10234.

Xu, Y. (2005). Revisiting the role of the fusiform face area in visual expertise. *Cerebral Cortex, 15,* 1234–1242.

3 The Nature of Attentional Modulation in V1

William James (1890) invited generations to contemplate the meaning of attention:

> Every one knows what attention is. It is the taking possession by the mind, in clear and vivid form, of one out of what seem several simultaneously possible objects or trains of thought. Focalization, concentration, of consciousness are of its essence.
>
> (pp. 403–404)

This description highlights that attention allows us to select and enhance information, and that this selected information enters awareness/consciousness.

This chapter focuses on whether visual-spatial attention modulates activity in V1 and extrastriate cortex (including V2, V3, and V4). As reviewed in Chapter 1, V1 is the first cortical region that mediates lower-level visual processing, while extrastriate cortex mediates higher-level visual processing. For decades, attention effects have been consistently observed in extrastriate cortex, but there has been intense debate regarding whether the magnitude of activity in V1 can also be increased by attention (note that this debate is related to an even older cognitive psychology debate regarding whether attention operates at early or late mental processing stages). Such attentional modulation of neural activity is thought to reflect a gain mechanism that amplifies the mental representation of an attended item or spatial location. The majority view on V1 attention effects has changed over time. It was initially thought that activity in V1 was not modulated by attention. Then, after V1 attention effects were consistently observed this view was reformulated to acknowledge attentional modulation of this region but that such attentional modulation could only occur relatively late in time via feedback from extrastriate cortex. This latter position, the current majority view, essentially maintains the position that V1 is not of primary importance during attention, as V1 modulation is thought to be driven by attention effects in extrastriate cortex. Proponents of the minority view have provided evidence that V1 attention effects can occur rapidly, which, if true, would indicate that this region is of central importance during this cognitive process.

Before turning to the evidence on both sides of the current debate, it should be mentioned that the majority view is grounded in the widespread belief that activity in V1 does not enter awareness. More broadly, indentifying whether a given region is associated with conscious processing or nonconscious processing (or both types of processing) is a central issue in cognitive neuroscience. The view that V1 activity does not contribute to awareness was represented by Crick & Koch (1995) who assumed: 1) the frontal cortex has a privileged role in visual awareness (given the biological usefulness of this brain region in planning and executing voluntary movements), and 2) a region must be directly connected to the frontal cortex for activity in that region to reach awareness. Working from these assumptions, Crick & Koch hypothesized that V1, having no direct connections to frontal cortex, did not contribute to awareness, while extrastriate cortical regions (including V2, V3, and V4), having direct connections to frontal cortex, were posited to contribute to awareness (Figure 3.1; see also, Figure 1.3).

The hypothesis that V1 does not contribute to awareness fits with empirical findings at the time that Crick & Koch's paper was published. For instance, during binocular rivalry in monkeys (where unique stimuli, such as horizontal red lines or vertical green lines, are presented to each eye and perception alternates between the stimuli) extrastriate cortex tracked the contents of awareness, and V1 responded to very finely spaced lines that are not perceived separately (i.e., V1 can process stimulus attributes that do not enter awareness). However, in a later review, Tong (2003) presented compelling evidence that V1 can reflect awareness including robust V1 binocular rivalry effects measured using fMRI in humans, V1 effects that tracked awareness of difficult-to-detect stimuli, and V1 ambiguous figure effects (where the perception of a special type of object,

Figure 3.1 *Visual processing hierarchy highlighting connections between visual processing regions and the prefrontal cortex. Visual information (light) is processed in the retina, the lateral geniculate nucleus (LGN), V1, and then higher visual cortical areas beginning in the extrastriate cortex (pathways are illustrated by vertical arrows). Prefrontal/premotor cortex has been argued to have a privileged role in awareness because these regions are involved in voluntary movement through the primary motor cortex (M1). It has been assumed that V1 activity does not enter awareness, as this region has no direct connections to the frontal cortex (illustrated to the right).*

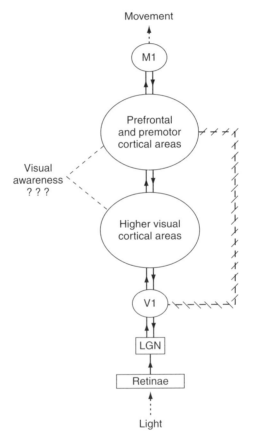

(Reprinted by permission from Macmillan Publishers Ltd: *Nature, 375,* Crick and Koch, copyright 1995.)

such as a rabbit-duck, alternates between two configurations). These latter findings indicated that activity in V1 could contribute to awareness, directly contradicting Crick & Koch's hypothesis. The evidence indicating that V1 can be involved in conscious processing is not surprising, as Crick & Koch's assumptions were speculative. That is, the assumption that the frontal cortex has a privileged role in awareness was based on the intuition that motor processing has a privileged role in consciousness (other cognitive processes, such as attention and memory, and the associated neural regions were ignored), and the second assumption that a direct connection to frontal cortex is necessary for a region to gain access to awareness had no basis. Of particular relevance, it is known that V1 connects directly to extrastriate area V2, which in turn connects directly to the frontal eye field within the frontal cortex (Figure 1.3). To illustrate the arbitrary nature of Crick & Koch's second assumption, why is a direct connection to frontal cortex sufficient for awareness while a connection with one additional junction not sufficient for awareness? These findings and arguments are touched on to underscore that, despite the widespread belief to the contrary, V1 has been associated with awareness. Rather than adopting arbitrary assumptions, the present chapter focuses on empirical evidence to assess the nature of attention effects in V1.

MAJORITY VIEW

No attention effects in V1

Moran & Desimone (1985) conducted a visual attention study in monkeys that to this day guides the interpretation of attention effects in V1 and extrastriate cortex. While recording from individual cells in V1, V4, and inferior temporal cortex, monkeys maintained fixation at a point and shifted attention between an effective stimulus, which produced a robust neural response in a given cell, and an ineffective stimulus, which produced almost no neural response in that cell (Figure 3.2, top). The monkey responded to indicate whether a stimulus presented at the attended location during sample and test periods were the same or different. It should be highlighted that the stimulus configuration did not change while cell responses were measured, such that any modulation of neural activity could be attributed to attention. This is true for all the attention studies that will be considered – the stimulus configuration is always identical across attention conditions to eliminate perceptual confounds. The attention index, a measure of attention effect, was computed by dividing the response rate of each cell when attention was directed away from the effective stimulus by the response rate

Figure 3.2 *Monkey single-cell attention effects in V4 but not in V1. Top, during fixation, attention was directed to an effective or ineffective stimulus within the receptive field (RF; key at the top, scale showing*

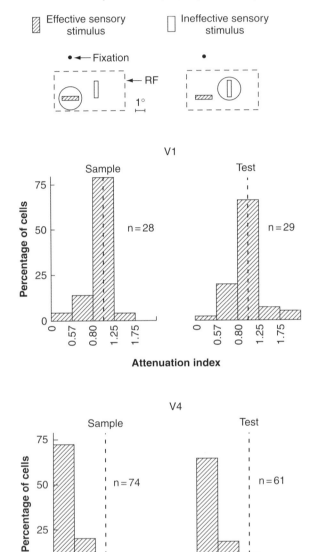

(From Moran and Desimone, 1985, Selective attention gates visual processing in the extrastriate cortex, Science, 229, 782–784. Reprinted with permission from AAAS.)

Figure 3.2   *(Continued) one degree of visual angle at the bottom; the locus of attention is illustrated by circles that were not shown during the experiment). Attention effects were measured using attention index values in V1 (middle) and V4 (bottom), where values near one indicate no attention effect and smaller values indicate a larger attention effect. The number of cells (n) from which activity was recorded is shown to the right of each panel.*

of that cell when attention was directed toward the effective stimulus. Attention index values close to a value of one indicate no attention effect, while attention index values less than a value of one indicate an attention effect.

In V1, cells had attention index values near one (Figure 3.2, middle), suggesting there was no attention effect in this region. In V4, there was a large attention effect when both stimuli were presented in the same receptive field, as indicated by attention index values less than one in the large majority of cells (Figure 3.2, bottom; ventral temporal cortex cells also showed a large attention effect). These findings indicated that attention modulates activity in extrastriate cortex, as early in the visual processing stream as V4, but does not modulate activity in V1. In a follow-up monkey study by Luck, Chelazzi, Hillyard, & Desimone (1997) that employed a similar paradigm, single-cell attention effects were measured in V1, V2, and V4. Attention modulated cells in V2 and V4, again when both stimuli were presented within the receptive field of each cell, but attention did not modulate activity in V1. Of importance, Luck et al. acknowledged that the receptive fields in V1 were so small that stimuli could not both be placed within a receptive field, a condition that was required in this study to produce attention effects in V2 and V4. Still, these results suggested that attention effects extended back to extrastriate region V2, but did not modulate activity in V1.

ERP findings from humans have provided convergent evidence that attention modulates activity in extrastriate cortex but does not modulate activity V1. In an ERP study conducted by Gomez Gonzales, Clark, Fan, Luck, & Hillyard (1994) participants maintained fixation at a cross in the centre of the screen, attended to stimuli in either the left visual field or the right visual field, and pressed a response button when the shapes above and below a line in the attended hemifield had the same form (a *form target*) or were the same distance from the line (a *distance target*; Figure 3.3, top). Attention effects were measured by comparing the ERP magnitude when attention was directed toward a non-target stimulus (a *standard*) in a given visual field wtih the ERP magnitude when attention was directed away from a standard in the same hemifield. As mentioned previously, the stimulus protocol and analysis procedure, as with all the studies considered, ensured that the perceptual properties across attention conditions were identical so that any differential effects could be attributed to attention. For example, the ERP magnitude when attention was directed toward right visual field standards was compared with the ERP magnitude when attention was directed away from right visual field standards. The analysis focused on ERPs generated from posterior scalp electrodes that reflect responses from V1 and extrastriate cortex. Of particular relevance, visual stimuli produce three robust ERP components that differ in their spatial-temporal profiles and underlying cortical sources (Jeffreys & Axford, 1972; Clark, Fan, & Hillyard, 1994; Di Russo, Martínez, Sereno, Pitzalis, & Hillyard, 2002). The C1 ERP component occurs rapidly (approximately 50 to 90 milliseconds after stimulus onset) and is generated by V1, which is known because the magnitude of this component reverses in polarity, changes from negative to positive, when stimuli are presented in the upper visual field versus the lower visual field, respectively. This polarity reversal occurs because V1 lies within the calcarine sulcus, where upper visual field stimuli in a given hemifield activate cortex on the lower bank of the sulcus in the contralateral hemisphere and lower visual field stimuli in the same hemfield activate cortex on the upper bank of the sulcus in the contralateral hemisphere (Figure 3.4). Extrastriate cortex also has a contralateral organization, where the right visual field maps onto the left hemisphere and the left visual field maps onto the right hemisphere. However, extrastriate cortex is located outside of the calcarine sulcus (Horton & Hoyt, 1991) such that the corresponding ERP components do not reverse in polarity as a function of visual field position. V1 and extrastriate cortex also have a *retinotopic* organization, like the retina, where adjacent positions in the visual field are mapped onto adjacent locations on cortex. The extrastriate P1 ERP component is positive in magnitude and occurs later in time (approximately 70 to 150 milliseconds), while the N1 component

Figure 3.3 *ERP attention effects in extrastriate cortex but not in V1. Top, while maintaining fixation, participants directed their attention to stimuli in the left visual field or the right visual field and detected infrequent targets. Bottom, ERP activity (microvolts per millisecond; scale at the bottom). Attention effects were measured by comparing ERP component magnitudes in occipital electrodes when stimuli were attended versus unattended (key at the bottom). The C1 component is generated in V1, the P1 component is generated in extrastriate cortex, and the N1 component appears to be generated in multiple cortical regions.*

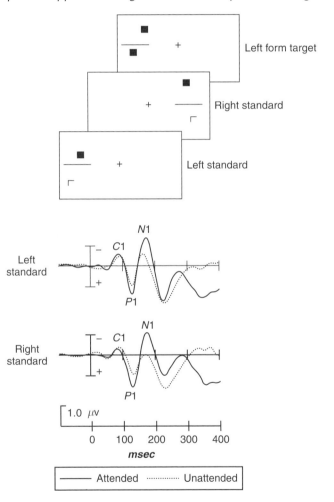

(With kind permission from Springer Science+Business Media: Brain Topography, Sources of attention-sensitive visual event-related potentials, 7, 1994, 41–51, Gomez et al., Figures 1 and 3.)

Figure 3.4 *Retinotopic organization of V1. Schematic coronal view of V1, which lies within the calcarine sulcus in the occipital lobe. V1 has a contralateral organization where the right visual field (illustrated to the upper right) maps onto the left hemisphere and the left visual field (not shown) maps onto the right hemisphere. The visual field representation is also inverted, where stimuli above the horizontal meridian (HM), in the upper visual field (1 and 2), are mapped onto the lower bank of the calcarine sulcus and stimuli below the horizontal meridian, in the lower visual field (3 and 4), are mapped onto the upper bank of the calcarine sulcus. V1 is organized such that upper and lower visual field stimuli are processed by cortex oriented in opposite directions such that the corresponding ERP C1 components reverse in polarity.*

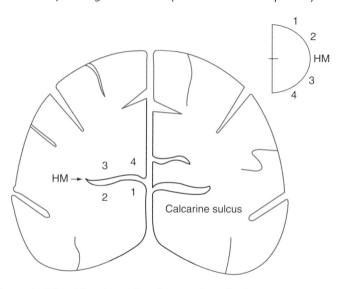

(Clark et al., Identification of early visual evoked potential generators by retinotopic and topographic analysis, 2, 3, 1994, 170–187. Copyright 1994 John Wiley & Sons, Inc. Reprinted with permission.)

is negative in magnitude, occurs even later in time, and appears to have multiple generators including extrastriate cortex and parietal cortex. Note that the C1, P1, and N1 ERP components all reflect neural activation, with polarity determined by the orientation of the underlying cortical sources (i.e., negative polarity does not imply neural deactivation). Because the N1 component has not been localized to a particular region of the brain, the P1 ERP component is the primary extrastriate component of interest in studies of visual-spatial attention. Although the C1 and P1 components can overlap in time, these components are separable in the following ways: 1) as described above, only the C1 component reverses in polarity as a function of stimulus position, and 2) the C1 component has a more symmetrical scalp electrode voltage distribution as compared with the early phase of the P1 that is primarily localized to scalp electrodes contralateral to the hemifield of stimulation (i.e., left visual field stimuli produce a predominantly right hemisphere P1 effect and right visual field stimuli produce a predominantly left hemisphere P1 effect). Now that the relevant ERP components have been reviewed, we can turn to the Gomez Gonzales et al. (1994) findings that attention increased the magnitude of the P1 and N1 components, but did not modulate the C1 component (Figure 3.3, bottom). The same pattern of results – attentional modulation of the P1 component but not the C1 component – has also been observed in other ERP studies of visual attention that were published in the same time period (Mangun, Hillyard, & Luck, 1993; Clark & Hillyard, 1996). These findings, like those of Moran & Desimone (1985), suggested that attention effects occur in extrastriate cortex but do not occur in V1.

Although the C1 and P1 ERP components have been localized to V1 and extrastriate cortex, respectively, the location of cortical activity that underlies a particular ERP component is inherently uncertain. This is due, in part, to the relatively coarse sampling of activity on the scalp during ERP recording, as electrodes typically have spacing of a few centimetres, thus limiting spatial resolution. The uncertainty in the location of the underlying cortical source(s) is referred to as the *inverse problem*, because a given ERP scalp voltage topography can be generated by many configurations of cortical sources (although this is less of a concern with the C1 component that reverses in polarity thus tethering it to V1). To address this issue, some investigators have combined ERP data, which has excellent temporal resolution but poor spatial resolution, with neuroimaging data (PET or fMRI), which has good or excellent spatial resolution but poor temporal resolution. In the first study of this kind, Heinze, Mangun, Burchert, Hinrichs, Scholz, Münte, Gös, Scherg, Johannes, Hundeshagen, Gazzaniga, & Hillyard (1994) integrated PET and ERPs to investigate visual attention effects (PET and ERP data were collected in separate sessions). During fixation, stimuli were rapidly flashed in both visual fields while participants attended to stimuli in the left visual field or the right visual field (Figure 3.5, top). Attention to the left visual field or the right visual field, each versus passive viewing (the baseline condition), produced

Figure 3.5 *Contralateral (retinotopic) visual attention PET and ERP effects. Top, while maintaining fixation, participants attended to stimuli in the left visual field or the right visual field (spotlights illustrate the attended location and were not shown during the experiment). Middle, contralateral PET attention effects produced by comparing activity associated with attention to stimuli in the visual field shown directly above versus the baseline condition (axial view, occipital pole at the bottom, key to the centre). Bottom, ERP scalp voltage topographies illustrating the contralateral P1 attention effect measured by comparing attention with stimuli in the visual field shown above versus the baseline condition (posterior view, key to the centre) and the corresponding voltage timecourses (microvolts per millisecond) at electrodes T02 and T01 (keys to the centre).*

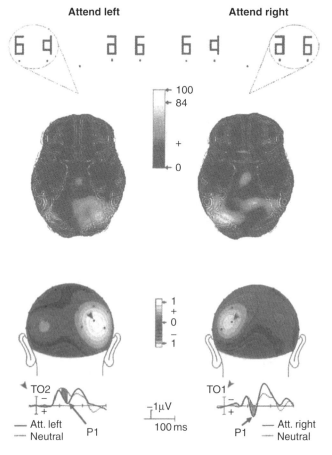

(Reprinted by permission from Macmillan Publishers Ltd: *Nature, 372,* Heinze et al., copyright 1994.)

PET activity in the contralateral extrastriate cortex (i.e., activity in the right extrastriate cortex and the left extrastriate cortex, respectively; Figure 3.5, middle). ERP activity also produced contralateral attention effects that specifically modulated the extrastriate cortex P1 component (Figure 3.5, bottom). V1 attention effects were not observed with PET or by modulation of the C1 ERP component that was measured from 50 to 80 milliseconds after stimulus onset. Subsequent studies that combined fMRI, which has better spatial resolution than PET, and ERPs found the same pattern of results, attentional modulation of extrastriate cortex but not V1 (Mangun, Buonocore, Girelli, & Jha, 1998; Martínez, Anllo-Vento, Sereno, Frank, Buxton, Dubowitz, Wong, Hinrichs, Heinze, & Hillyard, 1999).

Attention effects in V1 revealed

Although the preceding studies did not report attention effects in V1, such null findings may have occurred for a number of reasons that limited sensitivity, such as an insufficient number of trials or the employment of an insensitive analysis technique. As detailed above, Moran & Desimone (1985), based on single-cell monkey results, concluded that there were no attention effects in V1 as suggested by an attenuation index histogram centred at a value of one (Figure 3.2, middle). This is a reasonable conclusion, but it is possible that subtle V1 attention effects may have been missed and teasing out these effects might require a more sensitive analysis procedure. Providing some support for this possibility, inspection of Figure 3.2 (middle) shows a greater number of V1 cells with attention index values less than one than attention index values greater than one. If there were no V1 attention effects, the index values should have been symmetrically distributed about the value of one, which would have indicated that attention did not modulate the response in this region. However, a reanalysis of the data – conducted for this chapter and reported for the first time – showed that there were significantly more cells in the 0.57 to 0.80 attenuation index bins (ten cells) than in the 1.25 to 1.75 attenuation index bins (three cells; binomial test). It is notable that the bin widths were unequal, which may have biased the results; however, this is not of concern as a greater number of cells fell into the smaller bin (i.e., the results were in the opposite direction of what would be expected based on the relative bin sizes). This new finding indicates there were, in fact, V1 attention effects hidden in the results of the Moran & Desimone study. This finding directly contradicts two major conclusions of the original study: 1) that attention effects do not occur in V1, and 2) that attention effects require competing stimuli to be located within a cell's receptive field. The results of this reanalysis also underscore that when V1 attention effects are not observed a more sensitive analysis may be required to uncover such results.

In another monkey study, Motter (1993) recorded from cells in V1, V2, and V4 to measure attention effects. While maintaining fixation, one oriented bar was presented inside the receptive field of a cell (similar to Figure 3.2, top) and other oriented bars were presented outside of the receptive field at the same distance from fixation. On each trial, the stimulus configuration was constant and the monkey either attended to the bar within the receptive field of the cell or attended to a bar outside the receptive field. Attention effects were measured for each cell by comparing the response rate when attention was directed toward versus away from the bar within the cell's receptive field. Attention effects were observed in 39 percent of V2 cells and 45 percent of V4 cells. Critically, attention effects were also observed in 35 percent of V1 cells (Figure 3.6). In a subsequent monkey study, Roelfsema, Lamme, & Spekreijse (1998) also reported attention effects in V1.

In the late 1990s, fMRI studies began reporting attention effects in V1. Tootell, Hadjikhani, Hall, Marrett, Vanduffel, Vaughan, & Dale (1998) presented four flashing bars at the same distance from fixation (one in each quadrant of the visual field), and participants attended to one bar at a given time. The fMRI response was measured in early visual areas when attention was directed toward versus away from each bar. Contralateral attention effects were observed (similar to the previous PET results in Figure 3.5, middle), but with even greater spatial precision given that fMRI was used and the results were considered in reference to detailed retinotopic maps of V1 and extrastriate cortex. Attentional modulation was strongest in extrastriate regions V2 through V8, but they were also observed in V1 (Figure 3.7). Subsequent fMRI studies also reported retinotopically organized attention effects in V1 and extrastriate cortex (Brefczynski & DeYoe, 1999; Sasaki, Hadjikhani, Fischl, Liu, Marret, Dale, & Tootell, 2001; Slotnick, Schwarzbach, & Yantis, 2003).

Figure 3.6 *Monkey single-cell attention effects in V1. Response (spike rate, impulses per second, as a function of stimulus orientation) in four V1 cells when attention was directed toward the receptive field (black circles) or away from the receptive field (open circles).*

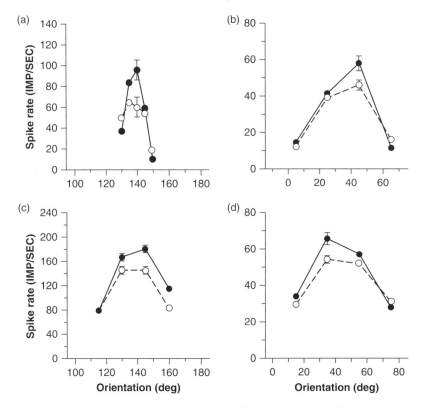

(Motter, 1993, Journal of Neurophysiology, 70, 909–919; reprinted with permission from The American Physiological Society.)

The findings described in this section indicate that attention effects occur in both extrastriate cortex and in V1. However, these findings are at odds with the commonly held view that V1 is not involved in conscious processing, as attention is intimately linked with consciousness.

V1 attention effects explained away

Likely driven by a desire to resolve the conflict between the general belief that V1 is not associated with conscious processing and the evidence of V1 attention effects, Steven Hillyard and colleagues hypothesized that V1 may be modulated by attention relatively

Figure 3.7 *fMRI attention effects in V1. Response (fMRI signal) in V1 and extrastriate cortical areas when attention was directed toward a stimulus or away from the stimulus (key at the bottom). Values greater than zero reflect attentional facilitation.*

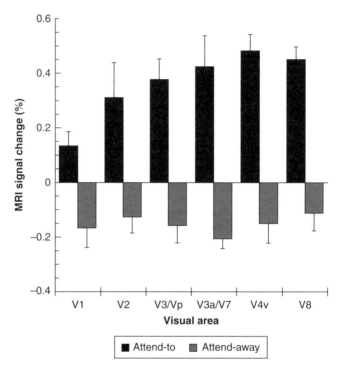

(Reprinted from Neuron, 21/6, Tootell et al., The retinotopy of visual spatial attention, Copyright 1998, with permission from Elsevier.)

late in time via feedback from extrastriate regions (Martínez et al., 1999). Martínez, DiRusso, Anllo-Vento, Sereno, Buxton, & Hillyard (2001) tested this hypothesis in an fMRI-ERP spatial attention study. While maintaining central fixation, participants attended to either the left visual field or the right visual field while checkerboard stimuli were flashed in one or the other hemifield. Attention effects corresponding to stimuli in each hemifield were measured by comparing activity with versus without attention. Consistent with previous findings, fMRI attention effects were observed in extrastriate cortex and V1, and corresponding ERP attention effects were observed in the extrastriate P1 and N1 components but not in the C1 component. Next, the investigators localized the cortical generators underlying the ERP C1 component that corresponded

Figure 3.8   *Late ERP source localization attention effects in V1. Left, activity of the V1 source (dipole 1) in addition to P1 and N1 sources (dipoles 2 through 7). Stimulus onset is marked by a short vertical line, activity with and without attention is shown in bold and thin lines, respectively, and times of interest are labeled (the time scale, in milliseconds, and key are at the bottom). Right, posterior view with corresponding dipole locations and orientations. Only left visual field responses are shown (the same pattern of results were observed with right visual field stimuli).*

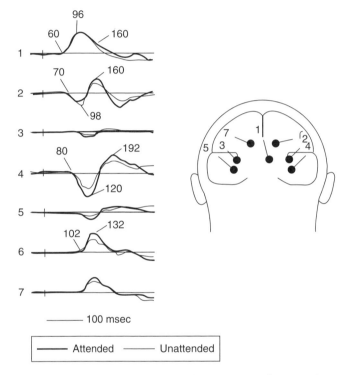

(Reprinted from Vision Research, 41/10–11, Martínez et al., Putting spatial attention on the map: Timing and localization of stimulus selection processes in striate and extrastriate visual areas, Copyright 2001, with permission from Elsevier.)

to the fMRI V1 activity, the P1 component that corresponded to fMRI extrastriate activity, and the N1 component. Each region of neural activity was localized based on the reasonable assumption that a circumscribed region of cortical activity can be represented by a dipole current source that has location, magnitude, and orientation. Such dipole activity is thought to reflect spatially separated positive and negative regions of active neurons (such as the cell bodies and axons) that are aligned perpendicular to the cortical surface (Nunez & Srinivasan, 2006). Their hypothesis was supported by the finding that attention did not modulate the magnitude of the V1 dipole source in the 60 to 100 milliseconds time interval that corresponded to the C1 component; however, a V1 attention effect was observed in the 152 to 184 milliseconds time interval (Figure 3.8; the top waveform corresponds to the V1 source).

This finding of relatively late attentional modulation of the C1 component was subsequently replicated in a number of studies (Noesselt, Hillyard, Woldorff, Schoenfeld, Hagner, Jäncke, Tempelmann, Hinrichs, & Heinze, 2002; Di Russo, Martínez, & Hillyard, 2003; Di Russo, Stella, Spitoni, Strappini, Sdoia, Galati, Hillyard, Spinelli, & Pitzalis, in press). Considered together, these results provided compelling evidence that attention can modulate V1, but that this modulation occurs relatively late in time due to feedback from extrastriate cortex, after the first wave of nonconscious processing in V1. This finding of relatively late V1 attentional modulation was appealing for multiple reasons. It resolved the seemingly inconsistent results from fMRI studies that indicated there was attentional modulation of V1 with earlier ERP studies that did not observe attentional modulation of the early C1 (V1) component. Moreover, these results fit with the view proposed by Crick & Koch that V1 was not centrally involved in conscious processing. That is, V1 could still be thought of as involved in rapid nonconscious processing, with modulation of this region occurring because it was recruited by higher-level regions relatively late in time. This constitutes the majority view today, and presumably is the primary reason why proponents of the majority view have almost completely stopped conducting research on this topic.

MINORITY VIEW

The story above, with all the loose ends tied up, has been satisfying for the large majority of those investigating the neural basis of attention. However, happy endings in cognitive neuroscience are often challenged by those who understand that brain operation is complex and doesn't follow simple rules (Chapter 9), or by those who happen to stumble upon the truth. Recently, there have been a handful of findings indicating that rapid attention effects can occur in V1. If such findings exist, they would contradict the popular notion that V1 modulation is strictly due to feedback from extrastriate regions and, more broadly, they would challenge the view that V1 is only involved in low-level nonconscious processing.

Kelly, Gomez-Ramirez, & Foxe (2008) hypothesized that previous ERP studies did not observe C1 attentional modulation because this component produces a less robust response and has a relatively high degree of variability in scalp location and polarity across participants that, if not considered, may have reduced sensitivity to C1 attention effects. In this study, before the attention session commenced, stimuli were presented to each participant at one of eight positions in the visual field at the same distance from fixation, and the pair of stimuli (one stimulus in the upper visual field and one stimulus in the diagonally opposite location in the lower visual field) that generated the highest C1 response within the 50 to 80 millisecond time range was employed for each participant. Moreover, again for each participant, the scalp location corresponding to these maximal C1 responses was also used in the attention session. In this way, both the optimal stimulus configuration and the optical scalp location were selected on an individual participant basis to maximize the C1 response. During the attention session, participants maintained central fixation and were cued to attend to one of two stimuli and detect targets that occurred on 30 percent of the trials. To further maximize sensitivity, as the C1 component is known to reverse in polarity depending on whether stimuli are in the upper visual field or the lower visual field, ERPs were generated by separately averaging all waveforms where the C1 component had either positive or negative polarity. Using these procedures, the C1 component was found to be strongly modulated by attention beginning 57 milliseconds after stimulus onset (Figure 3.9). As expected, the P1 component was also modulated by attention. These results support the hypothesis that previous failures to observe C1 attention effects may have been due to the relatively low signal strength and variability of this ERP component across participants.

Slotnick, Hopfinger, Klein, & Sutter (2002) reported ERP results that complemented the preceding findings in that rapid V1 effects were observed. While maintaining central fixation, each of 60 checkerboard stimuli rapidly and independently reversed in contrast (flickered) while participants attended to a small circle in the right visual field or the left visual field (Figure 3.10, left). The rapid

Figure 3.9   *Early ERP attention effects in V1. ERP activity (microvolts per millisecond) for stimuli in the upper visual field (light grey) and stimuli in the lower visual field (dark grey) when attended (solid lines) or unattended (dotted lines; key at the bottom). The C1 component is the initial peak that has negative and positive polarity corresponding to upper visual field stimuli and lower visual field stimuli, respectively.*

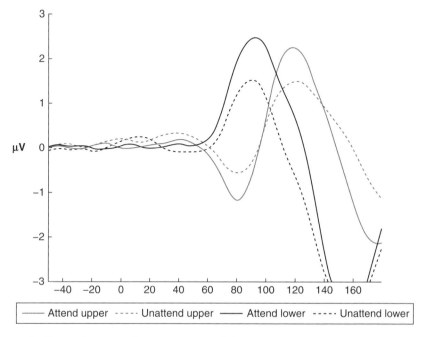

(Kelly et al., Spatial attention modulates initial afferent activity in human primary visual cortex, Cerebral Cortex, 2008, 18, 11, 2629–2636, by permission of Oxford University Press.)

flash ERP response to each stimulus reflected the C1 component, as indicated by the reverse in polarity as a function of stimulus position. For each stimulus location, the corresponding dipole magnitude with versus without attention served as a measure of attentional modulation. At the attended location, attentional modulation occurred in the 50 to 110 milliseconds epoch (Figure 3.10, left, region 1 is the stimulus with a black dot at the centre, and the corresponding attention effect is shown to the right). Of key importance, this effect did not change over time (i.e., the magnitude of attentional modulation did not differ between the 50 to 80 millisecond epoch and the 80 to 110 millisecond epoch). In addition, attention effects extended beyond the attended location to include the

Figure 3.10 *Early ERP source localization attention effects in V1. Left, illustration of 60 stimulus positions, each of which was simultaneously modulated with a flickering checkerboard. Participants fixated at the centre and attended to a small colour reversing dot in the right hemifield (illustrated in black) or the analogous position in the left hemifield (not shown). Right, V1 (C1 component) attentional modulation measured by the difference in dipole magnitude with or without attention corresponding to the stimulus at the attended location (region 1) or a set of stimuli around the attended location (region 2, bounded by the grey ellipse on the left).*

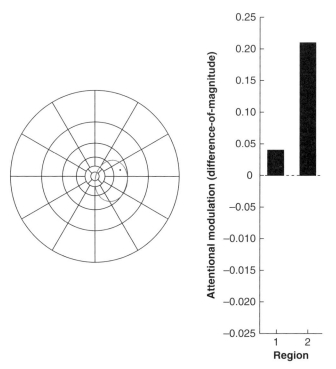

(Slotnick et al., 2002, Darkness beyond the light: Attentional inhibition surrounding the classic spotlight, NeuroReport, 13, 6, 773–778; reprinted with permission from Wolters Kluwer Health.)

fixation point (Figure 3.10, left, region 2 includes stimuli bounded by the grey ellipse, and the corresponding attention effect is shown to the right). These more spatially distributed attention effects did not occur in the 50 to 80 millisecond epoch, but rather came on line in the 80 to 110 millisecond epoch. These later attention effects may have reflected modulation of V1 via feedback from extrastriate cortical regions (although the timing of this effect is somewhat earlier than in the previously reported studies). It is also notable that the V1 modulation at the attended location was relatively small in magnitude as compared with the magnitude of the broader region of attentional facilitation (Figure 3.10, right; compare the magnitude of attentional modulation of region 1 to region 2). The broader region of attentional facilitation in V1 (corresponding to region 2) may reflect the relatively larger receptive field sizes in extrastriate cortex, which would be expected if this later modulation was due to a feedback mechanism.

Two other studies have reported attention effects in V1 that occurred early in time. Rauss, Pourtois, Vuilleumier, & Schwartz (2009) used an attentional load paradigm during ERP recording where the task at fixation was either easier (lower load) or harder (higher load). Considering that attentional resources are limited, during the low-load condition it can be assumed that a relatively greater degree of attention was allocated toward irrelevant peripheral stimuli. The C1 component, which reversed in polarity for upper visual field versus lower visual field stimuli, was found to be modulated by attention (although this modulation only occurred for stimuli presented in the upper visual field). McAdams & Reid (2005) conducted a single-cell monkey study where they correlated V1 cell firing rate with a *white-noise stimulus* made up of pixels that frequently changed luminance. V1 attention effects were observed as fast as 40 milliseconds after stimulus onset (although attentional modulation was not observed in firing rate).

It should be highlighted that none of the four previous studies that reported rapid attentional modulation in V1 used a standard spatial attention paradigm or analysis. This is not surprising, as earlier failures to observe rapid V1 attentional modulation suggest that these effects are relatively weak. As such, more sensitive experimental protocols and analysis techniques appear necessary to observe attentional modulation in V1. Of importance, rapid V1 attention effects are consistent with this region also being modulated later in time by feedback from extrastriate cortex. The complete body of evidence indicates that attentional modulation in V1 occurs earlier in time, without feedback from extrastriate cortex, and then additional attentional modulation of V1 occurs later in time via feedback from extrastriate cortex.

COUNTERPOINTS

As detailed above, the majority view of this controversy has gone through three phases. From the mid-1980s to the mid-1990s it was generally thought that there were no attention effects in V1, in the late 1990s there was compelling evidence indicating attention modulated V1, and from the early 2000s until today V1 modulation has been widely believed to occur relatively late in time. The most recent phase represents the current majority view in the field – attention effects occur in V1, but such modulation is due to feedback from higher-level extrastriate cortical regions. If the majority view is correct, the evidence supporting the minority view must be discounted in some way. Proponents of the majority view may simply ignore the findings that attention can rapidly modulate V1, given that such evidence has been observed only recently in a few studies. Proponents of the majority view may also acknowledge that rapid V1 attention effects might have been observed, but discount these findings because they have only been reported under non-standard stimulus and analysis conditions. This strategy of discounting minority view results was adopted in the mid-1990s after Motter (1993) reported the first attention effects in V1, but a growing body of evidence subsequently supported these findings and V1 attention effects became incorporated into the majority view.

It is, of course, the nature of majority views to persist, as they offer those in the field a framework to guide experiments and interpret results (Chapter 10). However, the majority view can stifle scientific progress if concrete evidence is ignored, or if the majority view has been largely accepted such that experiments that might challenge this view are not conducted. These negative consequences are currently in play with regard to the evidence that attention can rapidly modulate activity in V1. The four studies detailed above provide compelling evidence in support of the minority view, but this number of studies is limited and additional work must be conducted to replicate and extend these findings. Previously acquired ERP data from standard spatial attention studies could be reanalyzed, using procedures similar to that described by Kelly et al. (2008), to reduce between participant variability that may have washed out attention effects. Specifically, with any standard ERP data set, electrodes could be selected to maximize the C1 component magnitude and C1 component responses could be analyzed separately according to whether they had positive or negative polarity. Proponents of the majority view who want to maintain their viewpoint will not conduct such analyses, but those who are interested in determining whether or not attention can rapidly modulate activity in V1 will use these more sensitive techniques to assess whether there may be hidden V1 attention effects in their data.

As mentioned previously, the failure to observe rapid attention effects in V1, a core aspect of the majority view, is a null finding. There are numerous reasons that can explain a null finding, including an insufficient number of trials, a poor choice of stimulus, a task that is not sufficiently engaging, an insensitive analysis protocol, or large between participant variability. Any of these factors or, more likely, a combination of such factors may explain previous failures to observe rapid attention effects in V1. Critically, the evidence supporting the minority view has rejected this null hypothesis and illustrates that under certain stimulus and analysis conditions attention can rapidly modulate V1. These findings put the burden squarely on the proponents of the majority view, who must explain why their null findings have been rejected.

CONCLUSION

Proponents of the majority view believe that attentional modulation of V1 occurs relatively late in time due to feedback from extrastriate cortex. By contrast, evidence supporting the minority view indicates that attention can rapidly modulate V1 without feedback from extrastriate cortex. While there are only relatively few findings supporting the minority view, the corresponding empirical support is compelling and directly contradicts the majority view. It is expected that additional findings of rapid V1 attention effects will continue to be reported and that the majority view will again need revision.

SUGGESTED READINGS

Majority view

Heinze, H. J., Mangun, G. R., Burchert, W., Hinrichs, H., Scholz, M., Münte, T. F., Gös, A., Scherg, M., Johannes, S., Hundeshagen, H., Gazzaniga, M. S., & Hillyard, S. A. (1994). Combined spatial and temporal imaging of brain activity during visual selective attention in humans. *Nature, 372,* 543–546.

Di Russo, F., Martínez, A., & Hillyard, S. A. (2003). Source analysis of event-related cortical activity during visuo-spatial attention. *Cerebral Cortex, 13,* 486–499. Open access.

Minority view

McAdams, C. J., & Reid, R. C. (2005). Attention modulates the responses of simple cells in monkey primary visual cortex. *The Journal of Neuroscience, 25,* 11023–11033. Open access.

Kelly, S. P., Gomez-Ramirez, M., & Foxe, J. J. (2008). Spatial attention modulates initial afferent activity in human primary visual cortex. *Cerebral Cortex, 18,* 2629–2636. Open access.

REFERENCES

Brefczynski, J. A., & DeYoe, E. A. (1999). A physiological correlate of the 'spotlight' of visual attention. *Nature Neuroscience, 2,* 370–374.

Clark, V. P., & Hillyard, S. A. (1996). Spatial selective attention affects early extrastriate but not striate components of the visual evoked potential. *Journal of Cognitive Neuroscience, 8,* 387–402.

Clark, V. P., Fan, S., & Hillyard, S. A. (1994). Identification of early visual evoked potential generators by retinotopic and topographic analysis. *Human Brain Mapping, 2,* 170–187.

Crick, F., & Koch, C. (1995). Are we aware of neural activity in primary visual cortex? *Nature, 375,* 121–123.

Di Russo, F., Martínez, A., & Hillyard, S. A. (2003). Source analysis of event-related cortical activity during visuo-spatial attention. *Cerebral Cortex, 13,* 486–499.

Di Russo, F., Martínez, A., Sereno, M. I., Pitzalis, S., & Hillyard, S. A. (2002). Cortical sources of the early components of the visual evoked potential. *Human Brain Mapping, 15,* 95–111.

Di Russo, F., Stella, A., Spitoni, G., Strappini, F., Sdoia, S., Galati, G., Hillyard, S. A., Spinelli, D., & Pitzalis, S. (in press). Spatiotemporal brain mapping of spatial attention effects on pattern-reversal ERPs. *Human Brain Mapping.*

Gomez Gonzalez, C. M., Clark, V. P., Fan, S., Luck, S. J., & Hillyard, S. A. (1994). Sources of attention-sensitive visual event-related potentials. *Brain Topography, 7,* 41–51.

Heinze, H. J., Mangun, G. R., Burchert, W., Hinrichs, H., Scholz, M., Münte, T. F., Gös, A., Scherg, M., Johannes, S., Hundeshagen, H., Gazzaniga, M. S., & Hillyard, S. A. (1994). Combined spatial and temporal imaging of brain activity during visual selective attention in humans. *Nature, 372,* 543–546.

Horton, J. C., & Hoyt, W. F. (1991). Quadrantic visual field defects: A hallmark of lesions in extrastriate (V2/V3) cortex. *Brain, 114,* 1703–1718.

James, W. (1890). *The principles of psychology,* (Vol. 1). New York: Dover Publications, Inc.

Jeffreys, D. A., & Axford, J. G. (1972). Source locations of pattern-specific components of human visual evoked potentials. I. Component of striate cortical origin. *Experimental Brain Research, 16,* 1–21.

Kelly, S. P., Gomez-Ramirez, M., & Foxe, J. J. (2008). Spatial attention modulates initial afferent activity in human primary visual cortex. *Cerebral Cortex, 18,* 2629–2636.

Luck, S. J., Chelazzi, L., Hillyard, S. A., & Desimone, R. (1997). Neural mechanisms of spatial selective attention in areas V1, V2, and V4 of macaque visual cortex. *Journal of Neurophysiology, 77,* 24–42.

Mangun, G. R., Buonocore, M. H., Girelli, M., & Jha, A. P. (1998). ERP and fMRI measures of visual spatial selective attention. *Human Brain Mapping, 6,* 383–389.

Mangun, G. R., Hillyard, S. A., & Luck, S. J. (1993). Electrocortical substrates of visual selective attention. In D. E. Meyer & S. Kornblum (Eds.), *Attention and performance XIV, synergies in experimental psychology, artificial intelligence, and cognitive neuroscience* (pp. 219–243). Cambridge, MA: MIT Press.

Martínez, A., Anllo-Vento, L., Sereno, M. I., Frank, L. R., Buxton, R. B., Dubowitz, D. J., Wong, E. C., Hinrichs, H., Heinze, H. J., & Hillyard, S. A. (1999). Involvement of striate and extrastriate visual cortical areas in spatial attention. *Nature Neuroscience, 2,* 364–369.

Martínez, A., DiRusso, F., Anllo-Vento, L., Sereno, M. I., Buxton, R. B., & Hillyard, S. A. (2001). Putting spatial attention on the map: Timing and localization of stimulus selection processes in striate and extrastriate visual areas. *Vision Research, 41,* 1437–1457.

McAdams, C. J., & Reid, R. C. (2005). Attention modulates the responses of simple cells in monkey primary visual cortex. *The Journal of Neuroscience, 25*, 11023–11033.

Moran, J., & Desimone, R. (1985). Selective attention gates visual processing in the extrastriate cortex. *Science, 229*, 782–784.

Motter, B. C. (1993). Focal attention produces spatially selective processing in visual cortical areas V1, V2, and V4 in the presence of competing stimuli. *Journal of Neurophysiology, 70*, 909–919.

Noesselt, T., Hillyard, S. A., Woldorff, M. G., Schoenfeld, A., Hagner, T., Jäncke, L., Tempelmann, C., Hinrichs, H., & Heinze, H. J. (2002). Delayed striate cortical activation during spatial attention. *Neuron, 35*, 575–587.

Nunez, P. L., & Srinivasan, R. (2006). *Electric fields of the brain: The neurophysics of EEG* (2nd ed.). New York: Oxford University Press.

Rauss, K. S., Pourtois, G., Vuilleumier, P., & Schwartz, S. (2009). Attentional load modifies early activity in human primary visual cortex. *Human Brain Mapping, 30*, 1723–1733.

Roelfsema, P. R., Lamme, V. A., & Spekreijse, H. (1998). Object-based attention in the primary visual cortex of the macaque monkey. *Nature, 395*, 376–381.

Sasaki, Y., Hadjikhani, N., Fischl, B., Liu, A. K., Marrett, S., Dale, A. M., Tootell, R. B. (2001). Local and global attention are mapped retinotopically in human occipital cortex. Proceedings of the National Academy of Sciences of the United States of America, 98, 2077–2082.

Slotnick, S. D., Hopfinger, J. B., Klein, S. A., & Sutter, E. E. (2002). Darkness beyond the light: Attentional inhibition surrounding the classic spotlight. NeuroReport, 13, 773–778.

Slotnick, S. D., Schwarzbach, J., & Yantis, S. (2003). Attentional inhibition of visual processing in human striate and extrastriate cortex. *NeuroImage, 19*, 1602–1611.

Tong, F. (2003). Primary visual cortex and visual awareness. *Nature Reviews Neuroscience, 4*, 219–229.

Tootell, R. B. (2001). Local and global attention are mapped retinotopically in human occipital cortex. *Proceedings of the National Academy of Sciences of the United States of America, 98*, 2077–2082.

Tootell, R. B., Hadjikhani, N., Hall, E. K., Marrett, S., Vanduffel, W., Vaughan, J. T., & Dale, A. M. (1998). The retinotopy of visual spatial attention. *Neuron, 21*, 1409–1422.

4 Long-Term Memory and the Medial Temporal Lobe

Long-term memory refers to the retrieval of previously experienced information, but can also refer to the encoding of information or a stored representation. It is widely believed that retrieval from long-term memory relies on either the process of *recollection*, memory with specific detail, or *familiarity*, memory without any specific detail. To illustrate, if you were asked to recall where you had breakfast this morning, you might have a detailed memory that you ate while seated on your couch, which would reflect recollection, or you might be confident that you ate on the couch without retrieving any specific details, which would reflect familiarity. In the laboratory, *context memory* refers to memory for the context of a previously presented item and is assumed to reflect detailed recollection, while *item memory* refers to memory for the previously presented item itself and is assumed to be based on non-detailed familiarity.

There has been intense debate regarding two hypotheses of medial temporal lobe function that will be referred to as the *sub-region processing hypothesis* and the *system processing hypothesis*. The sub-region processing hypothesis, the majority view, assumes the medial temporal lobe sub-regions – the perirhinal cortex, the parahippocampal cortex, and the hippocampus – have separate functions during recollection and familiarity, where the perirhinal cortex mediates item processing, the parahippocampal cortex mediates context processing, and the hippocampus binds item

Figure 4.1   *Sub-region processing and system processing hypotheses of medial temporal lobe function. Left, the sub-region processing hypothesis specifies that the medial temporal lobe sub-regions – the perirhinal cortex (PRC), the parahippocampal cortex (PHC), and the hippocampus (HC) – have separate functions where the PRC processes item information, the PHC processes context information, and the HC binds item and context information (arrows illustrate the flow of information from the cortex to the medial temporal lobe sub-regions). This hypothesis predicts that the medial temporal lobe sub-regions will be differentially active during recollection and familiarity. Right, the system processing hypothesis specifies that the medial temporal lobe sub-regions operate together (indicated by the circular arrow) and predicts that each medial temporal lobe sub-region will be active to a similar degree during recollection and familiarity.*

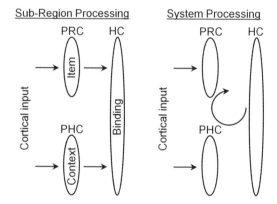

and context information (Figure 4.1, left; Diana, Yonelinas, & Ranganath, 2007; Ranganath, 2010). As such, this hypothesis predicts that medial temporal lobe sub-regions will be differentially active during context memory/recollection and item memory/familiarity.

By contrast, the system processing hypothesis, the minority view, assumes the medial temporal lobe sub-regions operate together (as a system) during both context memory/recollection and item memory/familiarity (Figure 4.1, right; Squire, Stark, & Clark, 2004; Squire, Wixted, & Clark, 2007). This hypothesis predicts that if a medial temporal lobe sub-region is active, the magnitude of activity within that sub-region should be the same or similar during context memory and item memory (although the magnitude of activity can vary across sub-regions). Distinguishing between these hypotheses

Figure 4.2   *MRI image of the medial temporal lobe.*
The left hippocampus body (HB) and the perirhinal cortex (PC, within the
parahippocampal gyrus) are outlined (partial coronal view). The
parahippocampal cortex (not shown) is located more posteriorly within
the parahippocampal gyrus.

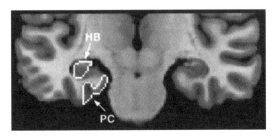

(Bernasconi et al., Mesial temporal damage in temporal lobe epilepsy:
A volumetric MRI study of the hippocampus, amygdala and
parahippocampal region, Brain, 2003, 126, Pt 2, 462–469, by
permission of Oxford University Press.)

fits within a central aim of cognitive neuroscience to identify the
functional role(s) of particular brain regions.

Evaluating these hypotheses depends on the specific anatomic
location of the relevant medial temporal lobe sub-regions.
Figure 4.2 shows the hippocampus in addition to the perirhinal
cortex within the parahippocampal gyrus (Bernasconi, Bernasconi,
Caramanos, Antel, Andermann, & Arnold, 2003). The hippocampus
runs in the anterior-posterior direction (into the page on the coronal view) and is flanked by the parahippocampal gyrus that also
runs in the anterior-posterior direction. The parahippocampal gyrus
contains the perirhinal cortex more anteriorly (toward the front
of the brain) and the parahippocampal cortex more posteriorly
(toward the back of the brain).

In an effort to increase the amount of relevant evidence in this
chapter, activity in the parahippocampal gyrus is assumed to reflect
activity in the parahippocampal cortex if the anterior-posterior spatial coordinate of parahippocampal gyrus activation falls within the
range of parahippocampal cortex activation coordinates reported
previously (Davachi, Mitchell, & Wagner, 2003; Woodruff, Johnson,
Uncapher, & Rugg, 2005; Ross & Slotnick, 2008; Yonelinas, Otten,
Shaw, & Rugg, 2005).

MAJORITY VIEW

Context memory-item memory activation evidence

Unless otherwise specified, all the evidence supporting the sub-region processing hypothesis has been obtained using fMRI. It should be mentioned that memory studies often employ very different stimuli and tasks, and that the term context is used very broadly to refer to an item's previous spatial location, its colour, or the task associated with an item during encoding. Of importance, despite the substantial differences in experimental protocols, memory findings have proven to be highly consistent across studies.

Cansino, Maquet, Dolan, & Rugg (2002) presented coloured objects in one of four quadrants during the encoding/study phase and participants classified each stimulus as artificial or natural (Figure 4.3). During the retrieval phase, old and new objects were presented at fixation and participants classified each item as old and previously in the "upper left," old and previously in the

Figure 4.3 *Stimulus protocol illustration. Left, example object. Top right, during the encoding/study phase, each object was presented in one quadrant. Bottom right, during the retrieval/test phase, objects were presented at fixation.*

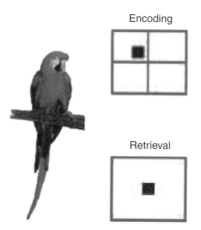

Encoding

Retrieval

(Cansino et al., Brain activity underlying encoding and retrieval of source memory, Cerebral Cortex, 2002, 12, 10, 1048–1056, by permission of Oxford University Press.)

"upper right," old and previously in the "lower left," old and previously in the "lower right," or "new." The comparison of accurate item memory and spatial location/context memory versus accurate item memory with inaccurate context memory (i.e., item memory alone) produced activity in the right hippocampus and the left parahippocampal cortex. This differential activation, produced by contrasting accurate item and context memory versus accurate item memory, supports the sub-region processing hypothesis of medial temporal lobe function. Note that studies in which the results could not be attributed to either recollection or familiarity were not considered in this chapter as such findings cannot be used to distinguish between the hypotheses of medial temporal lobe function. For instance, accurate item and context memory is often contrasted with completely forgotten items (i.e., responding "new" to a previously presented item), but activity associated with this contrast may be attributed to item memory, context memory, or both processes, making the interpretation of such results unclear. Davachi et al. (2003) investigated the role of medial temporal lobe sub-regions during memory encoding. During the study phase, words were presented and participants either generated a corresponding mental image or covertly (mentally, rather than aloud) read the word backwards. During the test phase, old and new words were presented and participants first classified each word as "old" or "new," and then "old" words were classified as previously in the "image" or "read" condition (based on memory for context). It should be highlighted that activity was measured during the study phase, before participants had produced responses during the test phase, such that study items were classified according to the subsequent response at test. For example, a particular item and its context at study may later be accurately remembered, and thus associated with subsequent accurate item and context memory. As will be illustrated repeatedly below, *subsequent memory* paradigms that measure memory activity during encoding have produced the same pattern of results as paradigms that measure memory activity during retrieval, thus encoding and retrieval results are considered together. Davachi et al. found that the left perirhinal cortex was associated with greater activity during subsequent accurate item memory than subsequent forgotten items (Figure 4.4, left panel). In addition, subsequent accurate item and context memory (context memory is synonymous with the term *source memory*) as

Figure 4.4   *Differential medial temporal lobe sub-region activity. Top, activity (percent signal change) in the labeled medial temporal lobe sub-regions associated with subsequent accurate item and context/source memory, subsequent accurate item memory only, and forgotten items (key to the right). Bottom, activity (in black) corresponding to the labeled regions directly above (coronal views).*

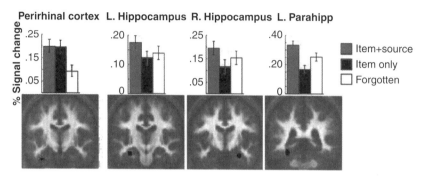

(Davachi et al.; Copyright (2003) National Academy of Sciences, U.S.A..)

compared with subsequent accurate item memory produced activity in the left and right hippocampus and the left parahippocampal cortex (Figure 4.4, middle and right panels).

Ranganath, Yonelinas, Cohen, Dy, Tom, & D'Esposito (2004) used words as stimuli and manipulated source by varying stimulus colour (and a corresponding task) at encoding. Subsequent accurate item and context memory versus subsequent accurate item memory produced activity in the right hippocampus and the right parahippocampal cortex. Weis, Specht, Klaver, Tendolkar, Willmes, Ruhlmann, Elger, & Fernández (2004) varied colour to manipulate the context of photos and observed that accurate item and context memory versus accurate item memory produced activity in the left hippocampus. Kensinger & Schacter (2006) used words and pictures as stimuli and varied context by manipulating the encoding task by asking participants to make an animate-inanimate judgment or a common-uncommon judgment. They found that subsequent accurate item and context memory versus subsequent accurate item memory was associated with activity in the left and right hippocampus and the right parahippocampal cortex. Ross & Slotnick (2008) presented abstract shapes in the left or right visual field during encoding, and found that accurate item and spatial location/context memory versus accurate item memory produced activity in the left and right hippocampus and the left parahippocampal cortex. Moreover, within the left perirhinal cortex there was a decrease in activity during accurate item memory as compared with forgotten items. Such item memory decreases in activation within perirhinal cortex during retrieval and item memory increases in activation within this region during encoding (Figure 4.4, left panel) have been consistently observed, although the reason behind this perirhinal polarity reversal is currently a mystery. Staresina & Davachi (2008) presented words with coloured backgrounds (context one) and manipulated task (context two), while Tendolkar, Arnold, Petersson, Weis, Brockhaus-Dumke, van Eijndhoven, Buitelaar, Fernández (2008) presented photos of landscapes with varied colour (context one) and shade (context two). In both studies, the left hippocampus produced a graded response during memorial encoding and retrieval, respectively, with the greatest magnitude of activity during accurate memory for two contexts, a lower magnitude of activity during accurate memory for one context, and the smallest magnitude of activity during accurate item memory. These findings of progressively increasing activity in the hippocampus with increasing amounts of information supports the view that this region binds information together, as a greater degree of binding would be required when more information is encoded or retrieved. Like Ross & Slotnick, Tendolkar et al. also reported that accurate item memory versus forgotten items produced a decrease in activity within the perirhinal cortex, which suggests that this region is involved in processing familiarity.

"Remember"-"know" activation evidence

The studies thus far have isolated the medial temporal lobe sub-regions associated with recollection by contrasting accurate item and context memory with accurate item memory and have isolated the sub-regions associated with familiarity by contrasting accurate item memory with forgotten items. This type of procedure can be described as *objective*, as it is based on behavioural accuracy. A *subjective* procedure has also been employed to investigate recollection and familiarity where, at test, a "remember" response corresponds to a memory associated with the subjective experience of specific detail while a "know" response corresponds to a memory that an item is familiar (i.e., associated with high confidence) but without any subjective experience of specific detail. The key distinction between "remember" and "know" responses is whether or not the participant has the subjective experience of detail. Even if a single detail is retrieved, participants are instructed to make a "remember" response. Of relevance, objective accuracy can be dissociated from subjective experience, as illustrated by accurate objective responses that are accompanied by the subjective experience of guessing.

Eldridge, Knowlton, Furmanski, Bookheimer, & Engle (2000) presented words in the study phase and then presented old and new words during the test phase. Participants first classified each item as "old" or "new," and then for "old" items made a "remember" or "know" response. The "remember" versus "know" contrast revealed activity in the left hippocampus and the right parahippocampal cortex. Woodruff et al. (2005) presented pictures or picture names during the study phase. During the test phase, old and new names were presented during the test phase and participants made a "remember," "know," or "new" response to each item. The "remember" greater than "know" contrast produced activity in the right hippocampus and the right parahippocampal cortex. Yonelinas et al. (2005) presented words at study and then presented old and new words at test. Participants made a "remember" response or, if an item was not associated with specific detail, made an old-new confidence judgment ranging from one to four (where one meant they were sure the item was "new" and four meant they were sure the item was "old"). The introduction of high confidence old responses in this study was an important aspect of the experimental design, as these items could be assumed to reflect familiarity based responses with relatively high memory strength (as compared with "know" responses that can reflect a broader range of memory strength), and thus were a more appropriate condition for comparison with high memory strength "remember" responses. The contrast between "remember" responses and the highest confidence familiarity responses produced activity in the left and right hippocampus and the left parahippocampal cortex. Montaldi, Spencer, Roberts, & Mayes (2006) used a similar procedure as in the previous study, where pictures of coloured scenes were shown during the study phase and old and new pictures were shown during the test phase. Participants made a "remember" response (which in this study was defined as memory for contextual detail that occurred without effortful retrieval), made a confidence judgment from one to three to convey very weak familiarity to strong familiarity, or responded "new." "Remember" responses versus the highest confidence familiarity responses produced activity in the left and right hippocampus. Consistent with previous findings, familiarity confidence rating increases (from one to three) were also associated with decreases in activity within the left and right perirhinal cortex.

The hippocampus, objective binding, and subjective experience

All the previous studies reported activity in the hippocampus by contrasting accurate item and context memory versus accurate item memory (to objectively isolate memory for context) or by contrasting "remember" responses versus "know"/high confidence familiarity responses (to isolate the subjective experience of memory for context). Objective memory for context, however, would be expected to correlate with the subjective experience of memory for context, as more accurate context memory responses should be associated with a higher rate of "remember" responses and less accurate context memory responses should be associated with a lower rate of "remember" responses. As such, the preceding evidence cannot be used to determine whether the hippocampus is associated with objective memory for context, the subjective experience of memory for context, or both aspects of memory. To distinguish between possibilities, Slotnick (2010a) conducted an experiment that employed both objective and subjective measures of item memory and context memory. During the study phase coloured or grey abstract shapes were presented (Figure 4.5, top). During the test phase old and new grey shapes were presented and participants classified each item as old and previously in "colour," old and previously in "grey," or "new," and then for "old" items made a "remember" or "know" response. Accurate item and context memory (item memory-hits and context memory-hits, HH) produced greater activity than accurate item memory (item memory-hits and context memory-misses, HM) in the left and right hippocampus (Figure 4.5, bottom left), and the hit-hit versus hit-miss difference in activity was greater than the "remember" (R) versus "know" (K) difference in activity (Figure 4.5, bottom right). In fact, "know" activity was greater than "remember" activity, in

Figure 4.5   *Evidence that the hippocampus mediates binding. Top, illustration of coloured or grey abstract shapes shown during the study phase (colour not shown). Bottom left, activity (in black) in the left hippocampus identified by contrasting accurate item and context memory (item memory-hits and context memory-hits, HH) versus accurate item memory (item memory-hits and context memory-misses, HM; coronal view). Bottom right, magnitude of activity associated with HH, HM, "remember" (R), and "know" (K) responses (percent signal change) in the hippocampal region to the left.*

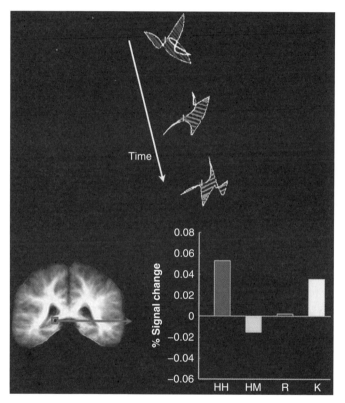

(Reprinted from NeuroImage, 49/2, Slotnick, 2010a, Does the hippocampus mediate objective binding or subjective remembering?, Copyright 2010, with permission from Elsevier.)

direct opposition to the pattern of activity predicted if the subjective experience of remembering was driving the response in the hippocampus. By comparison, the "remember" versus "know" contrast did not produce any activity in the hippocampus, but did produce activity in the left inferior parietal cortex. These results, along with previous findings, suggest that the hippocampus is associated with objective binding, while subjective aspects of memory depend on cortical regions outside of the medial temporal lobe such as the parietal cortex (Wheeler & Buckner, 2004; Montaldi et al., 2006) and the prefrontal cortex (Chua, Rand-Giovannetti, Schacter, Albert, & Sperling, 2004; Kao, Davis, & Gabrieli, 2005).

Lesion evidence

The results of the preceding fMRI studies provide compelling evidence that the hippocampus and parahippocampal cortex are associated with recollection, and that the perirhinal cortex is associated with familiarity. Further support for recollection based processing in the hippocampus has been provided by measuring behavioural performance in human patients with relatively selective damage to this region. Yonelinas, Kroll, Quamme, Lazzara, Sauvé, Widaman, & Knight (2002) evaluated 56 patients who had a brief episode of hypoxia (a lack of oxygen) that is thought to produce severe atrophy of the hippocampus but largely spare the parahippocampal gyrus. Memory for a list of words was tested using both recall, where participants produce as many words from a previously studied list as possible without any retrieval cues, and word recognition, where retrieval cues (old and new words) are provided. Patients were more impaired during the recall task than the recognition task (Figure 4.6, top). Given that recall is thought to rely on recollection to a greater degree than recognition, these results support the view that the hippocampus preferentially supports recollection. Yonelinas et al. conducted another experiment with four hypoxic patients with relatively selective damage to the hippocampus (H), five patients with relatively selective damage to the hippocampus and parahippocampal gyrus (H+), and control participants with no medial temporal lobe damage (C). Participants studied words and then at test were shown old and new words and made "remember," "familiar/know," or "new" responses. An estimate of recollection was computed as the proportion of old items that received "remember" responses minus the proportion of new items that received "remember" responses (which corrects for guessing). An estimate of familiarity was computed as the proportion of old items that were not remembered and received "know" responses minus the same estimate for new items (which corrects for guessing and assumes recollection and familiarity are independent processes). Compared with control participants, H+ patients had deficits in familiarity and recollection, but H patients only had a deficit in recollection (Figure 4.6, bottom). The results of these hypoxia patient experiments suggest that the hippocampus is specifically associated with recollection. However, it is tenuous to assume that recall taps into recollection to a greater degree than recognition. While it is reasonable to argue that recall (which does not involve retrieval cues) is relatively more difficult than recognition, difficulty does not necessarily correspond to the amount of details that are retrieved (for instance, detailed memories are often retrieved with little effort).

Figure 4.6 *Differential lesion results. Top, recall and recognition performance of hypoxia patients measured in z-scores (standard deviation units from control participant performance), with negative values of greater magnitude corresponding to more impaired performance. Bottom, familiarity and recollection estimates computed from "remember"-"know" responses for control participants (C), five patients with damage to the hippocampus and parahippocampal gyrus (H+), and four patients with damage to the hippocampus (H).*

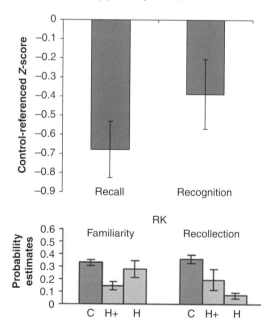

Furthermore, as discussed in more detail below, recognition may be associated with retrieval of detailed item or contextual information (recollection), thus recognition should not necessarily be assumed to rely on familiarity alone. As such, patient studies that only considered recall and recognition results were not considered.

Bowles, Crupi, Mirsattari, Pigott, Parrent, Pruessner, Yonelinas, & Köhler (2007) presented a case study of a patient with a left anterior temporal lobe lesion, due to surgical removal of a tumor in the amygdala that included the perirhinal cortex but spared the hippocampus and parahippocampal cortex. Memory for words was tested with a "remember"-"know" protocol. Estimates of recollection and familiarity indicated that this patient had a greater degree of recollection and a lower degree of familiarity than control participants.

The lesion evidence from both of the preceding studies suggests that the hippocampus (but not the perirhinal cortex) is necessary for the process of recollection and the perirhinal cortex (but not the hippocampus) is necessary for the process of familiarity. This double dissociation provides support for the sub-region processing hypothesis that complements the previous fMRI results.

MINORITY VIEW

There are those that believe the medial temporal lobe sub-regions are similarly engaged during recollection and familiarity. This position has been championed by Larry Squire. When considering the following findings, it is important to keep in mind that if a medial temporal lobe sub-region was similarly active during item memory and context memory, the contrast between these event types should not produce any differential activity in that sub-region. This line of research has focused on the role of the hippocampus, with the results taken to suggest that this region is similarly activated by recollection and familiarity. Gold, Smith, Bayley, Shrager, Brewer, Stark, Hopkins, & Squire (2006) conducted a subsequent memory fMRI experiment and a patient experiment. During the study phase of the fMRI experiment, words were each followed by a cue, "indoor" or "outdoor," and the participant imagined a corresponding scene associated with the word. During the test phase, old and new words were presented and participants classified each word as "old" or "new" and provided an item confidence rating ranging from one to three (where one meant "not sure," two meant "somewhat sure," and three meant "very sure"). For "old" words participants also classified the previous context ("indoor" or "outdoor") and provided a source confidence rating ranging from one to three. The contrast of subsequent accurate item and context memory versus subsequent accurate item memory did not produce any activity in the hippocampus, the parahippocampal cortex, or the perirhinal cortex. The contrast of subsequent accurate item memory with inaccurate source memory versus subsequent forgotten items did not produce any activity in the hippocampus either. However, the contrast of subsequent accurate item memory regardless of source accuracy versus subsequent forgotten items did produce activity in the left hippocampus and the right perirhinal cortex. Furthermore, subsequent accurate item and source memory and subsequent accurate item memory were associated with similar magnitudes of activity within each of these sub-regions (Figure 4.7, top). Of theoretical importance, this finding suggests that the hippocampus is involved during item memory/familiarity.

The second experiment included five amnesic patients: one following a cardiac arrest, two following drug overdose induced respiratory failure, one following kidney failure and toxic shock syndrome, and one with no known cause. Relatively selective hippocampal lesions were confirmed using MRI, with reductions in the hippocampal volume of both hemispheres ranging from 33 to 49 percent, which was more than three standard deviations smaller than the average volume of the control participants. The patients had little or no reduction in the volume of the parahippocampal gyrus, which was within two standard deviations from the average volume of the control participants. The patients with selective hippocampal lesions (H) and the first set of control participants (CON-1) studied 25 words three times. A second set of control participants (CON-2) studied 100 words one time to match the memory performance with the patients. Item memory performance was the hit rate (the probability of responding "old" to an old item) minus the false alarm rate (the probability of responding "old" to a new item, which corrected for guessing). Source memory performance was the probability of an accurate source response for items correctly classified as "old." Figure 4.7 (bottom) shows that the patients performed worse than the first control group and had similar performance levels as the second control

Figure 4.7 *Similar medial temporal lobe sub-region activity and lesion results. Top, medial temporal lobe activity (in black; coronal views) identified by the contrast subsequent accurate item memory regardless of source accuracy versus subsequent forgotten items and activation magnitudes associated with each event type (key to the right). Bottom, item memory (left) and source memory (right) behavioural performance (percent correct) for patients with damage primarily restricted to the hippocampus (H, initials adjacent to each square show individual patient performance), control participants using the same task (CON-1), and control participants using a more difficult task to match the level of patient performance (CON-2).*

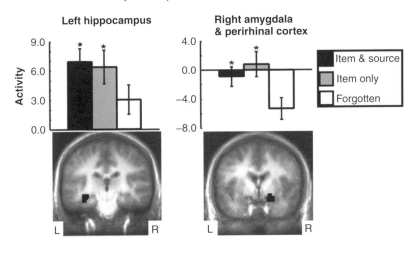

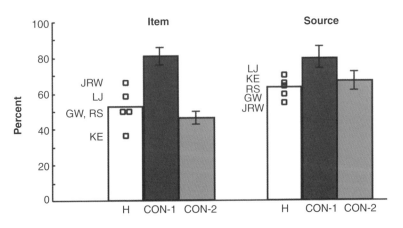

(Gold et al.; Copyright (2006) National Academy of Sciences, U.S.A.)

group during both the item memory task and the context memory task. These results suggest that the hippocampus is similarly involved during recollection and familiarity. Manns, Hopkins, Reed, Kitchener, & Squire (2003) investigated seven patients with relatively selective lesions to the hippocampus and sparing of the parahippocampal gyrus, including four of the five patients from the previous study. The patients had a similar impairment during recall as compared with recognition, although as mentioned previously it is uncertain whether these tasks should be assumed to reflect recollection and familiarity. Of greater importance, patient responses in a "remember"-"know" task were compared with the responses of two groups of control participants. One control group completed the same task as the patients and the other control group completed the test phase after a one week delay (to match memory performance with the patients). The patients had a similar degree of impairment in "remember" and "know" responses relative to control participant performance (Figure 4.8; if anything, for patients, "know" responses were relatively more impaired than "remember" responses). These findings failed to replicate the previously reported preferential deficit in recollection (Yonelinas et al., 2002), and suggest that that hippocampus is associated with both recollection and familiarity.

Song, Wixted, Hopkins, & Squire (2011) also reported impaired "remember" and "know" responses in the five patients with relatively selective hippocampal damage that participated in the Gold et al. (2006) study. The lesion evidence from the previous three studies support the view that the hippocampus is similarly involved in recollection and familiarity. To investigate why Yonelinas et al. (2002) might have previously observed greater impairment in recall as compared with recognition (Figure 4.6, top), Wixted & Squire (2004) reanalyzed the Yonelinas et al. data and found that the differential recall versus recollection results were due to inclusion of one aberrant recognition score of a control participant. When this score was removed from the analysis, patient recall performance and recognition performance were similarly impaired. This reanalysis indicates that the patient results of Yonelinas et al. were due to a control participant data outlier that should not have been included in the analysis, and had nothing to do with impaired patient performance.

Figure 4.8 *Similar hippocampal lesion results. Memory strength (d')
associated with "remember" and "know" responses for patients with
selective hippocampal lesions (H), control (CON) participants, and
control participants with an additional one week delay (1-WK CON;
key at the bottom).*

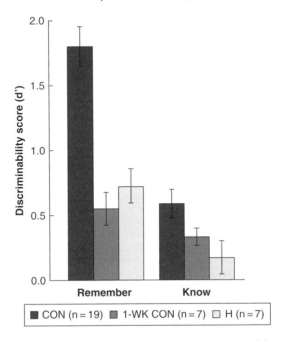

(Reprinted from Neuron, 37/1, Manns et al., Recognition memory
and the human hippocampus, Copyright 2003, with permission
from Elsevier.)

Kirwan, Wixted, & Squire (2008) conducted a subsequent memory fMRI study where words were presented during the study phase
and participants either made an animacy judgment (for green
words) or a size judgment (for red words). During the test phase, old
and new words were presented and participants made an item confidence rating ranging from one to six (where one meant "sure new,"
two meant "probably new," three meant "guess new," four meant
"guess old," five meant "probably old," and six meant "sure old")
and for words classified as "old" made a source confidence rating
ranging from one to six. Regions associated with subsequent accurate item memory were identified where activity linearly increased
with progressively higher item confidence ratings. Analysis was

Figure 4.9 *Item memory activity in the hippocampus and the perirhinal cortex. Subsequent item memory activity (in black) in the left hippocampus (L H), the right hippocampus (R H), and the right perirhinal cortex (R PRC; partial coronal view).*

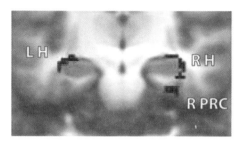

(Kirwan et al., 2008; The journal of neuroscience: the official journal of the Society for Neuroscience by SOCIETY FOR NEUROSCIENCE Copyright 2008. Reproduced with permission.)

restricted to items where source memory performance was at chance levels (i.e., source confidence "guess" ratings of three or four) to avoid a source memory strength confound. Kirwan et al. argued that the contrasts employed in previous studies did not adequately isolate these processes (which will be discussed in more detail below). The analysis revealed that activity in the left and right hippocampus and the right perirhinal cortex tracked subsequent item memory confidence ratings (Figure 4.9), suggesting that these regions were associated with item memory. A subsequent source memory analysis was conducted to identify activity that increased linearly with increasing source confidence ratings, with item memory ratings maintained at a confidence level of six to avoid an item memory strength confound. This analysis did not reveal any subsequent accurate context memory activity in the medial temporal lobe. However, activity in the prefrontal cortex tracked subsequent source memory confidence suggesting that this region, rather than the hippocampus, was involved in source memory.

COUNTERPOINTS

Table 4.1 illustrates the medial temporal lobe regions associated with recollection and familiarity that were identified using fMRI. Recollection was associated with the hippocampus in the large

Table 4.1 *fMRI activity associated with recollection and familiarity in the medial temporal lobe sub-regions (the hippocampus, HC, the perirhinal cortex, PRC, and the parahippocampal cortex, PHC)*

Study	Recollection			Familiarity		
	HC	PRC	PHC	HC	PRC	PHC
Cansino et al. (2002)	X		X			
Davachi et al. (2003)	X		X		X	
Ranganath et al. (2004)	X		X			
Weis et al. (2004)	X					
Kensinger & Schacter (2006)	X		X			
Ross & Slotnick (2008)	X		X		X	
Staresina & Davachi (2008)	X					
Tendolkar et al. (2008)	X				X	
Eldridge et al. (2000)	X		X			
Woodruff et al. (2005)	X		X			
Yonelinas et al. (2005)	X		X			
Montaldi et al. (2006)	X				X	
Slotnick (2010a)	X					
Gold et al. (2006)						
Kirwan et al. (2008)				X	X	

majority of studies, was associated with the parahippocampal cortex in approximately half of the studies, and was never associated with the perirhinal cortex. By contrast, familiarity was associated with the perirhinal cortex in a third of the studies, and was almost never associated with the hippocampus or the parahippocampal cortex.

The empirical evidence reported by proponents of the minority view has provided little support for the system processing hypothesis. Again, this hypothesis predicts that medial temporal lobe sub-regions will be similarly involved during recollection and familiarity. Kirwan et al. (2008) aimed to avoid a memory strength confound by keeping item memory or source memory confidence constant, based on the assumptions that accurate item memory and context memory reflect strong memory while accurate item memory alone reflects weak memory. Activity in the hippocampus and perirhinal cortex tracked item memory confidence, while no medial temporal lobe regions tracked source memory confidence. These distinct item memory and context memory results are at odds with the system processing hypothesis prediction of similar sub-region activation magnitudes. The fMRI evidence reported by Gold et al. (2006) also failed to support the system processing hypothesis as no medial temporal lobe sub-region activity was associated accurate item memory. Although the comparison between subsequent accurate item and context memory versus forgotten items did produce activity in the hippocampus and perirhinal cortex, this result can be discounted as this contrast confounds context memory and item memory (which is ironic because this is a major fault proponents of the minority view have found with the work of others). That the item memory contrast, which did not suffer from this confound, produced a null result indicates the procedures employed in this study had limited sensitivity.

While the fMRI evidence provides strong support for the sub-region processing hypothesis, patient results cannot convincingly distinguish between the system processing hypothesis and the sub-region processing hypothesis. The major problem with the patient data is that the lesions were almost all caused by an event that impacted the entire brain, such as a transient loss of oxygen due to cardiac arrest. If the brain outside of the medial temporal lobe is ignored, as it was by proponents of both the majority and minority views, the lesions might appear to selectively impact the hippocampus. However, the patient results reported could just as well have been caused by a lesion or lesions that occurred outside of this region. With this in mind, the patient results of Yonelinas et al. (2002), where recollection was impaired and familiarity was relatively spared (Figure 4.6), might have been due to a hippocampal lesion as was assumed, but could have been due to a prefrontal cortex lesion given that this region has been associated with memory confidence (Chua et al., 2004; Kao et al., 2005). The same reasoning can be used to question the patient evidence that has been taken to support the minority view. Furthermore, it is unclear whether a similar impairment in context memory and item memory in patients with selective hippocampal lesions actually supports the system processing hypothesis. Such a null finding may be due to any factor that limits sensitivity such as a relatively low number of trials, employment of a particular task, or the use of a particular analysis procedure. Of importance, null medial temporal lobe findings, whether based on lesion evidence or fMRI evidence, are not inconsistent with the sub-region processing hypothesis. By contrast, the differential medial temporal lobe evidence that has been consistently observed directly contradicts the system processing hypothesis. Thus, the empirical fMRI findings that have been taken to support the system processing hypothesis do not actually support this hypothesis, but are consistent with the sub-region processing hypothesis.

There are also theoretical reasons to question the system processing hypothesis. The memory strength explanation of differential medial temporal lobe results is a valid concern and should be taken seriously. However, there are a number of major problems with this explanation. First, contrary to the claim of minority view proponents, all the studies considered in this chapter that support the majority view did isolate item memory by maintaining context memory at chance levels, like Kirwan et al. (2008). Specifically, accurate item memory and inaccurate context memory was contrasted with inaccurate item memory and inaccurate context memory (forgotten items), such that source memory remained constant (i.e., inaccurate). Moreover, context memory was always isolated by comparing accurate item memory and accurate context memory versus accurate item memory and inaccurate context memory, such that item memory was maintained at a high level of performance, again like Kirwan et al. Thus, the critique that previous studies confounded item memory and context memory strength is not supported by the actual contrasts that were used. Second, the statement that context memory is stronger than item memory is not justified. The contrast of accurate item and context memory versus accurate item memory alone is employed to isolate the process of context memory, as item memory is subtracted out, thus context memory strength could be weaker than item memory strength. That is, while it is possible that context memory strength is greater than item memory strength under certain conditions, the opposite may also occur. It would seem prudent for future studies to include measures of context memory strength and item memory strength so that this factor can be taken into account when interpreting results. Third, proponents of the minority view often claim that item memory activity in the hippocampus can be taken as evidence against the sub-region processing hypothesis. However, item memory activity in the hippocampus is actually compatible with the sub-region processing hypothesis if the hippocampus serves a general binding function. From this perspective, the hippocampus can bind item and contextual information or this region can bind individual features that comprise an individual item, such as an item's colour and its shape. Such a general binding function deviates from an emphasis by proponents of the majority view on the role of the hippocampus in binding item and context information. However, of primary importance, this description still maintains that the hippocampus mediates binding of memorial information.

Although not directly related to the cognitive neuroscience debate, it is notable that neural evidence is often inappropriately taken to support a particular side of a separate debate in cognitive psychology. Specifically, most cognitive psychologists and cognitive neuroscientists believe recollection is a threshold process, where this process is engaged if memory strength is above a certain threshold and otherwise one has no memory and guesses. Others believe recollection is a continuous process, where there is no internal threshold and recollection reflects a range of memory strength from very weak to intermediate to very strong. Critically, brain evidence cannot distinguish between the threshold model and the continuous model of recollection, as recollection in both cases refers to detailed memories that are constructed by binding information. Thus, assuming the hippocampus mediates binding, both accounts predict that contrasting recollection and familiarity will activate this region. Although neural evidence cannot be used to distinguish between the threshold and continuous models of recollection, these models make district predictions with regard to behavioural performance. A growing body of behavioural evidence indicates recollection is a continuous process (Wixted, 2007). For instance, the shape of the receiver operating characteristic (ROC), a plot of the hit rate as a function of the false alarm rate (generated from confidence ratings), has provided some of the most compelling behavioural results. Specifically, the threshold recollection model predicts the ROC will be linear while the continuous recollection model predicts the ROC will be curved. Slotnick (2010b) found that ROCs generated from context memory-"remember" responses, which are based on recollection by any account, were curved (Figure 4.10), providing strong support for the continuous model of recollection. This related but separate debate is still playing out in cognitive psychology, and was touched on merely to emphasize that caution should

Figure 4.10   *Recollection based receiver operating characteristic (ROC) associated with context memory-"remember" responses.*

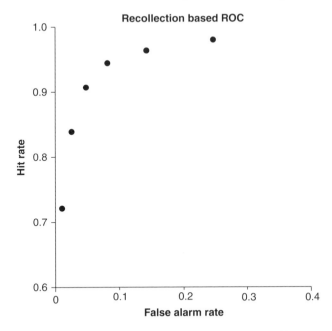

("Remember" source memory ROCs indicate recollection is a continuous process, Slotnick, Memory, 2010b, reprinted by permission of Taylor & Francis Ltd, http://www.tandf.co.uk/journals.)

be taken when it is claimed that neural evidence can distinguish between models of cognitive function.

CONCLUSION

The current body of evidence provides strong support for the sub-region processing hypothesis and directly contradicts the system processing hypothesis. Proponents of the minority view have made the valid argument that differential medial temporal lobe findings may be due to a strength confound; however, this argument does not account for the empirical results and it is not theoretically justified. It is anticipated that the strength confound argument will be discounted by future evidence, and that support for the sub-region processing hypothesis will continue to accumulate.

SUGGESTED READINGS

Majority view

Davachi, L., Mitchell, J. P., & Wagner, A. D. (2003). Multiple routes to memory: Distinct medial temporal lobe processes build item and source memories. *Proceedings of the National Academy of Sciences of the United States of America, 100,* 2157–2162. Open access.

Yonelinas, A. P., Otten, L. J., Shaw, K. N., & Rugg, M. D. (2005). Separating the brain regions involved in recollection and familiarity in recognition memory. *The Journal of Neuroscience, 25,* 3002–3008. Open access.

Minority view

Gold, J. J., Smith, C. N., Bayley, P. J., & Shrager, Y., Brewer, J. B., & Stark, C. E., Hopkins, R. O., & Squire, L. R. (2006). Item memory, source memory, and the medial temporal lobe: Concordant findings from fMRI and memory-impaired patients. *Proceedings of the National Academy of Sciences of the United States of America, 103,* 9351–9356. Open access.

Kirwan, C. B., Wixted, J. T., & Squire, L. R. (2008). Activity in the medial temporal lobe predicts memory strength, whereas activity in the prefrontal cortex predicts recollection. *The Journal of Neuroscience, 28,* 10541–10548. Open access.

REFERENCES

Bernasconi, N., Bernasconi, A., Caramanos, Z., Antel, S. B., Andermann, F., & Arnold, D. L. (2003). Mesial temporal damage in temporal lobe epilepsy: A volumetric MRI study of the hippocampus, amygdala and parahippocampal region. *Brain, 126,* 462–469.

Bowles, B., Crupi, C., Mirsattari, S. M., Pigott, S. E., Parrent, A. G., Pruessner, J. C., Yonelinas, A. P., & Köhler, S. (2007). Impaired familiarity with preserved recollection after anterior temporal-lobe resection that spares the hippocampus. *Proceedings of the National Academy of Sciences of the United States of America, 104,* 16382–16387.

Cansino, S., Maquet, P., Dolan, R. J., & Rugg, M. D. (2002). Brain activity underlying encoding and retrieval of source memory. *Cerebral Cortex, 12,* 1048–1056.

Chua, E. F., Rand-Giovannetti, E., Schacter, D. L., Albert, M. S., & Sperling, R. A. (2004). Dissociating confidence and accuracy: Functional magnetic resonance imaging shows origins of the subjective memory experience. *Journal of Cognitive Neuroscience, 16,* 1131–1142.

Davachi, L., Mitchell, J. P., & Wagner, A. D. (2003). Multiple routes to memory: Distinct medial temporal lobe processes build item and source memories. *Proceedings of the National Academy of Sciences of the United States of America, 100,* 2157–2162.

Diana, R. A., Yonelinas, A. P., & Ranganath, C. (2007). Imaging recollection and familiarity in the medial temporal lobe: A three-component model. *Trends in Cognitive Sciences, 11,* 379–386.

Eldridge, L. L., Knowlton, B. J., Furmanski, C. S., Bookheimer, S. Y., & Engel, S. A. (2000). Remembering episodes: A selective role for the hippocampus during retrieval. *Nature Neuroscience, 3,* 1149–1152.

Gold, J. J., Smith, C. N., Bayley, P. J., Shrager, Y., Brewer, J. B., Stark, C. E., Hopkins, R. O., & Squire, L. R. (2006). Item memory, source memory, and the medial temporal lobe: Concordant findings from fMRI and memory-impaired patients. *Proceedings of the National Academy of Sciences of the United States of America, 103,* 9351–9356.

Kao, Y. C., Davis, E. S., & Gabrieli, J. D. (2005). Neural correlates of actual and predicted memory formation. *Nature Neuroscience, 8,* 1776–1783.

Kensinger, E. A., & Schacter, D. L. (2006). Amygdala activity is associated with the successful encoding of item, but not source, information for positive and negative stimuli. *The Journal of Neuroscience, 26,* 2564–2570.

Kirwan, C. B., Wixted, J. T., & Squire, L. R. (2008). Activity in the medial temporal lobe predicts memory strength, whereas activity in the prefrontal cortex predicts recollection. *The Journal of Neuroscience, 28,* 10541–10548.

Manns, J. R., Hopkins, R. O., Reed, J. M., Kitchener, E. G., & Squire, L. R. (2003). Recognition memory and the human hippocampus. *Neuron, 37,* 171–180.

Montaldi, D., Spencer, T. J., Roberts, N., & Mayes, A. R. (2006). The neural system that mediates familiarity memory. *Hippocampus*, *16*, 504–520.

Ranganath, C. (2010). A unified framework for the functional organization of the medial temporal lobes and the phenomenology of episodic memory. *Hippocampus*, *20*, 1263–1290.

Ranganath, C., Yonelinas, A. P., Cohen, M. X., Dy, C. J., Tom, S. M, & D'Esposito, M. (2004). Dissociable correlates of recollection and familiarity within the medial temporal lobes. *Neuropsychologia*, *42*, 2–13.

Ross, R. S., & Slotnick, S. D. (2008). The hippocampus is preferentially associated with memory for spatial context. *Journal of Cognitive Neuroscience*, 20, 432–446.

Slotnick, S. D. (2010a). Does the hippocampus mediate objective binding or subjective remembering? *NeuroImage*, *49*, 1769–1776.

Slotnick, S. D. (2010b). "Remember" source memory ROCs indicate recollection is a continuous process. *Memory*, *18*, 27–39.

Song, Z., Wixted, J. T., Hopkins, R. O., & Squire, L. R. (2011). Impaired capacity for familiarity after hippocampal damage. *Proceedings of the National Academy of Sciences of the United States of America*, *108*, 9655–9660.

Squire, L. R., Stark, C. E., & Clark, R. E. (2004). The medial temporal lobe. *Annual Review of Neuroscience*, *27*, 279–306.

Squire, L. R., Wixted, J. T., & Clark, R. E. (2007). Recognition memory and the medial temporal lobe: A new perspective. *Nature Reviews Neuroscience*, *8*, 872–883.

Staresina, B. P., & Davachi, L. (2008). Selective and shared contributions of the hippocampus and perirhinal cortex to episodic item and associative encoding. *Journal of Cognitive Neuroscience*, *20*, 1478–89.

Tendolkar, I., Arnold, J., Petersson, K. M., Weis, S., Brockhaus-Dumke, A., van Eijndhoven, P., Buitelaar, J., & Fernández, G. (2008). Contributions of the medial temporal lobe to declarative memory retrieval: Manipulating the amount of contextual retrieval. *Learning & Memory*, *15*, 611–617.

Weis, S., Specht, K., Klaver, P., Tendolkar, I., Willmes, K., Ruhlmann, J., Elger, C. E., & Fernández, G. (2004). Process dissociation between contextual retrieval and item recognition. *NeuroReport*, *15*, 2729–2733.

Wheeler, M. E., & Buckner, R. L. (2004). Functional-anatomic corre-lates of remembering and knowing. *NeuroImage, 21,* 1337–1349.

Wixted, J. T. (2007). Dual-process theory and signal-detection theory of recognition memory. *Psychological Review, 114,* 152–176.

Wixted, J. T., & Squire, L. R. (2004). Recall and recognition are equally impaired in patients with selective hippocampal damage. *Cognitive, Affective, & Behavioral Neuroscience, 4,* 58–66.

Woodruff, C. C., Johnson, J. D., Uncapher, M. R., & Rugg, M. D. (2005). Content-specificity of the neural correlates of recollec-tion. *Neuropsychologia, 43,* 1022–1032.

Yonelinas, A. P., Kroll, N. E., Quamme, J. R., Lazzara, M. M., Sauvé, M. J., Widaman, K. F., & Knight, R. T. (2002). Effects of extensive temporal lobe damage or mild hypoxia on recollection and familiarity. *Nature Neuroscience, 5,* 1236–1241.

Yonelinas, A. P., Otten, L. J., Shaw, K. N., & Rugg, M. D. (2005). Separating the brain regions involved in recollection and famil-iarity in recognition memory. *The Journal of Neuroscience, 25,* 3002–3008.

5 Working Memory Segregation in the Frontal Cortex

Working memory refers to the active maintenance of information in the mind. For example, working memory is engaged when someone tells you their phone number and you mentally repeat it while searching for a piece of paper and a pen. Working memory is thought to be engaged during many other types of cognitive processes including attention (Chapter 3), long-term memory (Chapter 4), language (Chapter 6), and imagery (Chapter 7).

Visual working memory, the topic of this chapter, is thought by proponents of the majority view to mirror the what-where perceptual segregation in occipital-temporal and occipital-parietal cortex, respectively (Chapter 1), with these separate processing streams extending into the prefrontal cortex. Specifically, it has been hypothesized that the superior frontal sulcus within the dorsal prefrontal cortex is associated with working memory for spatial location, while the middle frontal gyrus and the inferior frontal cortex (which consists of the inferior frontal sulcus and the inferior frontal gyrus) within the ventral prefrontal cortex are associated with working memory for object identity (Figure 5.1). While this hypothesis has gained empirical support, it has been challenged by proponents of the minority view. This debate is of relevance to a broader issue in cognitive neuroscience regarding whether or not the prefrontal cortex – a region thought to mediate high-level control processing rather than low-level sensory processing – has some degree of sensory organization. If this is found to be the case, it would suggest that the prefrontal cortex is directly involved in sensory processing (in addition to mediating control processing).

Figure 5.1   *Prefrontal cortex regions of interest. Proponents of the majority view have hypothesized that spatial working memory is mediated by the superior frontal sulcus (SFS, which intersects the precentral sulcus, PCS) within the dorsal prefrontal cortex and that object working memory is mediated by the middle frontal gyrus (MFG) and the inferior frontal cortex (IFC, which consists of the inferior frontal sulcus and the inferior frontal gyrus) within the ventral prefrontal cortex (white ovals bound each region of interest; superior-lateral view, occipital pole to the right). Proponents of the minority view do not believe a spatial working memory-object working memory anatomic segregation exists in the prefrontal cortex.*

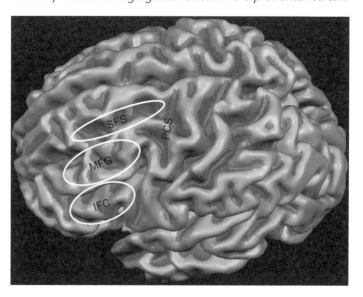

MAJORITY VIEW

Monkey evidence

Wilson, Scalaidhe, & Goldman-Rakic (1993) measured single-cell activity from monkey ventral prefrontal cortex and dorsal prefrontal cortex to assess whether these regions separately process object working memory and spatial working memory. During each object working memory trial, a visual pattern cue was briefly presented in the centre of the screen followed by a 2.5-second delay period. The monkeys then made a left or a right eye movement to indicate which pattern had been presented, based on a previously learned association between each pattern and the corresponding direction of eye movement. During each spatial working memory trial, a non-pattern stimulus was presented to the left or right of fixation followed by a 2.5-second delay period, and then the monkey made a left or right eye movement toward the spatial location of the previously presented stimulus. The results are illustrated by an individual neuron response in the ventral prefrontal cortex that was preferentially active during object working memory (Figure 5.2, top four panels) and an individual neuron response in the dorsal prefrontal cortex that was preferentially active during spatial working memory (particularly during spatial working

Figure 5.2 *Differential dorsal-ventral prefrontal cortex monkey single-cell results. Pattern/object working memory and spatial working memory (labeled at the centre) trials consisted of a cue period (C), a delay period, and a response (resp.) period with a left or right eye movement (labeled at the top). Activity (spikes per second as a function of time after cue offset) is shown from one neuron in the ventral prefrontal cortex (top four panels) and one neuron in the dorsal prefrontal cortex (bottom four panels).*

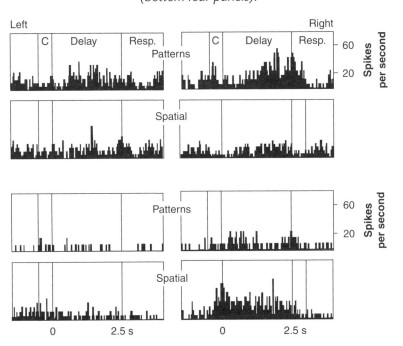

(From Wilson et al., 1993, Dissociation of object and spatial processing domains in primate prefrontal cortex, Science, 260, 1955–1958. Reprinted with permission from AAAS.)

memory of right visual field stimuli; Figure 5.2, bottom four panels). Across all 31 ventral prefrontal cortex neurons, 77 percent responded selectively during the object working memory delay period, 19 percent responded during both the object working memory delay period and the spatial working memory delay period, and 3 percent responded selectively during the spatial working memory delay period. The sustained prefrontal cortex activity during both object working memory and spatial working memory delay periods (Figure 5.2) suggests that a high rate of continuous neuronal firing is involved in maintaining the contents of working memory throughout this extended time period. It could be argued that working memory activity during the delay period reflected the preparation of the associated eye movement. However, eye movement preparation is mediated by the dorsal prefrontal cortex while object working memory was primarily associated with activity in the ventral prefrontal cortex, thus ruling out this potential confound.

These results suggest that the ventral prefrontal cortex mediates object working memory and the dorsal prefrontal cortex mediates spatial working memory. Levy & Goldman-Rakic (1999) bolstered the previous findings with evidence that lesions to monkey dorsal prefrontal cortex impaired spatial working memory performance but did not impair object working memory performance.

Human activation evidence

Human evidence has provided the majority of the support that the dorsal prefrontal cortex mediates spatial working memory and the ventral prefrontal cortex mediates object working memory. Courtney, Petit, Maisog, Ungerleider, & Haxby (1998) employed a working memory protocol where three faces were presented at different locations. Based on instructions, participants either maintained the face locations during the nine-second delay period (which required spatial working memory) or maintained the face identities during the delay period (which required object working memory), and then responded based on whether a test face matched the previously presented locations or faces (Figure 5.3, top right). Such a *match-nonmatch* task was used in all the subsequent working memory studies, unless otherwise specified. During control trials, scrambled faces were presented and participants were instructed not to maintain these stimuli in working memory during the delay period (Figure 5.3, top left). Note that if participants had engaged working memory in the control condition to a similar degree as the primary conditions, no working memory delay versus control delay activity would have been observed as it would have been subtracted out (Chapter 1); such activity was observed, which indicates that participants were able to follow instructions. Figure 5.3 (bottom) shows spatial working memory delay versus control delay activity (in white) and face/object working memory delay versus control delay activity (in dark grey) for a representative participant. Spatial working memory and object working memory activated both dorsal prefrontal cortex and ventral prefrontal cortex, to some degree, illustrating that each type of working memory is not strictly segregated to the dorsal prefrontal cortex or the ventral prefrontal cortex.

Of primary importance, across all participants, spatial working memory produced a greater magnitude and extent of activity in the left and right superior frontal sulcus, while object working memory produced a greater magnitude and extent of activity in the left inferior frontal cortex and a greater spatial extent (but not magnitude) of activity in the left middle frontal gyrus/cortex. Similar results were reported by Rowe & Passingham (2001), who reported that dot location/spatial working memory (with an 8.5- to 17.5-second delay period) produced activity in the left and right superior frontal sulcus, and Courtney, Ungerleider, Keil, & Haxby (1997) observed that face/object working memory (with an eight-second delay period) produced activity in the left and right middle frontal gyrus and the left and right inferior frontal gyrus.

Figure 5.3   (overleaf) *Differential dorsal-ventral prefrontal cortex activity. Top left, during the control condition three scrambled faces were each presented for two seconds at different locations, followed by a delay period (with no working memory task), and then participants made a response. Top right, the working memory tasks used the same stimulus protocol, except with intact faces. Participants either maintained the face spatial locations or face identities in working memory during the delay period. Bottom, spatial working memory activity and face/object working memory activity of one participant with regions of interest labeled (axial images, occipital pole at the bottom of each full image; key at the bottom).*

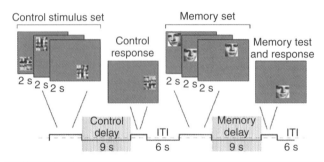

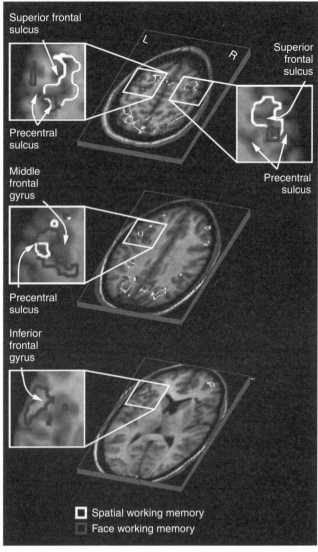

(From Courtney et al., 1998, An area specialized for spatial working memory in human frontal cortex, Science, 279, 1347–1351. Reprinted with permission from AAAS.)

Figure 5.4   *Illustration of an object working memory trial. Each trial consisted of an instruction cue, a three-second delay period (with a fixation cross), a three-second sample/encoding period, a nine-second delay period, a three-second test period, and a three-second inter-trial-interval (ITI).*

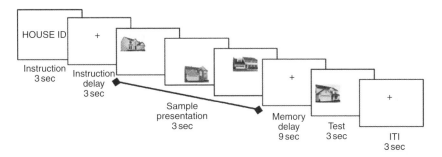

(Reprinted from Neuropsychologia, 41/3, Sala et al., Functional topography of a distributed neural system for spatial and nonspatial information maintenance in working memory, Copyright 2003, with permission from Elsevier.)

Courtney et al. (1998) also found that the location of spatial working memory activity within the superior frontal sulcus was on average seven millimetres anterior to the location of eye movement activity, which was located at the junction of the precentral sulcus and the superior frontal sulcus (see Figure 5.1 and Figure 5.3, bottom, partial image at the top left). This finding suggests that distinct regions of the dorsal prefrontal cortex mediate spatial working memory and eye movements.

Prefrontal working memory effects have also been investigated with other types of stimuli and tasks. Sala, Rämä, & Courtney (2003) presented an instruction cue followed by three faces or houses in one of 24 locations that were followed by a working memory delay period of nine seconds (Figure 5.4). On a given working memory trial, the instruction cue dictated whether house identity, face identity, spatial location, or nothing was to be maintained during the delay period. Across trials with faces or houses (experiment one) or for trials with houses alone (experiment two), spatial working memory produced greater activity than object working memory in the left and right superior frontal sulcus, while object working memory produced greater activity than spatial working memory in the left and right inferior frontal gyrus and the middle frontal gyrus. Sala &

Figure 5.5   *Illustration of a colour/angle working memory trial. Each trial consisted of an instruction cue (C for colour or R for rotation/angle), two coloured half-circles at encoding (colour is not shown), a 7.5-second working memory delay period, a test stimulus at retrieval, and a fixation period.*

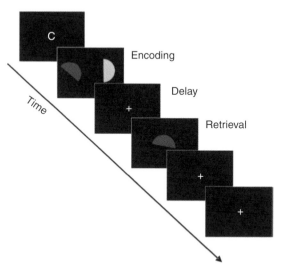

(Mohr et al., 2006; The journal of neuroscience: the official journal of the Society for Neuroscience by SOCIETY FOR NEUROSCIENCE Copyright 2006. Reproduced with permission.)

Courtney (2007) used a similar protocol with abstract patterns as stimuli and found that spatial working memory versus object working memory produced activity in the left and right superior frontal sulcus, while object working memory versus spatial working memory produced activity in the left middle frontal gyrus and the left inferior frontal gyrus. Landau, Garavan, Schumacher, & D'Esposito (2007) employed abstract shapes (irregular polygons) as stimuli in a similar paradigm, and found that object working memory versus spatial working memory produced activity in the left inferior frontal gyrus (no activity was observed in the dorsal prefrontal cortex or the ventral prefrontal cortex for the opposite contrast).

Mohr, Goebel, & Linden (2006) used a novel type of working memory stimulus, where either the colour of two half-circles (corresponding to object working memory) or the angle between the straight edges of the two half-circles (corresponding to spatial working memory) was maintained during the delay (Figure 5.5). Angle working memory versus colour working memory produced activity in the left and right superior frontal sulcus in addition to the right inferior frontal gyrus, while colour working memory versus angle working memory produced activity in the left inferior frontal sulcus. It is notable that this is the first instance when spatial working memory has been associated with activity in the ventral prefrontal cortex. However, as will be discussed in more detail below, working memory for certain stimulus types may tap into both spatial working memory and object working memory, which could explain the somewhat mixed pattern of activity observed in this study. Jackson, Morgan, Shapiro, Mohr, & Linden (2011) used the same experimental protocol as in the previous study, except for a shorter working memory delay period of two seconds, and reported that angle working memory versus colour working memory only produced activity in the left and right superior frontal sulcus, while colour working memory versus angle working memory produced activity in the left inferior frontal gyrus. Of importance, angle working memory activated the left and right superior frontal sulcus in both of the preceding studies, which suggests that activity in this region was relatively more robust as compared with the inferior frontal gyrus activity reported by Mohr et al. (2006).

The preceding fMRI findings provide compelling support for the majority view. Specifically, spatial working memory was found to consistently produce activity in the superior frontal sulcus within the dorsal prefrontal cortex, and object working memory was found to consistently produce activity in the inferior frontal cortex within the ventral prefrontal cortex.

Human TMS evidence

Mottaghy, Gangitano, Sparing, Krause, & Pascual-Leone (2002) assessed whether different regions of the prefrontal cortex are necessary for spatial working memory and object working memory. TMS was applied at 1 pulse per second (1 Hertz) for ten minutes to the left superior frontal sulcus region, the left middle frontal gyrus region, or the left inferior frontal gyrus region. This standard TMS protocol disrupts processing in the targeted cortical region for at least five minutes. The target regions were confirmed using MRI in five of the eight participants. Consistent with the previous fMRI findings, TMS to the left superior frontal sulcus region temporarily impaired

Figure 5.6 *Differential TMS results. Spatial working memory performance (percent correct; left panels) and face/object working memory performance (middle panels) with no TMS (base), immediately after TMS (post 1), five minutes after TMS (post 2), and ten minutes after TMS (post 3). Behavioural results are separated into rows by the site of TMS application (right), the left superior frontal sulcus region (labeled DM, dorsomedial), the left middle frontal gyrus region (labeled DL, dorsolateral), and the left inferior frontal gyrus region (labeled V, ventral). Asterisks mark impaired performance. The nasion (N), tragus (T), and primary motor cortex (M), anatomic landmarks, are also labeled.*

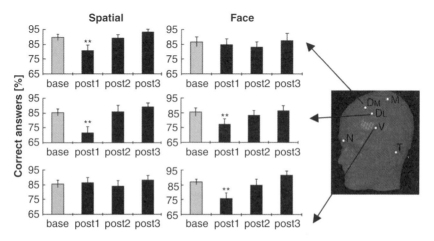

(Mottaghy et al., Segregation of areas related to visual working memory in the prefrontal cortex revealed by rTMS, Cerebral Cortex, 2002, 12, 4, 369–375, by permission of Oxford University Press.)

spatial working memory but not face/object working memory performance (Figure 5.6, top panels), and TMS to the left inferior frontal gyrus region temporarily impaired object working memory but not spatial working memory performance (Figure 5.6, bottom panels). TMS to the left middle frontal gyrus region impaired both spatial working and object working memory (Figure 5.6, middle panels), but this finding is difficult to interpret as it could reflect that this region mediates both types of working memory or it could reflect incidental stimulation of the superior frontal sulcus region due to the limited spatial resolution of TMS.

These differential TMS findings are of particular relevance as they complement the previous fMRI findings in that the dorsal prefrontal cortex was found to be necessary for spatial working memory and the ventral prefrontal cortex was found to be necessary for object working memory.

MINORITY VIEW

Some investigators have failed to report evidence that spatial working memory and object working memory are associated with the dorsal prefrontal cortex and the ventral prefrontal cortex, respectively. Bradley Postle has been the primary proponent of this view. It should be mentioned that only studies that isolated spatial working memory or object working memory, which are of relevance to distinguishing between the hypotheses under investigation, were considered in this section.

Postle, Berger, Taich, & D'Esposito (2000a) assessed whether spatial working memory activity is anterior to eye movement activity, as claimed by Courtney et al. (1998). Of importance, the one-dimensional (horizontal) eye movement task employed by Courtney et al. was distinct from the two-dimensional (horizontal and vertical) stimulus locations used in their spatial working memory task. Postle et al. correctly argued that a two-dimensional eye movement task would be more appropriate for comparison with a two-dimensional spatial working memory task. The following conditions were employed in the Postle et al. study: one-dimensional eye movements (free saccades), two-dimensional eye movements (guided saccades), maintenance of a spatial-temporal sequence in working memory, and working memory manipulation (Figure 5.7, top). The manipulation condition will not be discussed as it is not relevant to the present debate. Replicating Courtney et al., spatial working memory versus one-dimensional eye movements (free saccades) produced activity in the superior frontal sulcus in four of the five participants (Figure 5.7, bottom left; the black dots within the white shaded regions). However, spatial working memory versus two-dimensional eye movements (guided saccades) did not produce activity in the superior frontal sulcus in any of the participants (Figure 5.7, bottom right).

This latter null finding suggests that the superior frontal sulcus is not specialized for spatial working memory but is rather associated with both spatial working memory and two-dimensional eye movements.

Figure 5.7 *Null working memory versus eye movement results. Top, on each trial, participants made one-dimensional eye movements (free saccades; the corresponding stimulus display is not shown), two-dimensional eye movements (guided saccades) toward each of the six spatial cues that sequentially turned black (indicated by arrows, and followed by the instruction fixate), encoded the spatial-temporal cue order and maintained this information during the delay period (indicated by the instruction forward), or encoded the spatial-temporal cue order and*

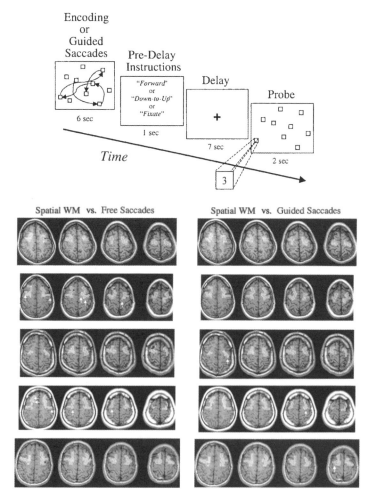

(Postle et al., Activity in human frontal cortex associated with spatial working memory and saccadic behavior, 2000a, 12, Supplement 2, Journal of Cognitive Neuroscience, 2–14; Reprinted by permission of MIT Press Journals; Copyright 2000.)

Figure 5.7   *(Continued) manipulated the contents of working memory according to the instruction (e.g., down-to-up). Working memory delay periods were followed by a probe to assess whether that number corresponded to that location's order in the working memory sequence. Bottom left, activity (black dots) within the superior frontal sulcus (shaded white) associated with spatial working memory (WM) versus one-dimensional eye movements (free saccades) in five participants (one participant per row; axial views, more superior to the right, occipital pole at the bottom of each image). Bottom right, activity in the same participants associated with spatial working memory versus two-dimensional eye movements (guided saccades).*

Hamidi, Tononi, & Postle (2008) used TMS to investigate the degree to which different prefrontal cortex and parietal cortex regions are necessary for spatial working memory. Each trial consisted of an encoding period with four dots at different spatial locations (one dot in each quadrant of the visual field), a three-second delay period, and a one dot probe. TMS was applied at 10 Hertz to a target region in the left or right hemisphere during the entire delay period (Figure 5.8, top), or no TMS was applied (which was a measure of baseline performance). TMS to the middle frontal gyrus on the ventral bank of the superior frontal sulcus (within the dorsolateral prefrontal cortex) impaired spatial working memory accuracy as compared with no TMS. However, this impairment (i.e., the difference in accuracy value) did not significantly differ from the impairment produced by TMS versus no TMS to the postcentral gyrus (the stimulated control region; Figure 5.8, bottom). Of importance, due to the limited spatial resolution of this technique, TMS to the middle frontal gyrus can be assumed to have also stimulated the superior frontal sulcus. Hamidi et al. took this null difference across regions to suggest that the dorsolateral prefrontal cortex, which includes the superior frontal sulcus, is not necessary for spatial working memory.

Both of the preceding studies failed to support the hypothesis that the dorsal prefrontal cortex is specialized for spatial working memory. More broadly, these findings could be taken to suggest that spatial working memory and object working memory are not

Figure 5.8 *Null TMS results. Top, 10 Hertz TMS was applied during the entire spatial working memory delay period to the middle frontal gyrus on the ventral bank of the superior frontal sulcus (within the dorsolateral prefrontal cortex, dlPFC), the frontal eye field (FEF), the postcentral gyrus (PCG), the superior parietal lobule (SPL), or the intraparietal sulcus (IPS; occipital pole at the right). Bottom, spatial working memory accuracy (proportion correct) with TMS (black bars) or with no TMS (white bars) applied to the specified region. The asterisk indicates a significant TMS effect.*

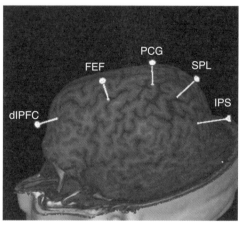

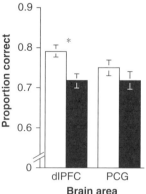

(Reprinted from Brain Research, 1230, Hamidi et al., Evaluating frontal and parietal contributions to spatial working memory with repetitive transcranial magnetic stimulation, Copyright 2008, with permission from Elsevier.)

processed separately in the dorsal prefrontal cortex and the ventral prefrontal cortex.

COUNTERPOINTS

While the studies that supported the minority view did not report evidence that spatial working memory was associated with the dorsal prefrontal cortex, it is important to keep in mind that these are null results. Such null findings do not constitute evidence, but reflect an absence of evidence and thus should not be taken to refute a hypothesis. Real evidence contradicts and thus excludes a hypothesis, as eloquently stated by Bacon (1620):

> Only when the *rejection* and *exclusion* has been performed in proper fashion will there remain (at the bottom of the flask, so to speak) an affirmative form, solid, true and well-defined (the volatile opinions having now vanished into smoke).
>
> (p. 127)

Bacon's point is that a hypothesis can only be rejected when evidence is observed that contradicts it. For instance, the studies that support the majority view have provided consistent evidence that the dorsal prefrontal cortex is preferentially associated with spatial working memory and the ventral prefrontal cortex is preferentially associated with object working memory. These findings repeatedly contradicted the null hypothesis that spatial working memory and object working memory are not processed separately in the prefrontal cortex. By comparison, null findings do not contradict the hypothesis that there are separate prefrontal cortex pathways for spatial working memory and object working memory. If only null findings had been consistently observed this might suggest that no differential findings exist; but that is not the case. It must be underscored that there are numerous reasons for a null finding such as the use of a particular stimulus set, the employment of a certain task, an unexpected cognitive strategy, an insensitive data acquisition technique, an insensitive method of analysis, an insufficient number of participants, unmotivated participants, between participant variability, and human error. In a circumstance where the null hypothesis has been consistently rejected, as it has by results supporting the majority view, the burden rests on those that believe the null hypothesis is correct to explain why the null hypothesis has been repeatedly contradicted.

As detailed above, Postle et al. (2000a) reported that there was no spatial working memory greater than two-dimensional saccade activity in the superior frontal sulcus (Figure 5.7, bottom right). Slotnick (2005) assessed whether this null finding may have been due to the limited sensitivity of the general linear model analysis employed by Postle et al. that may have relied upon an incorrect fMRI activation profile in the prefrontal cortex. The data from Postle et al. was reanalyzed using timecourse analysis, which does not assume a specific fMRI activation profile. Specifically, activation timecourses associated with spatial working memory and two-dimensional eye movements (saccades) were extracted from regions of interest within the superior frontal sulcus and the precentral sulcus of each participant (Figure 5.9, top). A comparison of spatial working memory activity versus two-dimensional saccade activity, across all participants, revealed preferential spatial working memory activity in the superior frontal sulcus (Figure 5.9, bottom). This reanalysis shows that the null results of Postle et al. (2000a) were not due to a lack of spatial working memory specific activity in the superior frontal sulcus, but were due to the employment of a method of analysis that was not sufficiently sensitive to detect the spatial working memory specific activity that existed in the dorsal prefrontal cortex.

The null TMS findings of Hamidi et al. (2008) can also be discounted due to the TMS target location. While spatial working memory has been consistently associated within the posterior superior frontal sulcus, Hamidi et al. targeted the anterior aspect of the middle frontal gyrus, which would not be expected to impair spatial working memory performance. That is, a null finding would be expected as a region that was not associated with spatial working memory was targeted, so this null finding is not relevant to the current debate.

Stimulus factors may also blur the spatial working memory and object working memory distinction and produce null findings. As detailed above (Figure 5.4), Sala et al. (2003) observed a pattern of results supporting the majority view. However, additional stimulus effects were revealed when object working memory trials were separated as a function of stimulus type and contrasted against one

Figure 5.9 *Differential working memory versus eye movement results. Top left, cortical surface of a participant with regions of interest demarcated by white circles and distances (in centimetres) from the junction of the superior frontal sulcus (SFS) and the precentral sulcus (PCS) labeled in white (top view, occipital pole at the bottom). Top right, activation timecourses extracted from two regions of interest (percent signal change as a function of seconds after working memory delay onset or saccade onset, each marked by a white vertical line). Spatial working memory delay activity and two-dimensional saccade activity extracted from two regions of interest are shown*

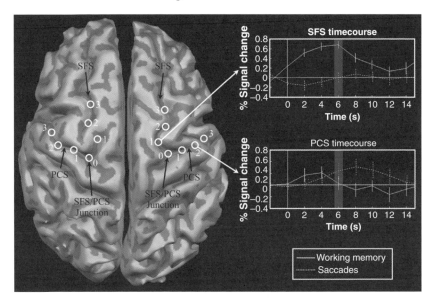

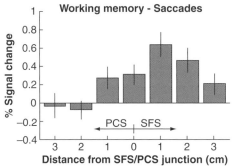

(Spatial working memory specific activity in dorsal prefrontal cortex? Disparate answers from fMRI beta-weight and timecourse analysis, Slotnick, Cognitive Neuropsychology, 2005, reprinted by permission of Taylor & Francis Ltd, http://www.tandf.co.uk/journals.)

Figure 5.9   *(Continued) in solid and dotted lines, respectively (key to the bottom right). Activation magnitudes at six seconds following event onset that were used in the analysis are highlighted in grey. Bottom, difference-of-activation magnitudes, across participants, between spatial working memory and two-dimensional saccades for each region of interest.*

---

another. Face working memory versus house working memory activated the left inferior frontal gyrus (within the ventral prefrontal cortex), while house working memory versus face working memory activated the right middle frontal gyrus and the left and right superior frontal sulcus (within both the ventral prefrontal cortex and the dorsal prefrontal cortex). Yee, Roe, & Courtney (2010) employed a colour or abstract shape working memory paradigm and found that colour working memory versus abstract shape working memory activated the inferior frontal gyrus, while abstract shape working memory versus colour working memory activated the middle frontal gyrus and the superior frontal sulcus. The results of the two previous studies suggest that certain stimuli, such as houses or abstract shapes, that are associated with more detailed spatial processing, might produce less segregated or null findings. Of importance, stimulus factors appear to produce relatively minor effects that have had little impact on the differential spatial working memory versus object working memory effects observed in the dorsal prefrontal cortex and the ventral prefrontal cortex.

Task factors may also produce null findings. The present analysis aimed to only include studies that employed tasks where the cognitive processes engaged could be attributed to either spatial working memory or object working memory. In the study by Mohr et al. (2006) discussed above, either half-circle colours or half-circle edge angles were maintained in working memory (Figure 5.5). Angle working memory activity was reported in the left and right superior frontal sulcus and colour working memory activity was reported in the left inferior frontal sulcus, in support of the majority view. However, angle working memory also activated the right inferior frontal gyrus, which is seemingly at odds with the view that spatial working memory is associated with the dorsal prefrontal cortex. The angle working memory task employed could have relied on maintenance of the two half-circle angles (i.e., spatial working memory) as was assumed, but could have relied on maintenance of a unified V shape formed by the angles (i.e., object working memory) or could have engaged both of these cognitive strategies. That is, participants may have relied on object working memory to some degree during the spatial working memory task, which may explain why inferior frontal gyrus activity was observed during a putative spatial working memory task. The *n-back* task, in which a sequence of items is continually presented and the current item in the sequence is compared with a certain number of items (n) earlier (Figure 5.10), has also produced null spatial-object working memory dorsal-ventral prefrontal cortex results (Postle, Stern, Rosen, & Corkin, 2000b). Although the n-back task requires working memory, this task also involves continually updating and purging the contents of working memory, which can be very cognitively demanding. The additional

Figure 5.10   *Illustration of the n-back task. Left, spatial 2-back task, where dots were sequentially presented and participants were instructed to respond when a dot location matched the location presented two items earlier (the arrow indicates a correct response). Right, analogous object 2-back task, where participants were instructed to respond based on matching object shape.*

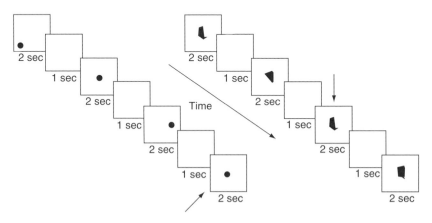

(Reprinted from NeuroImage, 11/5, Postle et al., 2000b, An fMRI investigation of cortical contributions to spatial and nonspatial visual working memory, Copyright 2000, with permission from Elsevier.)

cognitive processes required for this task, as compared with the working memory tasks employed by the studies considered in this chapter, would be expected to increase the magnitude and extent of activity in the prefrontal cortex. This additional activity may have washed out any differential prefrontal cortex effects that could have been observed. In support of this possibility, inclusion of n-back working memory studies in a meta-analysis completely overshadowed a robust left hemisphere lateralized verbal working memory effect such that it was undetectable (Smith & Jonides, 1999). Null prefrontal cortex effects have also been reported during a *"what"-then-"where"* task that involved a spatial working memory task and an object working memory task that immediately followed one another and shared an intermediate stimulus or location (Postle & D'Esposito, 1999). Based on the immediate temporal proximity of these tasks coupled with the shared stimulus or location that directly linked them, it is not surprising that differential effects were not observed. This mixed experimental design likely fostered the engagement of both spatial working memory and object working memory during both types of working memory delay periods. These examples illustrate two tenets of cognitive neuroscience research – if tasks do not isolate the cognitive processes of interest or are too demanding, null effects should be expected. Such null results do not reflect a lack of an effect, but rather reflect a failure to conduct a thoughtful *cognitive analysis* during the experimental design phase, where the cognitive processes engaged by a particular task are identified via introspection (which is necessary to correctly employ subtractive logic; Chapter 1). In light of the consistent rejection of the null hypothesis, the fact that many spatial working memory-object working memory prefrontal cortex null findings have been reported suggests that cognitive analysis is not conducted enough in cognitive neuroscience, at least by some working memory investigators. It is hoped that this discussion will promote more detailed cognitive analysis by cognitive neuroscientists.

Table 5.1 summarizes all the fMRI results considered. Across studies, spatial working memory has been most consistently associated with the superior frontal sulcus within the dorsal prefrontal cortex and was almost never associated with the ventral prefrontal cortex. By contrast, object working memory has been most consistently associated with the inferior frontal cortex within the ventral prefrontal cortex and was never associated with the dorsal

Table 5.1   *fMRI activity associated with spatial working memory (spatial WM) and object working memory (object WM) in the superior frontal sulcus (SFS), the middle frontal gyrus (MFG), and the inferior frontal cortex (IFC). Stimuli consisted of faces (F), dots (D), houses (H), patterns (P), shapes (sh.), colours (C), angles (A), and squares (sq.), and the asterisk marks a reanalysed study*

Study	Stimuli	Spatial WM			Object WM		
		SFS	MFG	IFC	SFS	MFG	IFC
Courtney et al. (1998)	F	X				X	X
Rowe et al. (2001)	D	X					
Courtney et al. (1997)	F					X	X
Sala et al. (2003)	F/A	X				X	X
Sala et al. (2007)	P	X				X	X
Landau et al. (2007)	sh.						X
Mohr et al. (2006)	C/A	X		X			X
Jackson et al. (2011)	C/A	X					X
Postle et al. (2000a)	sq.						
Postle et al. (2000a)*	sq.	X					

prefrontal cortex. The preponderance of evidence supporting the majority view, coupled with the methodological, stimulus, and task factors that can explain all of the observed null findings, is sufficient to reject the null hypothesis.

If the null hypothesis was correct, proponents of the minority view would need to explain the findings of the majority view. However, proponents of the minority have not provided any viable explanation for why the null hypothesis has been consistently rejected. This stands in contrast to the valid memory strength argument that has been put forth by proponents of the minority view in the long-term memory controversy (Chapter 4).

Meta-analyses of working memory studies have consistently shown: 1) the left prefrontal cortex is preferentially associated with verbal working memory and the right prefrontal cortex is preferentially associated with spatial working memory, and 2) the dorsal prefrontal cortex is preferentially associated with manipulating the contents of working memory and the ventral prefrontal cortex is preferentially associated with maintaining the contents of working memory (D'Esposito, Aguirre, Zarahn, Ballard, Shin, &

Lease, 1998; Smith & Jonides, 1999; Fletcher & Henson, 2001). One of these meta-analyses also showed that the dorsal prefrontal cortex is preferentially associated with spatial working memory and the ventral prefrontal cortex is preferentially associated with object working memory (Smith & Jonides, 1999). The relatively less consistent support for a spatial working memory-object working memory dorsal prefrontal cortex-ventral prefrontal cortex distinction may be due to a relatively less distinct segregation in the prefrontal cortex, or may be due to the employment of paradigms that have fostered null findings. Furthermore, these meta-analyses did not consider the body of evidence that has accumulated in the last decade that has provided very strong support for the majority view.

Of additional relevance, it is often assumed that the dorsal prefrontal cortex and the ventral prefrontal cortex mediate either spatial working memory and object working memory or that these regions mediate working memory manipulation and working memory maintenance. However, the assumption that the prefrontal cortex has a fixed processing organization, with only a single region associated with a single function, is inconsistent with the known flexible processing organization of this region (Miller, 2000). More generally, the belief that a particular region is linked to a single cognitive function ignores the known complexity of brain function (Chapter 9). Based on the current body of evidence, the dorsal prefrontal cortex appears to mediate both spatial working memory and working memory manipulation, while the ventral prefrontal cortex appears to mediate both object working memory and working memory maintenance.

CONCLUSION

In support of the majority view, there is an abundance of evidence that the dorsal prefrontal cortex is associated with spatial working memory and the ventral prefrontal cortex is associated with object working memory. Proponents of the minority view have embraced null findings, and have offered no viable explanation for the evidence supporting the majority view. By contrast, all the null findings that have been taken to support the minority view can be attributed to methodological, stimulus, or task limitations. Unless proponents of the minority view can provide an explanation for the mounting evidence in support of the majority view, which seems very unlikely, it is anticipated that this controversy will fade away with time.

SUGGESTED READINGS

Majority view

Courtney, S. M., Petit, L., Maisog, J. M., Ungerleider, L. G., & Haxby, J. V. (1998). An area specialized for spatial working memory in human frontal cortex. *Science, 279,* 1347–1351. Open access.

Slotnick, S. D. (2005). Spatial working memory specific activity in dorsal prefrontal cortex? Disparate answers from fMRI beta-weight and timecourse analysis. *Cognitive Neuropsychology, 22,* 905–920.

Minority view

Postle, B. R., Berger, J. S., Taich, A. M., & D'Esposito, M. (2000a). Activity in human frontal cortex associated with spatial working memory and saccadic behavior. *Journal of Cognitive Neuroscience, 12 Supplement 2,* 2–14.

Hamidi, M., Tononi, G., & Postle, B. R. (2008). Evaluating frontal and parietal contributions to spatial working memory with repetitive transcranial magnetic stimulation. *Brain Research, 1230,* 202–210. Open access.

REFERENCES

Bacon, F. (1620). *The new organon.* L. Jardine & M. Silverthorne (Eds.). New York: Cambridge University Press.

Courtney, S. M., Petit, L., Maisog, J. M., Ungerleider, L. G., & Haxby, J. V. (1998). An area specialized for spatial working memory in human frontal cortex. *Science, 279,* 1347–1351.

Courtney, S. M., Ungerleider, L. G., Keil, K., & Haxby, J. V. (1997). Transient and sustained activity in a distributed neural system for human working memory. *Nature, 386,* 608–611.

D'Esposito, M., Aguirre, G. K., Zarahn, E., Ballard, D., Shin, R. K., & Lease, J. (1998). Functional MRI studies of spatial and nonspatial working memory. *Cognitive Brain Research, 7,* 1–13.

Fletcher, P. C., & Henson, R. N. (2001). Frontal lobes and human memory: Insights from functional neuroimaging. *Brain, 124,* 849–881.

Hamidi, M., Tononi, G., & Postle, B. R. (2008). Evaluating frontal and parietal contributions to spatial working memory with repetitive transcranial magnetic stimulation. *Brain Research, 1230,* 202–210.

Jackson, M. C., Morgan, H. M., Shapiro, K. L., Mohr, H., & Linden, D. E. (2011). Strategic resource allocation in the human brain supports cognitive coordination of object and spatial working memory. *Human Brain Mapping, 32,* 1330–1348.

Landau, S. M., Garavan, H., Schumacher, E. H., & D'Esposito, M. (2007). Regional specificity and practice: Dynamic changes in object and spatial working memory. *Brain Research, 1180,* 78–89.

Levy, R., & Goldman-Rakic, P. S. (1999). Association of storage and processing functions in the dorsolateral prefrontal cortex of the nonhuman primate. *The Journal of Neuroscience, 19,* 5149–5158.

Miller, E. K. (2000). The prefrontal cortex and cognitive control. *Nature Reviews Neuroscience, 1,* 59–65.

Mohr, H. M., Goebel, R., & Linden, D. E. (2006). Content- and task-specific dissociations of frontal activity during maintenance and manipulation in visual working memory. *The Journal of Neuroscience, 26,* 4465–4471.

Mottaghy, F. M., Gangitano, M., Sparing, R., Krause, B. J., & Pascual-Leone, A. (2002). Segregation of areas related to visual working memory in the prefrontal cortex revealed by rTMS. *Cerebral Cortex, 12,* 369–375.

Postle, B. R., & D'Esposito, M. (1999). "What"-then-"where" in visual working memory: An event-related fMRI study. *Journal of Cognitive Neuroscience, 11,* 585–597.

Postle, B. R., Berger, J. S., Taich, A. M., & D'Esposito, M. (2000a). Activity in human frontal cortex associated with spatial working memory and saccadic behavior. *Journal of Cognitive Neuroscience, 12 Supplement 2,* 2–14.

Postle, B. R., Stern, C. E., Rosen, B. R., & Corkin, S. (2000b). An fMRI investigation of cortical contributions to spatial and nonspatial visual working memory. *NeuroImage, 11,* 409–423.

Rowe, J. B., & Passingham, R. E. (2001). Working memory for location and time: Activity in prefrontal area 46 relates to selection rather than maintenance in memory. *NeuroImage, 14*, 77–86.

Sala, J. B., & Courtney, S. M. (2007). Binding of what and where during working memory maintenance. *Cortex, 43*, 5–21.

Sala, J. B., Rämä, P., & Courtney, S. M. (2003). Functional topography of a distributed neural system for spatial and nonspatial information maintenance in working memory. *Neuropsychologia, 41*, 341–356.

Slotnick, S. D. (2005). Spatial working memory specific activity in dorsal prefrontal cortex? Disparate answers from fMRI beta-weight and timecourse analysis. *Cognitive Neuropsychology, 22*, 905–920.

Smith, E. E., & Jonides, J. (1999). Storage and executive processes in the frontal lobes. *Science, 283*, 1657–1661.

Wilson, F. A., Scalaidhe, S. P., & Goldman-Rakic, P. S. (1993). Dissociation of object and spatial processing domains in primate prefrontal cortex. *Science, 260*, 1955–1958.

Yee, L. T., Roe, K., & Courtney, S. M. (2010). Selective involvement of superior frontal cortex during working memory for shapes. *Journal of Neurophysiology, 103*, 557–563.

6 The Visual Word Form Area

Language comprehension and language production are mediated, in part, by the left posterior superior temporal gyrus (*Wernicke's area*) and the left posterior inferior frontal gyrus (*Broca's area*), respectively (Figure 6.1). Thus, it is not surprising that reading visually presented words, which involves language comprehension and language production, produces activity in these regions (Price, 2000). Visual word processing also produces activity in a well circumscribed region of the left occipito-temporal sulcus bordering the fusiform gyrus (McCandliss, Cohen, & Dehaene, 2003). This region has been labeled the *visual word form area* and is referred to as the *VWFA* (Cohen, Dehaene, Naccache, Lehéricy, Dahaene-Lambertz, Hénaff, & Michel, 2000).

It is the majority view that the VWFA is specialized for processing visual words and word-like stimuli (such as the pseudo-word "zib") independent of language, case, or spatial location. However, proponents of the minority view have questioned whether visual word processing is localized to the VWFA and whether this region selectively processes visually presented words. This debate, like the fusiform face area debate (Chapter 2), is relevant to the general issue of whether an individual region of the brain can be specialized for a single cognitive process.

MAJORITY VIEW

Activation evidence

fMRI studies have provided compelling support for the existence of the VWFA. It should be mentioned that ERP evidence is not considered in this chapter as VWFA activity is always accompanied by activation in other cortical regions making the localization

Figure 6.1 *Regions associated with language processing. The left posterior superior temporal gyrus (LPSTG, Wernicke's area), the left posterior inferior frontal gyrus (LPIFG, Broca's area), and the visual word form area (VWFA; outlined by white ovals).*

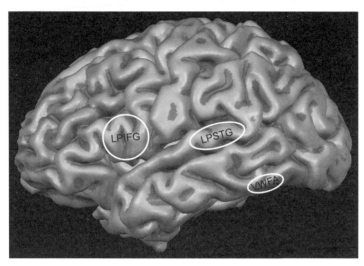

of the underlying neural sources inherently uncertain. Stanislas Dehaene and Laurent Cohen are the primary proponents of the majority view.

Cohen et al. (2000) presented a series of ten common nouns in the left visual field, ten common nouns in the right visual field, or participants maintained central fixation with no task. Participants were instructed to name each word covertly (mentally, rather than aloud). Word processing in both the left visual field versus fixation and the right visual field versus fixation produced activity in the VWFA, with no activity in the homologous region of the right hemisphere (Figure 6.2). These results indicate that activation of the VWFA does not depend on stimulus position in the visual field. Word processing also produced activity in the left posterior inferior frontal gyrus and the left superior temporal gyrus.

Dehaene, Naccache, Cohen, Le Bihan, Mangin, Poline, & Riviére (2001) presented nouns or blank screens (referred to in this study as *blanks*) that were temporally separated from *masks* such that the words were visible (Figure 6.3, top left), or presented nouns or blanks temporally adjacent to masks such that the words were not visible (Figure 6.3, top right). Of relevance, masks that share visual features and are presented at the same spatial location and

Figure 6.2 *Activity associated with visual word processing. Visual word processing versus fixation (in black; lateral views, occipital poles toward the centre) during left visual field stimulation (top) and during right visual field stimulation (bottom) produced activity in the VWFA (shown at the centre of each circle).*

Stimulated hemifield

Left

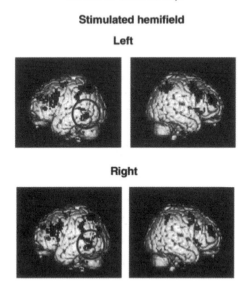

Right

(Cohen et al., The visual word form area: Spatial and temporal characterization of an initial stage of reading in normal subjects and posterior split-brain patients, Brain, 2000, 123, Pt 2, 291–307, by permission of Oxford University Press.)

in immediate temporal proximity of a stimulus can disrupt perceptual processing of the stimulus such that it is not consciously processed. In the first experiment, participants covertly named each word that was perceived. Visible words versus blanks produced activity in the VWFA and also produced activity in the left inferior frontal cortex. It might be expected that masked words would not activate the VWFA, if this region only mediates conscious processing. However, masked words versus blanks also produced activity in the VWFA, although the magnitude of activity in this region was only 8.6 percent of that associated with visible words. This suggests that the VWFA is activated, to some degree, regardless of conscious experience. Dehaene et al. also conducted a repetition priming experiment to assess whether VWFA activity would be modulated as a function of word case. Repetition priming typically

Figure 6.3   *VWFA case-independent repetition priming effects. Top, stimulus protocol for the first experiment, where words or blanks were immediately preceded and followed by blanks (left) such that the words were visible, or words or blanks were immediately preceded and followed by masks (right) such that the words were not visible. Bottom left, activity (in black) associated with repetition priming in the VWFA (axial view, occipital pole at the bottom). Bottom right, magnitude of activation (percent signal change) in the VWFA associated with the same or different target words in the same or different case.*

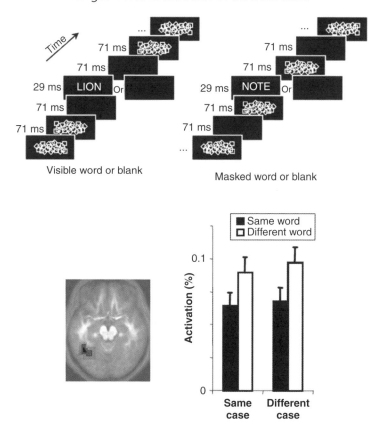

(Reprinted by permission to Macmillan Publishers Ltd: *Nature Neuroscience, 4,* Dehaene et al., copyright 2001.)

refers to a relative reduction in neural activity associated with repeated (old) items as compared to new items, thought to reflect more fluent processing of repeated items (perhaps corresponding to a relative decrease in the number of neurons involved in processing repeated items). The previous paradigm was modified such that each masked word (Figure 6.3, top right) was followed by a visible word (presented for half a second) that was either the same (old) or different (new) in either the same case or a different case. For example, the masked word "NOTE" might be followed by the visible lower case word "note," which would correspond to the same word-different case condition. Neural priming effects occurred in the VWFA (Figure 6.3, bottom left) as same (old) words were associated with a lower magnitude of activity as compared to different (new) words, and these VWFA effects did not depend on word case (Figure 6.3, bottom right).

Dehaene, Le Clec'H, Poline, Le Bihan, & Cohen (2002) further refined the processing characteristics of the VWFA. Participants were sequentially presented with pairs of words (from the categories tools, body parts, action verbs, animals, and numbers) or pseudo-words (such as the word "wug") that followed the rules of language with regard to orthography (i.e., they were word-like strings of letters) and phonology (i.e., they sounded like words). Words were also presented either visually, an upper case word followed by a lower case word, or auditorily, in two different male voices. Participants decided whether or not the same word was repeated in each pair of words, regardless of changes in case or voice. Thus, this design manipulated stimulus category (words, pseudo-words), stimulus modality (visual, auditory), and repetition type (same, different). The contrast of written stimuli (words and pseudo-words) and spoken stimuli produced activity in the entire occipital-temporal ventral visual processing stream including the VWFA (Kronbichler, Hutzler, Wimmer, Mair, Staffen, & Ladurner, 2004, also reported word and pseudo-word activation of the VWFA in addition to the left inferior frontal gyrus). Dehaene et al. also reported that spoken stimuli versus written stimuli did not activate the VWFA. Furthermore, extraction of event-related activity in the VWFA showed that words and pseudo-words produced a similar response magnitude in this region (Figure 6.4). Auditory words produced little if any activation of the VWFA, which suggests that this region is associated with stimuli presented in the visual modality. Moreover, the VWFA responded similarly to word or word-like stimuli (pseudo-words), which suggests this region responds to letter strings at the orthographic-phonologic level of processing that precedes the lexical (word meaning) level of processing. Cohen, Lehéricy, Chochon, Lemer, Rivaud, & Dahaene (2002) further tested the degree to

Figure 6.4   *VWFA word and pseudo-word activation. VWFA activation timecourses (percent signal change per second) associated with words from the labeled categories and pseudo-words presented visually (in dark grey, marked with triangles) or auditorily (in black, marked with circles).*

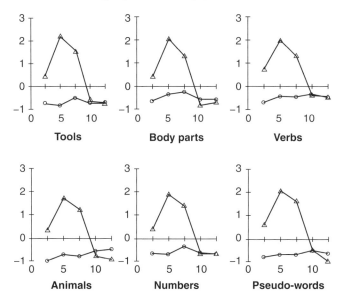

(Dehaene et al., 2002, The visual word form area: A prelexical representation of visual words in the fusiform gyrus, NeuroReport, 13, 3, 321–325, reprinted with permission from Wolters Kluwer Health.)

which the VWFA processes prelexical stimuli and found that consonant strings such as "dtwtpm" (versus checkerboards) also activated this region (in addition to Broca's area). However, words did produce a greater magnitude of activation than consonant strings in the VWFA. Vigneau, Jobard, Mazoyer, & Tzourio-Mazoyer (2005) similarly assessed the VWFA response to processing words and nonwords (including consonant strings, vowel strings, and words from a completely unfamiliar language that differed in orthographic structure) and found that word and non-word reading produced a similar magnitude of activity in this region. Word reading also produced activity in the left posterior inferior frontal gyrus and the left posterior superior temporal gyrus. Replicating Dehaene et al. (2002), Vigneau et al. also reported that auditory presentation of words did not produce activity in the VWFA.

The previous studies employed French or German stimuli, which are alphabetic scripts. Liu, Zhang, Tang, Mai, Chen, Tardif, & Luo (2008) evaluated the response of the VWFA with Chinese stimuli. Participants were presented with relatively large or small real characters (analogous to words), pseudo-characters (analogous to pseudo-words), artificial characters (analogous to strings of scrambled letter fragments), and checkerboards (Figure 6.5, left). In comparison with the pseudo-words employed in previous studies, pseudo-characters are orthographically legal but cannot be pronounced, such that orthographic without phonologic processing was isolated in this study by comparing pseudo-characters with artificial characters. Participants classified each stimulus as either "large" or "small" (to motivate vigilance). Both the contrast of real characters with artificial characters and the contrast of pseudo-characters with artificial characters produced activity in the VWFA (Figure 6.5, right). That pseudo-characters activated the

Figure 6.5 *VWFA real character and pseudo-character activation. Left, Chinese stimuli that varied in size (labeled) used to evaluate VWFA processing. Right, activity (in light grey) associated with real characters versus artificial characters (top) and pseudo-characters versus artificial characters (bottom; left lateral, top, and right lateral views are shown from left to right). The arrow points to VWFA activity.*

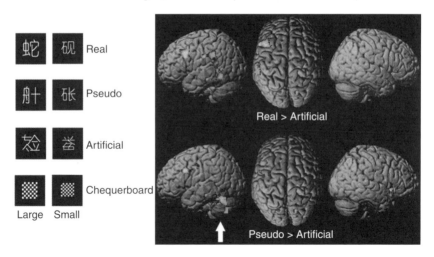

(Reprinted from NeuroImage, 40/3, Liu et al., The Visual Word Form Area: Evidence from an fMRI study of implicit processing of Chinese characters, Copyright 2008, with permission from Elsevier.)

VWFA suggests that orthographic without phonologic processing is sufficient to activate this region. In addition, real characters (but not pseudo-characters) versus artificial characters produced activity in the left posterior inferior frontal gyrus and the left posterior superior temporal gyrus.

Szwed, Dehaene, Kleinschmidt, Eger, Valabrègue, Amadon, & Cohen (2011) obtained results that complimented the previous findings by presenting degraded words and degraded objects that were either intact or scrambled. The contrast between words and scrambled words as compared with objects and scrambled objects, which subtracted out low-level features, produced activity in the VWFA and the left superior temporal gyrus. The VWFA activity reported suggests that this region responds to words to a greater degree than objects.

Considering all the previous findings, the VWFA can be described as involved in word and pseudo-word processing to a greater degree than non-word processing.

Lexical or prelexical processing in the VWFA?

As mentioned previously, the VWFA responds to pseudo-words that follow the rules of language but have no meaning, which suggests the VWFA processes stimuli at the prelexical level. Glezer, Jiang, & Riesenhuber (2009) distinguished between a prelexical hypothesis that specifies the VWFA should be similarly responsive to words or pseudo-words and a lexical hypothesis that specifies the VWFA is specialized for word processing but not pseudo-word processing. The lexical hypothesis predicts that the VWFA is specifically tuned to words, which should produce spatially localized high-magnitude responses in this region, while pseudo-words should produce more spatially distributed low-magnitude responses. By this account, VWFA neurons that process words such as "harm," "term," and "tarp" might all weakly respond to the orthographically similar pseudo-word "tarm" that summed together could give the appearance of a strong and selective response to this pseudo-word. As such, the fMRI response in the VWFA might be equivalent to words and pseudo-words in this scenario, but only individual words selectively drive the VWFA response. By contrast, the prelexical hypothesis predicts a spatially localized high-magnitude response in the VWFA for both words and pseudo-words. Glezer et al. argued that previous fMRI paradigms may not have been sufficiently sensitive to distinguish between the lexical and prelexical hypotheses. As such, a repetition priming paradigm, where the magnitude of visual processing activity is reduced during repetition of the same versus different items, was employed to more accurately probe the VWFA response to words and pseudo-words. Participants were presented with word and pseudo-word pairs each consisting of a *prime* and a *target* and pressed a response button whenever an infrequently occurring fruit or vegetable word occurred (to encourage detailed stimulus processing). Prime and targets were either the same, differed by one letter (1L), or were different (Figure 6.6, top). Both the lexical hypothesis and the prelexical hypothesis predict

Figure 6.6 *Support for the lexical hypothesis of VWFA processing. Top, illustration of repetition priming protocol for real word (RW) and pseudo-word (PW) pairs. Each trial consisted of a prime word followed by a target word that was the same, differed by one letter (1L), or was different. Bottom left, VWFA activity (in white; axial, sagittal, and coronal views are shown clockwise from the bottom left). Bottom right, VWFA activity (percent signal change) associated with real word and pseudo-word pairs as a function of condition.*

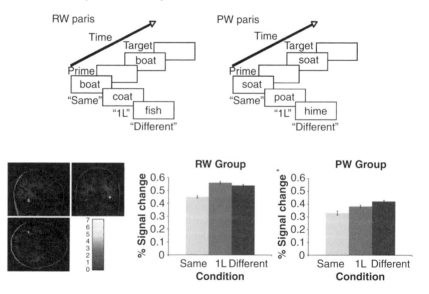

(Reprinted from Neuron, 62/2, Glezer et al., Evidence for highly selective neuronal tuning to whole words in the "visual word form area," Copyright 2009, with permission from Elsevier.)

that VWFA activity associated with target processing should have the lowest magnitude in the same condition and the highest magnitude in the different condition for both real words and pseudo-words (reflecting standard repetition priming effects). Critically, the lexical and prelexical hypotheses make different predictions with regard to the magnitude VWFA activity produced in the 1L conditions. If the lexical hypothesis is correct and the VWFA is tuned specifically to words, the 1L word condition should not produce priming effects because the meaning of the words do not match, while the 1L pseudo-word condition should produce priming effects because the pseudo-words match to some degree. The prelexical hypothesis assumes that words and pseudo-words are processed by the VWFA in the same way and predicts the same pattern of priming effects in the 1L word condition and the 1L pseudo-word condition. VWFA activity associated with words and pseudo-words showed the expected priming effects (Figure 6.6, bottom), with same words producing activity of a lower magnitude than different words. In support of the lexical hypothesis of VWFA processing, there were no priming effects in the 1L word condition but there were priming effects in the 1L pseudo-word condition. These results suggest that the VWFA operates at the lexical level rather than the orthographic level. However, is should be highlighted that these results were observed in a single study, and the role of the VWFA in word, pseudo-word, and non-word processing is still a topic of active investigation. That is, whether the VWFA is involved in processing at the lexical or the prelexical level is independent of the present debate.

Considering all of the evidence thus far, the VWFA can be described as responsive to visually presented words (and possibly pseudo-words) regardless of language, case, or spatial location.

Lesion evidence

Patient evidence has also been employed to assess the role of the VWFA in word processing. Cohen, Martinaud, Lemer, Lehéricy, Samson, Obadia, Slachevsky, & Dehaene (2003) reported six patients who had overlapping lesions of the VWFA (Figure 6.7) and selective difficulty reading words (alexia), which is of direct relevance as reading involves visual word processing. Gaillard, Naccache, Pinel, Clémenceau, Volle, Hasboun, Dupont, Baulac, Dahaene, Adam, & Cohen (2006) reported a patient with a lesion

Figure 6.7   *Overlap of lesions in six patients with selective word reading difficulty (lowest to highest degree of overlap shown from dark grey to light grey; sagittal and coronal views are shown to the left and right, respectively).*

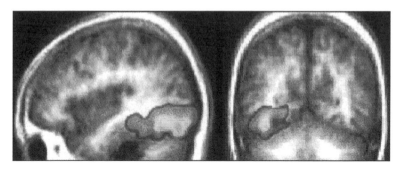

(Cohen et al., Visual word recognition in the left and right hemispheres: Anatomical and functional correlates of peripheral alexias, Cerebral Cortex, 2003, 13, 12, 1313–1333, by permission of Oxford University Press.)

largely restricted to the VWFA who also had a very selective reading impairment, as indicated by intact verbal language production, verbal language comprehension, object recognition, place recognition, and face recognition. These patient results complement the previous fMRI findings and suggest that the VWFA is necessary for word processing, thus providing further support for the majority view that the VWFA is a specialized region for visual word processing.

MINORITY VIEW

If the visual word form area exists, this label dictates it is localized in a single region of the brain that is highly selective for processing words or word-like stimuli in the visual modality. More generally (as discussed in Chapter 2), when a spatially restricted region of cortex is given a name that describes a single processing function, a very strong claim is made that rests on the following criteria: 1) localizability – that type of processing is only mediated by that single circumscribed region, and 2) selectivity – that region mediates that single processing function and is not involved in other kinds of processing. If neither of these criteria is met, there is little if any justification to label that region according to that specific cognitive function. The evidence in this section supports the minority view that the VWFA does not survive the criterion of localizability or the criterion of selectivity.

Using fMRI, the proponents of the majority view conducted contrasts to isolate the regions associated with visual word processing. If there was a VWFA, these contrasts should have produced activity that was completely or at least largely restricted to this region. However, visual word and word-like processing not only produced activity in the VWFA, but produced activity outside of this region as well (see Figure 6.2 and Figure 6.5). Proponents of the majority view have largely ignored activations outside the VWFA, but that does not mean these activations do not exist. Table 6.1 shows that the left posterior inferior frontal gyrus (Broca's area) and the left posterior superior temporal gyrus (Wernicke's area; Figure 6.1) were co-activated with the VWFA in many of the preceding fMRI studies. The key point is that the VWFA was never activated in isolation – Broca's area was activated in the large majority of these studies, Wernicke's area was activated in half of these studies, and many other regions (not included in Table 6.1) were activated as well. These results indicate that visual word form processing involves many cortical regions, rather than being strictly localized to the VWFA as this region's name implies.

Proponents of the minority view have challenged the notion that the VWFA selectively responds to words. Price & Devlin (2003) showed that the VWFA responded to word reading, as expected, but also responded to naming objects versus saying "OK" to objects, naming the colour of gratings versus saying "OK" to gratings,

Table 6.1 *fMRI activity associated with visually presented words, pseudo-words, and letter strings in the visual word form area (VWFA), the left inferior frontal gyrus (LIFG), and the left superior temporal gyrus (LSTG)*

Study	Stimuli	VWFA	LIFG	LSTG
Cohen et al. (2000)	Words	X	X	X
Dehaene et al. (2001)	Words	X	X	
Dehaene et al. (2002)	Words/Pseudo-words	X		
Kronbichler et al. (2004)	Words/Pseudo-words	X	X	
Cohen et al. (2002)	Words/Letter strings	X	X	
Vigneau et al. (2005)	Words	X	X	X
Liu et al. (2008)	Words	X	X	X
Szwed et al. (2011)	Words	X		X

Figure 6.8 *VWFA activation by visual word processing and other types of processing. Activity in the VWFA (marked by the white crosshairs) associated with reading (words and pseudowords versus rest or words and pseudowords versus false fonts shown in grey and white, respectively), object naming, colour naming, nonobject action decisions, and repeating auditory words (axial views, occipital pole at the bottom of each image).*

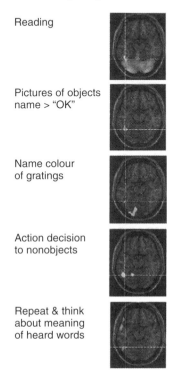

Reading

Pictures of objects name > "OK"

Name colour of gratings

Action decision to nonobjects

Repeat & think about meaning of heard words

(Reprinted from NeuroImage, 19/3, Price and Devlin, The myth of the visual word form area, Copyright 2003, with permission from Elsevier.)

making action ("twist" or "pour") decisions to nonobjects versus making perception decisions to nonobjects, and repeating and thinking about auditory words versus saying "OK" to noise bursts (Figure 6.8). As the VWFA was activated by objects, gratings, and nonobjects, these findings indicate that this region is not selective for visual word forms. Moreover, auditory words also activated the VWFA, which suggests this region does not selectively process stimuli presented in the visual modality. Thus, this set of results challenges whether the VWFA selectively processes words and whether this region selectively processes visual stimuli, the only two processing characteristics of this region according to its label.

Starrfelt & Gerlach (2007) used PET to examine the selectivity of the VWFA. Participants viewed words or pictures of objects and identified the colour (white or yellow) or the category (natural or artificial) of each stimulus. Participants were also presented with objects and nonobjects composed of object parts and classified each stimulus accordingly. The VWFA was activated by words, as expected, but this region was also activated by pictures during the category identification task and by objects and nonobjects during the object-nonobject decision task (Figure 6.9, left). Consistent with previous findings that word processing is preferentially lateralized to the left hemisphere, the right hemisphere VWFA homologue produced a weaker response to words than the VWFA but did respond to objects in some conditions (Figure 6.9, right).

As described previously, Szwed et al. (2011) used a contrast analysis and reported that words versus scrambled words as compared to objects versus scrambled objects produced activity in the VWFA, which was taken to support the majority view. However, Szwed

Figure 6.9 *VWFA activation by visual words and objects. Left, VWFA activity (regional cerebral blood flow, rCBF, measured with PET) associated with colour (col) or category (cat) identification of words (W) or pictures (P) of objects, and associated with an object-nonobject decision task (ODT). Right, activity in the right hemisphere VWFA homologue associated the same conditions.*

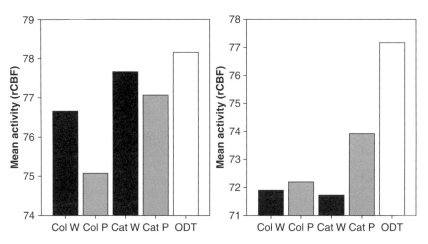

(Reprinted from NeuroImage, 35/1, Starrfelt and Gerlach, The visual what for area: Words and pictures in the left fusiform gyrus, Copyright 2007, with permission from Elsevier.)

et al. also conducted a region of interest analysis that uncovered object activity in the VWFA. Specifically, the VWFA responded to a greater degree to words than scrambled words, responded to a greater degree to objects than scrambled objects, and responded similarly to both objects and words (Figure 6.10). Although the contrast analysis results and the region of interest analysis results appear to be inconsistent, the peak location of the activity produced by the contrast was over two standard deviations anterior to the known location of the VWFA, while the location of activity used for the region of interest analysis was less than one standard deviation from the VWFA (McCandliss et al., 2003). These findings indicate that only the region of interest analysis results correspond to the VWFA, while the contrast analysis results produced activity in a more anterior ventral fusiform region. Thus, the findings of Szwed et al. provide additional support that the VWFA is involved in both word and object processing.

The preceding studies found that both word and non-word stimuli, including objects, activated the VWFA, which suggests this

Figure 6.10 *Similar magnitude of VWFA activation by visual words and objects. Left, left hemisphere occipital-temporal cortex with regions of interest marked by spheres (partial lateral view, occipital pole to the right). The VWFA corresponds to the leftmost region of interest. Right, VWFA activity associated with words, scrambled words, objects, and scrambled objects (key at the bottom).*

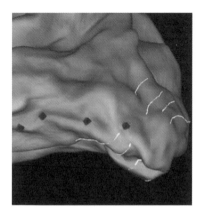
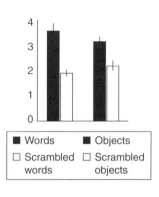

(Reprinted from NeuroImage, 56/1, Szwed et al., Specialization for written words over objects in the visual cortex, Copyright 2011, with permission from Elsevier.)

region is associated with processing some feature that is common to these event types (and is reminiscent of the findings indicating that the FFA is involved in processing complex visual features that are shared by faces and objects; Chapter 2). Woodhead, Wise, Sereno, & Leech (2011) investigated this possibility by assessing whether the VWFA was associated with processing stimuli with relatively high spatial frequency components. High spatial frequency refers to sharp or more closely spaced features that make up letters/words, while low spatial frequency refers to blurry or more widely spaced features. Participants viewed whole-screen greyscale sine-wave gratings, consisting of alternating light and dark bands, that varied in spatial frequency from very low (widely spaced bands) to very high (closely spaced bands). A comparison of high spatial frequency gratings with low spatial frequency gratings produced activity in the VWFA. This finding suggests that the VWFA may not be driven by words or word-like stimuli, but rather may respond to any stimulus that has high frequency components (i.e., closely spaced features), such as words or objects.

Hillis, Newhart, Heidler, Barker, Herskovits, & Degaonkar (2005) conducted a study of 80 left hemisphere stroke patients to investigate the degree to which the VWFA and other language processing regions were associated with word processing. Patients were tested within 24 hours after the stroke onset and MRI was used to determine if a region was disrupted, as indicated by hypoperfusion (reduced blood flow) or neural infarct (death). There was no correlation between VWFA disruption and written word comprehension, which requires visual word processing. Note that if the VWFA was necessary for visual word processing, even at the prelexical level, word comprehension would have been impaired because lower-level visual word processing must precede higher-level word comprehension (e.g., individual letter identification must precede extraction of a word's meaning). That is, a lesion earlier in the word processing stream would disrupt all later stages of word processing, yet VWFA lesions did not impair word comprehension. However, written word comprehension was correlated with disruption of the left posterior superior temporal gyrus (Wernicke's area). The latter finding indicates that the left posterior superior temporal gyrus is more important for visual word processing than the VWFA.

The previous fMRI results indicate that the VWFA not only processes visual words, but can also be activated by objects, non-objects, and colour gratings when the stimulus is held constant and the task is manipulated. The VWFA was also activated by auditory words versus noise and objects versus scrambled objects. Moreover, in multiple studies, the VWFA responded similarly to visual words and objects. The patient study also reported no correlation between lesions to the VWFA and visual word processing. These findings pose many serious challenges to the majority view that the VWFA is selective for processing visual words.

COUNTERPOINTS

Proponents of the majority view have argued that the VWFA is selective for processing visual words or word-like stimuli by providing alternative explanations for some of the contradictory evidence reported above. Evidence has been discounted based on the paradigms employing blocked designs, where many stimuli of a given event type are sequentially presented in an extended block of time such that the corresponding contrasts are susceptible to global attention or vigilance differences across blocks (Cohen et al., 2002). That is, it could be argued that participants may have been more vigilant during certain blocks, which could have produced vigilance activity in the VWFA. This is a valid criticism of blocked designs. However, vigilance is a global process and such an argument predicts a global increase in neural activity with numerous activations that are non-specifically distributed throughout the brain. The results reported by Price & Devlin (2003), by comparison, illustrated a very limited number of activations (Figure 6.8), which rules out such a vigilance explanation. Even if a vigilance explanation might explain away all the blocked results, it does not apply to the studies that employed event-related designs – where event types were intermixed such that the potential vigilance confound does not apply – and also found that the VWFA was not selective for visually presented words. In a separate argument, proponents of the majority view have accurately pointed out that VWFA activity produced by words presented in the auditory modality (Figure 6.8, bottom image) could trigger visual imagery of the words, particularly during tasks that foster word visualization, and thus should not be taken as evidence against the visual selectivity of this region. Cohen, Jobert, Le Bihan, & Dehaene (2004) tested this empirically in an fMRI study where participants were presented with words in the auditory modality and detected either sounds, where the auditory representation should be maintained, or corresponding letters, where transformation from an auditory to a visual representation would be beneficial for task performance. It was predicted that the VWFA should have been relatively more active during the visual feature detection task. However, the VWFA was found to have a similar magnitude of activation during the sound detection and letter detection tasks. This null finding may have been due to insufficient sensitivity and thus weakens, but does not rule out, the argument that words presented in the auditory modality may activate the VWFA due to word visualization. Of importance, even if this explanation is correct, it might account for the VWFA for auditory words but does not account for the evidence that visual objects have activated the VWFA to the same or similar degree as visual words.

Still, there have been only a limited number of studies supporting the minority view such that these findings may be largely ignored by proponents of the majority view at this time. Additional empirical studies need to be conducted to further assess the degree of selectivity in the VWFA.

With regard to VWFA localization, purported activation of this region can be discounted if it is too distant from its known location (McCandliss et al., 2003). Ben-Shachar, Dougherty, Deutsch, & Wandell (2007) attempted to localize the VWFA anatomically within the posterior occipito-temporal sulcus. However, words produced similar responses in the left and right hemispheres, which is at odds with the differential pattern of responses that have been consistently observed in the VWFA and its right hemisphere homologue (Figure 6.2 and Figure 6.9). Moreover, the region identified was more than two standard deviations posterior to the known location of the VWFA. As such, this study almost certainly investigated the processing characteristics of an extrastriate region posterior to the VWFA. Reinke, Fernandes, Schwindt, O'Craven, & Grady (2008) similarly assumed the VWFA was localized to a region that was far more posterior than the known anatomic location of this region. These findings highlight that the correct identification of the VWFA and its right hemisphere homologue should include comparisons of the spatial coordinates and activation profiles to the highly consistent findings that have been previously reported.

Of importance, all the minority view studies considered in this chapter localized the VWFA to within one standard deviation from the known anatomic location of this region, which side steps a potential argument that the VWFA might have been incorrectly localized in these studies.

Of additional relevance to word processing localization, proponents of the majority view would need to explain why the VWFA is nearly always co-activated with the left inferior frontal gyrus and often co-activated with the left superior temporal gyrus to convincingly argue for the existence of the this region. As word processing has been associated with activity in multiple areas, what is the justification for selecting a single region out of many active regions and labeling it as the single area mediating that function? It seems very unlikely that a convincing answer will materialize.

CONCLUSION

The VWFA processes words and word-like stimuli presented in the visual modality. However, visual word processing also appears to involve other cortical regions such as the left inferior frontal gyrus and the left superior temporal gyrus. Moreover, the VWFA does not appear to be selective for visual word processing, as this region also responds to other stimulus types such as objects. While the amount of evidence challenging the localization and selectivity of the VWFA is currently limited, the burden lies with the proponents of the VWFA to provide convincing justification for the continued use of this label.

SUGGESTED READINGS

Majority view

Dehaene, S., Naccache, L., Cohen, L., Le Bihan, D., Mangin, J. F., Poline, J. B., & Rivière, D. (2001). Cerebral mechanisms of word masking and unconscious repetition priming. *Nature Neuroscience, 4,* 752–758.

Glezer, L. S., Jiang, X., & Riesenhuber, M. (2009). Evidence for highly selective neuronal tuning to whole words in the "visual word form area." *Neuron, 62,* 199–204. Open access.

Minority view

Szwed, M., Dehaene, S., Kleinschmidt, A., Eger, E., Valabrègue, R., Amadon, A., & Cohen, L. (2011). Specialization for written words over objects in the visual cortex. *NeuroImage, 56,* 330–344.

Woodhead, Z. V., Wise, R. J., Sereno, M., & Leech, R. (2011). Dissociation of sensitivity to spatial frequency in word and face preferential areas of the fusiform gyrus. *Cerebral Cortex, 21,* 2307–2312. Open access.

REFERENCES

Ben-Shachar, M., Dougherty, R. F., Deutsch, G. K., & Wandell, B. A. (2007). Differential sensitivity to words and shapes in ventral occipito-temporal cortex. *Cerebral Cortex, 17,* 1604–1611.

Cohen L., Dehaene, S., Naccache, L., Lehéricy, S., Dehaene-Lambertz, G., Hénaff, M. A., & Michel, F. (2000). The visual word form area: Spatial and temporal characterization of an initial stage of reading in normal subjects and posterior split-brain patients. *Brain, 123,* 291–307.

Cohen, L., Jobert, A., Le Bihan, D., & Dehaene, S. (2004). Distinct unimodal and multimodal regions for word processing in the left temporal cortex. *NeuroImage, 23,* 1256–1270.

Cohen, L., Lehéricy, S., Chochon, F., Lemer, C., Rivaud, S., & Dehaene, S. (2002). Language-specific tuning of visual cortex? Functional properties of the Visual Word Form Area. *Brain, 125,* 1054–1069.

Cohen, L., Martinaud, O., Lemer, C., Lehéricy, S., Samson, Y., Obadia, M., Slachevsky, A., & Dehaene, S. (2003). Visual word recognition in the left and right hemispheres: Anatomical and functional correlates of peripheral alexias. *Cerebral Cortex, 13,* 1313–1333.

Dehaene, S., Le Clec'H, G., Poline, J. B., Le Bihan, D., & Cohen, L. (2002). The visual word form area: A prelexical representation of visual words in the fusiform gyrus. *NeuroReport, 13,* 321–325.

Dehaene, S., Naccache, L., Cohen, L., Le Bihan, D., Mangin, J. F., Poline, J. B., & Rivière, D. (2001). Cerebral mechanisms of word masking and unconscious repetition priming. *Nature Neuroscience, 4,* 752–758.

Gaillard, R., Naccache, L., Pinel, P., Clémenceau, S., Volle, E., Hasboun, D., Dupont, S., Baulac, M., Dehaene, S., Adam, C., & Cohen, L. (2006). Direct intracranial, fMRI, and lesion evidence for the causal role of left inferotemporal cortex in reading. *Neuron, 50,* 191–204.

Glezer, L. S., Jiang, X., & Riesenhuber, M. (2009). Evidence for highly selective neuronal tuning to whole words in the "visual word form area." *Neuron, 62,* 199–204.

Hillis, A. E., Newhart, M., Heidler, J., Barker, P., Herskovits, E., & Degaonkar, M. (2005). The roles of the "visual word form area" in reading. *NeuroImage, 24,* 548–559.

Kronbichler, M., Hutzler, F., Wimmer, H., Mair, A., Staffen, W., & Ladurner, G. (2004). The visual word form area and the frequency with which words are encountered: Evidence from a parametric fMRI study. *NeuroImage, 21,* 946–953.

Liu, C., Zhang, W. T., Tang, Y. Y., Mai, X. Q., Chen, H. C., Tardif, T., & Luo, Y. J. (2008). The Visual Word Form Area: Evidence from an fMRI study of implicit processing of Chinese characters. *NeuroImage, 40,* 1350–1361.

McCandliss, B. D., Cohen, L., & Dehaene, S. (2003). The visual word form area: Expertise for reading in the fusiform gyrus. *Trends in Cognitive Sciences, 7,* 293–299.

Price, C. J. (2000). The anatomy of language: Contributions from functional neuroimaging. *Journal of Anatomy, 197,* 335–359.

Price, C. J., & Devlin, J. T. (2003). The myth of the visual word form area. *NeuroImage, 19,* 473–481.

Reinke, K., Fernandes, M., Schwindt, G., O'Craven, K., & Grady, C. L. (2008). Functional specificity of the visual word form area: General activation for words and symbols but specific network activation for words. *Brain and Language, 104,* 180–189.

Starrfelt, R., & Gerlach, C. (2007). The visual what for area: Words and pictures in the left fusiform gyrus. *NeuroImage, 35,* 334–342.

Szwed, M., Dehaene, S., Kleinschmidt, A., Eger, E., Valabrègue, R., Amadon, A., & Cohen, L. (2011). Specialization for written words over objects in the visual cortex. *NeuroImage, 56,* 330–344.

Vigneau, M., Jobard, G., Mazoyer, B., & Tzourio-Mazoyer, N. (2005). Word and non-word reading: What role for the visual word form area? *NeuroImage, 27*, 694–705.

Woodhead, Z. V., Wise, R. J., Sereno, M., & Leech, R. (2011). Dissociation of sensitivity to spatial frequency in word and face preferential areas of the fusiform gyrus. *Cerebral Cortex, 21*, 2307–2312.

7 Can Visual Mental Images be Pictorial?

A visual image refers to a mental representation of an object or scene. The nature of visual imagery has been debated for decades, but the candidate hypotheses have remained the same. The pictorial imagery hypothesis, the majority view, predicts that visual images can be depictive, with visual details and spatial relationships like visual perception, and thus predicts activity in early visual processing regions such as V1 (Figure 7.1, left). The symbolic imagery hypothesis, the minority view, predicts that visual images are not depictive but rather are represented more symbolically, as with language (Chapter 6), and thus should activate word processing regions but not early visual processing regions (Figure 7.1, right). These hypotheses illustrate that visual imagery can be related to perception and language processing. Imagery has also been linked to working memory, corresponding to the active maintenance of the image, and can also rely on long-term memory, if previously experienced objects or events are imagined. Given that visual imagery has been associated with a number of cognitive processes, this debate has broad implications. The pictorial imagery hypothesis and the symbolic imagery hypothesis have been evaluated empirically, as only the pictorial imagery hypothesis predicts that visual imagery can produce activity in early visual areas such as V1, the first visual cortical processing region that is involved in detailed visual-spatial processing. While there is compelling evidence supporting the pictorial imagery hypothesis, proponents of the minority view have provided empirical evidence and theoretical arguments in support of the symbolic imagery hypothesis that continue to foster debate.

Figure 7.1 *Pictorial and symbolic hypotheses of imagery. Top, if a visual stimulus, such as the painting* Stairway at Auvers *by van Gogh (1890), is studied and then imagined there are two hypotheses regarding the nature of mental imagery. Left, the pictorial imagery hypothesis predicts the image can be depictive, with visual details and spatial relationships. Such a visual-spatial representation is predicted to activate early visual regions including V1 (white shaded oval), but may also activate higher-level regions associated with shape, category, or word processing (lateral view, occipital pole at the right). Right, the symbolic imagery hypothesis predicts that an image is represented symbolically, such as by a verbal description that would activate word processing regions (white shaded oval) but would not activate early visual regions such as V1.*

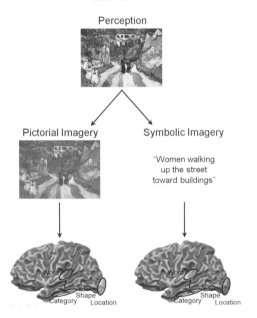

MAJORITY VIEW

The imagery debate has been reformulated multiple times. An initial debate within cognitive psychology and a subsequent debate within cognitive neuroscience will be briefly considered, followed by a detailed evaluation of the evidence pertaining to the current debate within cognitive neuroscience. Stephen Kosslyn has been the major proponent of the pictorial imagery hypothesis throughout all phases of this debate.

Behavioural evidence

Behavioural measures were first used in the field of cognitive psychology in an effort to distinguish between the pictorial imagery hypothesis and the symbolic imagery hypothesis. In a study by Kosslyn, Ball, & Reiser (1978), participants first memorized a fictional map of an island with a hut, a tree, a rock, a well, a lake, sand, and grass (Figure 7.2, top). Then, the map was removed, participants heard the names of object pairs (e.g., "sand" and "hut"), imagined a little black dot moving as quickly as possible in the shortest path between each pair of objects, and pressed a button. Reaction time was highly correlated with the distance between objects (Figure 7.2, bottom), which suggested participants visualized the map during the task (i.e., the mental images were depictive). However, as discussed below, the images might have actually been symbolic in nature, as response time could have been correlated with distance because participants had *tacit knowledge* that it should take longer to mentally scan greater distances. This tacit knowledge argument was used to question cognitive psychology evidence that supported the pictorial imagery hypothesis, and led, in part, to the next phase of the imagery debate.

Activation evidence

To address the limitations of behavioural evidence, proponents of the pictorial imagery hypothesis turned to cognitive neuroscience. Specifically, only the pictorial imagery hypothesis predicts that imagery can activate early visual areas such as V1 (Figure 7.1). Moreover, if such activation was observed it would be resistant to a tacit knowledge argument because V1 activation is not under volitional control (although the evidence in Chapter 3 indicates activity in this region can reflect conscious processing). Kosslyn & Thompson (2003) conducted a meta-analysis of 39 neuroimaging studies of visual imagery and found that approximately half of these studies reported activity in early visual regions, including V1 (Brodmann area 17) and extrastriate cortex (Brodmann area 18; Figure 1.6). As detailed below, imagery activity in V1 has also been observed in approximately half of the individual participants evaluated, which is consistent with the group results. These findings indicate that visual imagery effects are weaker or more variable across participants than the robust visual perception effects that have been

Figure 7.2 *Behavioural evidence that imagery is pictorial. Top, fictional map of an island that was memorized and then imagined. Bottom, speed of mentally scanning between objects on the imagined map as a function of distance (seconds per centimetre).*

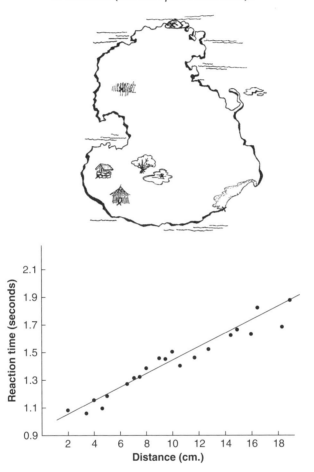

(Kosslyn et al., Visual images preserve metric spatial information: Evidence from studies of image scanning, Journal of Experimental Psychology: Human Perception and Performance, 4, 1, 47–60, 1978, published by the American Psychological Association, reprinted with permission.)

consistently observed at the individual participant and group level of analysis. Kosslyn & Thompson also found that early visual region activity was more often observed in studies that employed techniques with higher sensitivity, which supports the previous point, and studies that employed tasks with more detailed visualization.

These findings provide compelling evidence that visual imagery can activate early visual regions, in support of the pictorial imagery hypothesis. However, as discussed below, proponents of the minority view have argued that early visual activity could be epiphenomenal (i.e., having no functional value, as is typically the case with the sound of a car engine). This is a valid argument as cortical-cortical projections are known to exist between temporal cortex and early visual regions (Figure 1.3), thus symbolic imagery activity in temporal cortex could feedback and incidentally activate V1 and extrastriate cortex.

Lesion evidence

Kosslyn, Pascual-Leone, Felician, Camposano, Keenan, Thompson, Ganis, Sukel, & Alpert (1999) conducted a PET-TMS experiment to assess whether imagery activity in V1 was epiphenomenal. Participants first memorized sets of bars within each quadrant that had variable length, width, tilt, and spacing (Figure 7.3, left). Then, they heard the labels (numbers) of two quadrants identifying the target sets of bars and the dimension to be compared and responded to indicate whether the first target set was greater in that dimension. As in other studies, visual imagery produced PET activity in V1 (Brodmann area 17) and extrastriate cortex (Brodmann areas 18 and 19; Figure 7.3, middle). In a separate experiment in the same study, 1 Hertz TMS was applied to the occipital pole for ten minutes to temporarily disrupt processing in V1 (the real TMS condition) or was applied after lowering the coil three centimetres and rotating it 90 degrees to ensure cortex was not stimulated (the sham TMS condition). Real TMS versus sham TMS preferentially impaired performance on the visual imagery task and a corresponding visual perception task, as indicated by the relatively slower response times following real TMS (Figure 7.3, right). These findings show that V1 is necessary for visual imagery, providing compelling support for the pictorial imagery hypothesis.

Retinotopic activation evidence

The most recent and current form of the imagery debate has focused on the precise spatial layout of the visual image in V1. This region lies within the medial occipital cortex on the upper and lower banks of the calcarine sulcus and has a retinotopic organization of the visual field, where adjacent positions in the visual field are

Figure 7.3   *Activation and TMS evidence that imagery is pictorial. Left, four sets of bars that were memorized and then imagined. Middle, visual imagery activity (in light grey/white) within V1 (Brodmann area 17) and extrastriate cortex (Brodmann areas 18 and 19; coronal view). Right, response time (in milliseconds) for individual participants (numbered) during the perception task and the imagery task following real TMS to V1 that temporary disrupted processing in this region or sham TMS that did not disrupt processing in this region.*

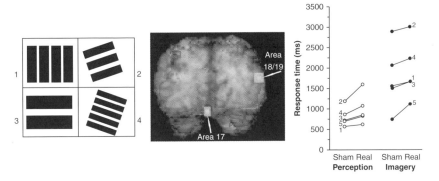

(From Kosslyn et al., 1999, The role of area 17 in visual imagery: Convergent evidence from PET and rTMS, Science, 284, 167–170. Reprinted with permission from AAAS.)

mapped onto adjacent locations on the cortical surface. Holmes (1945) created a detailed retinotopic map of V1 primarily based on comparisons between the spatial location and extent of perceptual deficits in the visual field and the site of V1 damage caused by gunshot wounds incurred during World War I (Figure 7.4). Of relevance, the right visual field is mapped onto V1 in the left hemisphere, while the left visual field is mapped onto V1 in the right hemisphere. Furthermore, the central visual field (near fixation) is mapped onto more posterior V1 (close to the occipital pole), while the peripheral visual field (far from fixation) is mapped onto more anterior V1 (away from the occipital pole). That is, the topographic organization of the visual field in V1 is left-right reversed and central-to-peripheral visual field positions are mapped posterior-to-anterior. This retinotopic map has proven to be remarkably accurate, except that the amount of cortex allocated to the central visual field was underestimated (Horton & Hoyt, 1991).

Proponents of the majority view have capitalized on this topographic organization, as only the pictorial imagery hypothesis predicts that visual imagery at a particular spatial location should

Figure 7.4 *Illustration of the left hemisphere retinotopic map in V1 (left; medial view, occipital pole at the left). Regions of V1 are marked with shapes according to the corresponding positions in the right visual field (right; fixation is at the centre of the crosshairs, and radial and eccentric angles, in degrees, are demarcated by straight lines and semi-circles, respectively).*

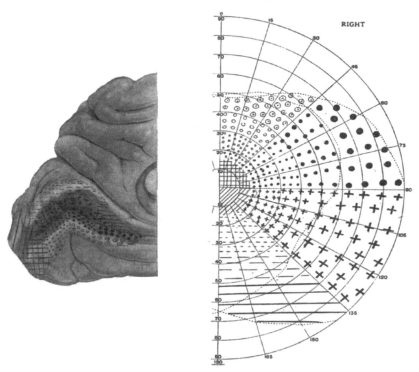

(Holmes, The organization of the visual cortex in man, Figure 5, 348–361, 1945, reprinted with permission of The Royal Society.)

produce retinotopic activity in V1. Such activity cannot be explained with a tacit knowledge argument, as it is nonsensical to argue that participants have any knowledge of the retinotopic organization of V1 or, as mentioned previously, have the ability to volitionally modulate activity in this region. Moreover, it would be difficult to argue that a specific pattern of retinotopic activity in V1 is epiphenomenal, as activity in this region reflects highly detailed visual-spatial processing that is inconsistent with the non-detailed symbolic processing that would be driving such epiphenomenal activity via a feedback mechanism. Only studies that reported retinotopic imagery effects in V1 are considered, as this evidence has provided the most compelling support for the pictorial imagery hypothesis.

Kosslyn, Alpert, Thompson, Maljkovic, Weise, Chabris, Hamilton, Rauch, & Buonanno (1993) used PET to assess whether visual imagery produced retinotopic activation of V1. Participants heard names of letters along with cue words asking whether the corresponding uppercase letter was composed solely of straight lines, was left-right symmetrical, had at least one horizontal or vertical straight line down the full length of one of its four sides, or had exactly two end points that did not meet any other lines. In the small letter imagery condition participants were instructed to imagine the letters at the smallest possible visible size, while in the large letter imagery condition participants were instructed to imagine the letters at the largest possible visible size. Consistent with the known retinotopic organization of V1 (Figure 7.4), the contrast of large letter imagery and small letter imagery produced activity in more anterior V1 (corresponding to the peripheral visual field

Figure 7.5 *Anterior-posterior (retinotopic) V1 activation evidence that imagery is pictorial. Right hemisphere illustration with V1 activity produced by the large letter imagery versus small letter imagery contrast and the small letter imagery versus large letter imagery contrast (sagittal view, occipital pole at the right; key to the bottom right). Tick marks indicate distance (in millimetres) from the anterior commissure, an anatomic landmark.*

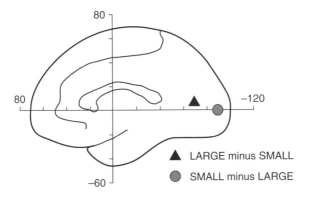

(Kosslyn et al., Visual mental imagery activates topographically organized visual cortex: PET investigations, 1993, 5, 3, Journal of Cognitive Neuroscience, 263–287; Reprinted by permission of MIT Press Journals; Copyright 1993.)

representation), while the contrast of small letter imagery and large letter imagery produced activity in more posterior V1 (corresponding to the central visual field representation; Figure 7.5). Kosslyn, Thompson, Kim, & Alpert (1995) reported a similar posterior-to-anterior shift in the location of V1 PET activity that corresponded to imagery of small, medium, and large objects.

Using fMRI, visual imagery has been shown to produce even more detailed retinotopic activity in V1 and early extrastriate cortex. Klein, Dubois, Mangin, Kherif, Flandin, Poline, Denis, Kosslyn, & Le Bihan (2004) presented participants with black and white flickering checkerboard wedges that were either horizontally oriented or vertically oriented in addition to a unique tone that was linked to each orientation in the visual perception condition (Figure 7.6, top). Note that flickering stimuli, as compared to non-flickering stimuli, produce a more robust response in visual processing regions. In the visual imagery condition, only tones were presented and, for each tone, participants were instructed to imagine the corresponding horizontally oriented flickering checkerboard wedges or vertically oriented flickering checkerboard wedges. In approximately half of the participants, visual perception and visual imagery of horizontally oriented wedges versus vertically oriented wedges produced activity in V1, near the base of the calcarine sulcus

Figure 7.6 *Detailed retinotopic activation evidence that imagery is pictorial. Top, during the visual perception condition, horizontally (horiz.) oriented or vertically (vert.) oriented stimuli (stim.), flickering checkerboard wedges, and linked tones were presented. During the visual imagery condition, only tones were presented and participants imagined the corresponding oriented checkerboard wedges. Middle, individual participant (S1) right hemisphere (RH) results. Regions of interest are identified in the left panels (posterior-medial view), with V1 consisting of the regions labeled 3 and 4, between the two upper light grey solid lines, and the approximate location of the calcarine sulcus demarcated by the white dashed line separating these regions. Middle and right panels, activity associated with the horizontal wedge versus vertical wedge contrasts (labeled to the left) for the perception condition and the imagery condition (labeled at the top; significance values are indicated by the greyscale bar to the right, with black reflecting greater significance). Bottom, results for the same participant in the left hemisphere (LH), with V1 between the two middle light grey solid lines.*

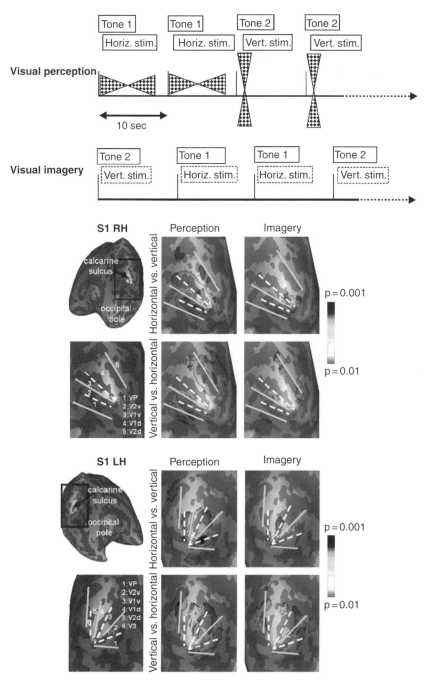

(Reprinted from Cognitive Brain Research, 22/1, Klein et al., Retinotopic organization of visual mental images as revealed by functional magnetic resonance imaging, Copyright 2004, with permission from Elsevier.)

(Figure 7.6, middle and bottom, white dashed line separating regions 3 and 4), while visual perception and visual imagery of vertically oriented wedges versus horizontally oriented wedged produced activity at the V1/V2 border and other vertical meridian representations (Figure 7.6, middle and bottom, light grey solid lines). These activations are consistent with the known retinotopic organization of V1 (Figure 7.4). Slotnick, Thompson, & Kosslyn (2005) conducted a similar fMRI study where participants imagined two flickering checkerboard wedges slowly rotating about the fixation point, and also reported detailed retinotopic V1 activity in half of the participants.

Additional depictive evidence

The preceding findings indicate that visual imagery can produce retinotopic activity in V1, providing strong support for the pictorial imagery hypothesis. Convergent evidence that imagery can be depictive has also stemmed from behavioural evidence and patient lesion findings. Pearson, Clifford, & Tong (2008) conducted a binocular rivalry experiment, where a green vertical grating was presented to the left eye and a red horizontal grating was presented to the right eye. Under these conditions, participants only perceive one grating at any given time, with the percept alternating in time such that each grating is observed with an approximately equal (50 percent) probability. To assess the degree of orientation specificity during visual imagery and visual perception, a horizontal red grating or a vertical green grating was either perceived or imagined, and then binocular rivalry gratings that varied in orientation relative to the initial grating orientation were presented (Figure 7.7, left; rivalry gratings were always oriented perpendicular to one another). Of relevance, it had previously been shown that participants were biased to perceive a particular binocular rivalry grating more often when it matched a previously perceived or imagined grating, referred to as *perceptual facilitation*. Visual perception and visual imagery produced similar orientation specific effects, with the greatest degree of perceptual facilitation when the orientation of the initial grating and the corresponding binocular rivalry grating matched (Figure 7.7, right). These orientation specific imagery effects can be assumed to reflect processing in V1 to some degree, as only the earliest visual regions (V1, V2,

Figure 7.7 *Orientation specific binocular rivalry-imagery effects. Left, in the perception condition either a red horizontal grating or a green vertical grating (illustrated in light grey and dark grey, respectively) was presented to the left eye (LE) or the right eye (RE), then the binocular rivalry gratings were presented with the same orientation (0 degrees) or different orientations relative than the initial grating. The imagery condition had the same protocol except that participants imagined the initial green vertical grating or red horizontal grating based on a cue (G or R). Right, for both the perception condition and the imagery condition (key at the top), the percentage of trials that the binocular rivalry grating was perceived in a configuration that corresponded to the initial grating (perceptual facilitation) as a function of the orientation difference between these gratings (in degrees, deg).*

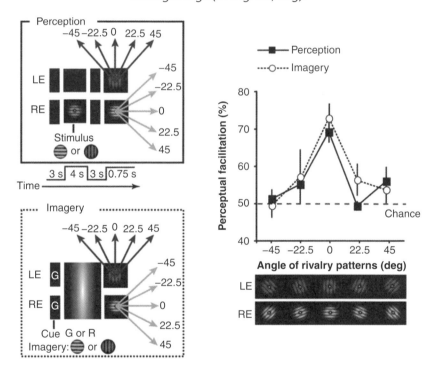

(Reprinted from Current Biology, 18/13, Pearson et al., The functional impact of mental imagery on conscious perception, Copyright 2008, with permission from Elsevier.)

and V3) are orientation selective (Tootell, Hadjikhani, Vanduffel, Liu, Mendola, Sereno, & Dale, 1998; Vanduffel, Tootell, Schoups, & Orban, 2002).

Farah, Soso, & Dasheiff (1992) tested the spatial extent of visual imagery in a patient before and after their entire right occipital lobe was removed in an effort to treat seizures. The patient and a group of control participants were instructed to imagine each of 12 objects such as a "kitten" or a "car" at the normal size, bring the imagined object closer while keeping it clear, stop moving it when it was as close as possible but the image was not overflowing (i.e., extending outside of the imagined visual field), and then report their corresponding distance to the object. The maximum extent of the imagined visual field, measured in degrees of visual angle, was computed based on an estimate of the actual size of each object and the reported distance to that object during imagery. Pre-operatively, the patient's visual field extent during imagery did not differ from that of control participants; however, post-operatively, the patient had a reduced visual field extent during imagery in the horizontal dimension but not the vertical dimension (Figure 7.8). This selective reduction in the horizontal visual field is precisely that predicted based on the retinotopic organization of V1, as the full extent of the horizontal visual field requires processing by both hemispheres while the full extent of the vertical visual field is processed separately in each hemisphere (Figure 7.4).

Figure 7.8 *Retinotopic lesion evidence. Maximum size of the visual image in an epilepsy patient, measured horizontally and vertically, both pre-operatively (pre-op) and post-operatively (post-op), following removal of the entire right occipital lobe.*

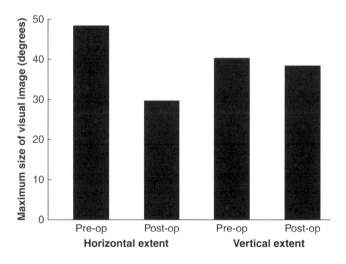

While the orientation specific and retinotopic imagery effects in the two preceding studies cannot be definitely attributed to V1, the results are consistent with this possibility and provide convergent evidence that imagery can be depictive.

MINORITY VIEW

The symbolic imagery hypothesis, the minority view, has been supported by both empirical results and theoretical arguments. As mentioned previously, approximately half of visual imagery neuroimaging studies have reported activity in V1 and early extrastriate cortex (Kosslyn & Thompson, 2003), which means the other half of imagery studies have not reported activity in V1. Many investigators have taken such null findings in V1 to suggest that visual imagery is not depictive (e.g., Roland & Gulyás, 1994). To illustrate, Mellet, Tzourio, Crivello, Joliot, Denis, & Mazoyer (1996) used PET to identify the neural regions associated with a mental cube assembly task, during which auditory word cues indicated the direction of subsequently added cubes to construct each of four objects (Figure 7.9, top). Participants reported using vivid visual imagery while performing this task. They were also able, with reasonable accuracy, to select the matching sequence of objects from four sets of objects. The control task consisted of words presented auditorily that sounded similar to the cues in the cube assembly task but had low imagery value and no directional content. A comparison between the cube assembly task and the control task produced no activity in V1 or in the surrounding extrastriate cortex (Figure 7.9, bottom, such activity would have been apparent to the left, near the occipital pole). This finding suggests that V1 is not necessarily activated during visual imagery, even when participants report vivid visual experience.

Zago, Corti, Bersano, Baron, Conti, Ballabio, Lanfranconi, Cinnante, Costa, Cappellari, & Bresolin (2010) reported a patient who had sudden blindness in both visual fields and was found to have complete lesions of V1 in both hemispheres (Figure 7.10). Visual imagery was assessed by asking questions about the structural characteristics of letters (e.g., top or bottom larger), animals (e.g., ear shape), objects (e.g., sharp or rounded), and colours (e.g., hue comparison). Despite a severe impairment in visual perception, the

Figure 7.9 *Null imagery effects in V1 and extrastriate cortex. Top, in the visual imagery condition participants imagined one cube (illustrated in dark grey), sequentially added 11 cubes according to auditory word cues presented twice per second (key to the right), visualized the object for five seconds, and then constructed the next object. Bottom, activity associated with imagery (sagittal view illustration; occipital pole at the left).*

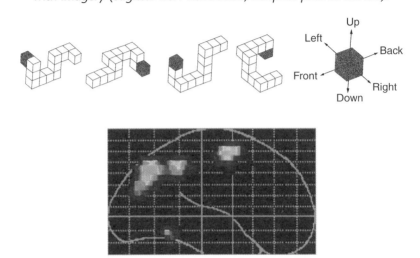

(Mellet et al., 1996; The journal of neuroscience: the official journal of the Society for Neuroscience by SOCIETY FOR NEUROSCIENCE Copyright 1996. Reproduced with permission.)

patient had no impairment in any of the 16 visual imagery tasks, as compared with control participant performance. These results suggest that processing in V1 is not necessary for visual imagery.

Zenon Pylyshyn (2002) has made theoretical arguments to discount the evidence supporting the pictorial imagery hypothesis. As mentioned above, he has argued that depictive imagery evidence may be due to tacit knowledge, where participants simulate what would happen during visual perception. If depictive imagery results were eliminated by asking participants to use a different strategy, referred to as *cognitive penetrability*, it could be argued that pictorial evidence does not reflect a core aspect of mental imagery. To evaluate this possibility, different task instructions were used in the previously described fictional island experiment in which participants imagined a dot moving between object pairs and a strong correlation was observed between reaction time and mental distance traversed (Kosslyn et al., 1978). Specifically, rather than imagining

Figure 7.10   *Computed tomography (x-ray) image of a blind patient with complete V1 lesions in both hemispheres (lesions are shown in darker grey near the bottom; axial view, occipital pole at the bottom).*

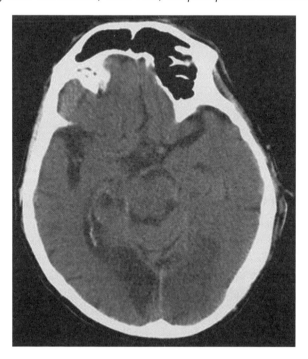

(Zago et al., 2010, A cortically blind patient with preserved visual imagery, Cognitive and Behavioral Neurology, 23, 1, 44–48, reprinted with permission from Wolters Kluwer Health.)

a dot moving between objects, as in the original experiment (see Figure 7.2), Pylyshyn instructed participants that there were lights at each object on the map and if a light went out at one object it would instantly go on at the other object. With these instructions, no relationship between reaction time and between-object distance was observed. This null finding suggests that the previous results could be attributed to task factors, rather than reflecting depictive visual imagery. Pylyshyn also pointed out that early visual activity associated with imagery could be epiphenomenal, as mentioned previously. If this is the case, imagery activity in V1 should not be taken to support the pictorial imagery hypothesis. In a separate argument, Pylyshyn pointed out that seemingly depictive imagery results may be attributed to selectively attending to specific regions of space. That is, selective attention to one region of space is known to increase the magnitude of activity in the corresponding retinotopic region of V1 (Chapter 3), and thus could produce the identical pattern of activity that has been attributed to depictive visual imagery. Pylyshyn's arguments are all valid and have challenged the empirical evidence supporting the pictorial imagery hypothesis. Armed with these arguments, Pylyshyn has made the strong claim that there is insufficient evidence to reject the symbolic imagery hypothesis.

COUNTERPOINTS

Before considering additional points, it is important to make explicit that the majority position states that imagery *can* be depictive but can also be symbolic, while the minority position maintains that imagery *cannot* be depictive and is thus always symbolic (Figure 7.1). It is notable that if the minority position were relaxed such that imagery could sometimes be depictive, there would be no difference between these hypotheses and the imagery debate would cease to exist (but this is unlikely to happen anytime soon).

The empirical evidence and theoretical positions that have been put forth by proponents of the minority view can be largely discounted. Proponents of the minority view have focused on the absence of activity in V1 and early extrastriate cortex that has been reported in approximately half of the empirical studies (Kosslyn & Thompson, 2003). However, as underscored in Chapter 5, null findings can be due to numerous factors such as the employment of a task that does not sufficiently engage the cognitive process of interest, a technique with insufficient sensitivity, an insufficient number of participants, or between participant variability. Of relevance, the evidence supporting the majority view has shown that visual imagery *can* produce activity in V1 – not that activity is always observed in this region – which is exactly what the pictorial imagery hypothesis predicts. Said another way, the symbolic imagery hypothesis predicts null findings for all studies and all participants, but this prediction has been contradicted by the observed V1 imagery effects in numerous studies.

With regard to the argument that V1 activity during visual imagery might be epiphenomenal, temporary disruption of V1 using TMS impaired visual imagery (Kosslyn et al., 1999), in direct opposition to this possibility. Still, this is a single result, thus the necessity of V1 during visual imagery could be bolstered by additional lesion studies.

The tacit knowledge argument has also been addressed empirically. While such an argument may explain behavioural results, it cannot explain the neuroimaging findings. Specifically, there is no basis to argue that tacit knowledge could be engaged to produce the retinotopic patterns of V1 activity that have been reported during imagery, as participants have no knowledge of the retinotopic layout of V1 nor do they have the ability to volitionally activate specific regions of V1. It can be assumed that Pylyshyn (2002) followed a similar line of reasoning when stipulating the type of neuroimaging evidence that would support the pictorial imagery hypothesis:

> In order to support such a view, it is important not only that such topographically organized areas be involved in imagery, but also that their involvement be of the right sort – that the way their topographical organization is involved reflects the spatial properties of the image.
>
> (p. 175)

Exactly this type of topographic evidence was subsequently reported in the form of retinotopic activity in V1 during visual imagery (Klein et al., 2004; Slotnick et al., 2005), thus providing support for the pictorial imagery hypothesis by Pylyshyn's own criterion.

It is more difficult to discount the spatial attention explanation of evidence that has been taken to support the pictorial imagery hypothesis. Disentangling these cognitive processes is particularly tricky as visual imagery involves imagining an object at a specific spatial location, visual attention can be allocated to the identical spatial location without visual imagery, and both processes would be expected to increase activity in V1. For instance, in the Klein et al. (2004) study, participants were instructed to imagine the flickering wedges at the horizontal meridian or at the vertical meridian (Figure 7.6). However, attention to the same spatial locations without visual imagery could have also produced the retinotopic pattern of V1 activity observed (Chapter 3). In an effort to address this issue, Slotnick et al. (2005) compared retinotopic activity associated with visual imagery of rotating flickering wedges with retinotopic activity associated with an attention control condition in which the same spatial locations were attended without imagery. In support of the pictorial imagery hypothesis, visual imagery produced a greater magnitude of retinotopic activity in V1 than visual attention. However, it could still be argued that a relatively greater degree of attention was allocated during the imagery condition than during the attention control condition, which could have produced the greater magnitude of retinotopic activity that was observed in the imagery condition. Future work will be needed to separate visual attention and visual imagery effects, or to quantify the degree to which visual attention modulates V1 activity during visual imagery tasks. Thus, although the null empirical findings, the tacit knowledge argument, and the epiphenomenal argument can be discounted, the attention explanation for depictive imagery activity in V1 remains a serious concern.

CONCLUSION

There is a preponderance of evidence that visual imagery can be depictive, which supports the pictorial imagery hypothesis and contradicts the symbolic imagery hypothesis. However, the spatial attention account of depictive imagery results has yet to be adequately addressed. Still, all the visual imagery evidence to date supports or is consistent with the pictorial imagery hypothesis. Therefore, it is anticipated that when visual imagery and visual attention are disentangled, the pictorial imagery hypothesis will gain further support.

SUGGESTED READINGS

Majority view

Kosslyn, S. M., Pascual-Leone, A., Felician, O., Camposano. S., Keenan, J. P., Thompson, W. L., Ganis, G., Sukel, K. E., & Alpert, N. M. (1999). The role of area 17 in visual imagery: Convergent evidence from PET and rTMS. *Science, 284*, 167–170.

Slotnick, S. D., Thompson, W. L., & Kosslyn, S. M. (2005). Visual mental imagery induces retinotopically organized activation of early visual areas. *Cerebral Cortex, 15*, 1570–1583. Open access.

Minority view

Pylyshyn, Z. W. (2002). Mental imagery: In search of a theory. *Behavioral and Brain Sciences, 25*, 157–182.

Mellet, E., Tzourio, N., Crivello, F., Joliot, M., Denis, M., & Mazoyer, B. (1996). Functional anatomy of spatial mental imagery generated from verbal instructions. *The Journal of Neuroscience, 16*, 6504–6512. Open access.

REFERENCES

Farah, M. J., Soso, M. J., & Dasheiff, R. M. (1992). Visual angle of the mind's eye before and after unilateral occipital lobectomy. *Journal of Experimental Psychology: Human Perception and Performance, 18*, 241–246.

Holmes, G. (1945). The organization of the visual cortex in man. *Proceedings of the Royal Society of London. Series B, Biological Sciences, 132*, 348–361.

Horton, J. C., & Hoyt, W. F. (1991). The representation of the visual field in human striate cortex: A revision of the classic Holmes map. *Archives of Ophthalmology, 109*, 816–824.

Klein, I., Dubois, J., Mangin, J. F., Kherif, F., Flandin, G., Poline, J. B., Denis, M., Kosslyn, S. M., & Le Bihan, D. (2004). Retinotopic organization of visual mental images as revealed by functional magnetic resonance imaging. *Cognitive Brain Research, 22*, 26–31.

Kosslyn, S. M., & Thompson, W. L. (2003). When is early visual cortex activated during visual mental imagery? *Psychological Bulletin, 129*, 723–746.

Kosslyn, S. M., Alpert, N. M., Thompson, W. L., Maljkovic, V., Weise, S. B., Chabris, C. F., Hamilton, S. E., Rauch, S. L., & Buonanno, F. S. (1993). Visual mental imagery activates topographically organized visual cortex: PET investigations. *Journal of Cognitive Neuroscience, 5*, 263–287.

Kosslyn, S. M., Ball, T. M., & Reiser, B. J. (1978). Visual images preserve metric spatial information: Evidence from studies of image scanning. *Journal of Experimental Psychology: Human Perception and Performance, 4,* 47–60.

Kosslyn, S. M., Pascual-Leone, A., Felician, O., Camposano. S., Keenan, J. P., Thompson, W. L., Ganis, G., Sukel, K. E., & Alpert, N. M. (1999). The role of area 17 in visual imagery: Convergent evidence from PET and rTMS. *Science, 284,* 167–170.

Kosslyn, S. M., Thompson, W. L., Kim, I. J., & Alpert, N. M. (1995). Topographical representations of mental images in primary visual cortex. *Nature, 378,* 496–498.

Mellet, E., Tzourio, N., Crivello, F., Joliot, M., Denis, M., & Mazoyer, B. (1996). Functional anatomy of spatial mental imagery generated from verbal instructions. *The Journal of Neuroscience, 16,* 6504–6512.

Pearson, J., Clifford, C. W., & Tong, F. (2008). The functional impact of mental imagery on conscious perception. *Current Biology, 18,* 982–986.

Pylyshyn, Z. W. (2002). Mental imagery: In search of a theory. *Behavioral and Brain Sciences, 25,* 157–182.

Roland, P. E., & Gulyás, B. (1994). Visual imagery and visual representation. *Trends in Neurosciences, 17,* 281–287.

Sereno, M. I., & Dale, A. M. (1998). Functional analysis of primary visual cortex (V1) in humans. *Proceedings of the National Academy of Sciences of the United States of America, 95,* 811–817.

Slotnick, S. D., Thompson, W. L., & Kosslyn, S. M. (2005). Visual mental imagery induces retinotopically organized activation of early visual areas. *Cerebral Cortex, 15,* 1570–1583.

Tootell, R. B., Hadjikhani, N. K., Vanduffel, W., Liu, A. K., Mendola, J. D., Vanduffel, W., Tootell, R. B., Schoups, A. A., & Orban, G. A. (2002). The organization of orientation selectivity throughout macaque visual cortex. *Cerebral Cortex, 12,* 647–662.

van Gogh, V. (1890). *Stairway at Auvers* [Painting]. St. Louis, MO: Saint Louis Art Museum.

Zago, S., Corti, S., Bersano, A., Baron, P., Conti, G., Ballabio, E., Lanfranconi, S., Cinnante, C., Costa, A., Cappellari, A., & Bresolin, N. (2010). A cortically blind patient with preserved visual imagery. *Cognitive and Behavioral Neurology, 23,* 44–48.

8

The Neural Basis of Processing Animacy

When you see animate others, such as two people, they can be evaluated to provide information regarding the type of social interaction in which they are engaged or to assess whether you might interact with them. Proponents of the majority view have hypothesized that such social processing is mediated by regions in the *social network* of the brain (Figure 8.1, left) that includes the medial prefrontal cortex and the cingulate cortex (which are thought to be involved in self-reflection), the amygdala (which is involved in emotion processing), and the superior temporal sulcus and the fusiform gyrus (which process biological motion and biological form, respectively; Adolphs, 2001; Wheatley, Milleville, & Martin, 2007). Proponents of the minority view have hypothesized that social processing is mediated by regions of the *mirror network* (Figure 8.1, right) that includes the inferior frontal gyrus, just anterior to and including the ventral premotor cortex, and the anterior inferior parietal lobule (Rizzolatti & Craighero, 2004; Rizzolatti & Fabbri-Destro, 2008). To illustrate mirror network processing, when an observer sees another person performing an action, such as grasping an object, the observer's hand region in the ventral premotor cortex activates as if the observer is grasping the object as well. Mirror network activity is thought to be important for understanding the intentions of others, a key aspect of social processing, via the simulation of an observed action. The social network hypothesis and the mirror network hypothesis make distinct predictions regarding the neural regions that mediate animacy/social processing and thus can be tested empirically.

Figure 8.1 *Social network and mirror network regions. Left, the social network includes the medial prefrontal cortex (mPFC), the cingulate cortex (CC), the amygdala (amyg.), the superior temporal sulcus (STS), and the fusiform gyrus (FG; medial and lateral views are shown at the top and bottom, respectively). Right, the mirror network includes the inferior frontal gyrus (IFG) and the anterior inferior parietal lobule (IPL).*

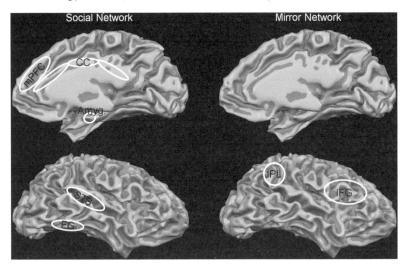

MAJORITY VIEW

A preponderance of evidence indicates that the social network is involved in processing animacy. It should be mentioned that the neural basis of animacy/social processing is often investigated using stimuli that are associated with both social and non-social processing. For example, emotional faces have been used to study social processing; however, these stimuli are imbued with emotional content making it uncertain whether the corresponding neural activity reflects social processing or emotional processing. As such, studies that have confounded social and non-social processing are not considered.

Before turning to the neuroimaging evidence, a classic study by Heider & Simmel (1944) will be briefly considered, as their stimulus protocol has served as a model for many studies in social cognitive neuroscience. Participants viewed a short (approximately two-minute) film in which a large triangle, a small triangle, and a circle moved in an environment consisting of a rectangle with a section that opened or closed like the door of a room (Figure 8.2).

Figure 8.2   *Heider and Simmel movie frame. Single frame of a movie in which shapes (a big triangle, a small triangle, and a circle) moved about an environment consisting of a rectangular room with a door.*

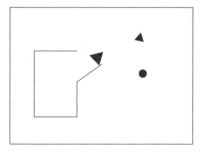

(Heider and Simmel; From *American Journal of Psychology*. Copyright 1944 by the Board of Trustees of the University of Illinois. Used with permission of the author and the University of Illinois Press.)

This movie should be watched before proceeding to appreciate the high degree of social interaction conveyed by these simple moving shapes – it is posted online at http://www.pnas.org/content/ 101/19/7487/suppl/DC1#F1 (Heberlein & Adolphs, 2004, Supporting Movie 1). In anthropomorphic terms, the movie includes scenes such as the big triangle and a small triangle fighting, the big triangle chasing the circle inside the room, and the small triangle and circle dancing together (and possibly kissing). Of importance, these shapes have no inherent animate or social attributes, but are interpreted as such based only on their patterns of movement.

Activation evidence

Over half a century after the Heider and Simmel study was published, Martin & Weisberg (2003) presented participants with moving shapes during fMRI to investigate the neural regions associated with social processing. Each of the 24 movies lasted 21 seconds and were created from shapes (such as circles, triangles, and squares) to show either social actions or mechanical actions. Social actions included a baseball game, dancing, fishing, scaring, playing on a seesaw, playing on a slide, swimming, and sharing (Figure 8.3, top, illustrates sharing). Mechanical actions, which were meaningful but had no social content, served as the primary control condition and included billiards, bowling, pinball, a canon, a crane, a steam shovel, a conveyer belt, and a paper shredder. Shapes from either

Figure 8.3 *(Opposite) Social processing activates social network regions. Top, movie frames illustrating sharing. An adult (large circle) gives ice cream cones to three children (small circles), a child drops their ice cream, and then another child shares their ice cream with that child. Bottom, social processing activity (in black; left panels) and corresponding activation timecourses (right panels; percent signal change as a function of time), with regions labeled at the top, in the static shapes condition (stills), the social action condition (soc), the random motion condition with social stimuli (Rs), the mechanical action condition (mech), and the random motion condition with mechanical stimuli (Rm).*

---

the social movies or the mechanical movies that were in random motion or were static, which did not convey social information, served as additional control conditions. Participants were instructed to make a meaningful interpretation before viewing each social movie or mechanical movie, and were instructed not to interpret the random motion or static displays (to avoid the interpretation of random motion as meaningful). Movies interpreted as social versus mechanical produced activity in regions of the social network including the right ventromedial prefrontal cortex, the right amygdala, the left and right superior temporal sulcus, and the left and right fusiform gyrus (Figure 8.3, bottom left panels). Activation timecourses showed that these regions produced little activity when participants viewed shapes in random motion or static shapes (Figure 8.3, bottom right panels).

Castelli, Happé, Frith, & Frith (2000) also used movies with moving shapes, but employed PET to investigate the neural regions associated with viewing different forms of social interaction. Each of 12 movies lasted 34 to 45 seconds and consisted of a big red triangle and a small blue triangle. There were three types of movie: 1) *mental attribution* that involved persuading, bluffing, mocking, and surprising, 2) *physical attribution* that involved dancing, chasing, imitating, and leading, and 3) *random movement* that involved bouncing off the walls or drifting. The mental attribution and physical attribution conditions, which both involved social interaction, versus the random movement condition produced activity in the social network including the left medial prefrontal cortex, the left and right amygdala/temporal poles, the left and right superior temporal sulcus, and the left and right fusiform gyrus.

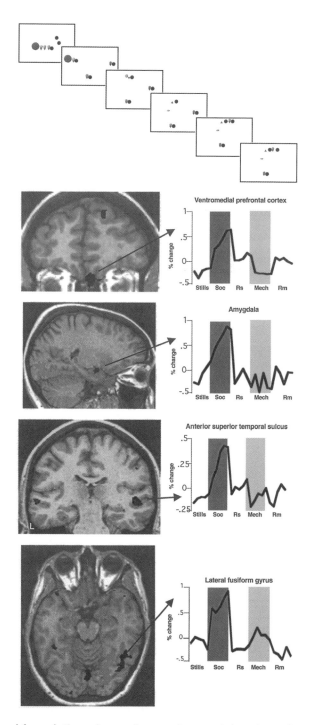

(Neural foundations for understanding social and mechanical concepts, Martin and Weisberg, *Cognitive Neuropsychology*, 2003, reprinted by permission of Taylor & Francis Ltd, http://www.tandf.co. uk/journals.)

Santos, Kuzmanovic, David, Rotarska-Jagiela, Eickhoff, Shah, Fink, Bente, & Vogeley (2010) presented movies of two moving three-dimensional spheres during fMRI. The first sphere moved toward the second sphere (the approach condition) or did not move in that direction, and then the second sphere moved toward the first sphere (the respond condition) or did not move in that direction. Approach movement always had a time delay to convey animate behaviour. Participants rated the animacy of each movie from one to four (where one meant "physical," two meant "rather physical," three meant "rather personal," and four meant "personal"). Similar to previous comparisons between animate versus inanimate conditions, regions were identified in which the magnitude of activity increased with increasing animacy ratings. This analysis revealed activity in the social network including the right medial prefrontal cortex, the right anterior cingulate cortex, the left superior temporal sulcus, and the left fusiform gyrus. Of additional relevance, the opposite pattern of activity, where the magnitude of activity decreased with increasing animacy ratings, was observed in mirror network regions including the right anterior inferior parietal lobule and the right inferior frontal gyrus (Figure 8.4). These findings support the social network hypothesis and directly contradict the mirror network hypothesis of animacy processing.

Figure 8.4 *Increasing animacy ratings are associated with decreasing mirror network activity. Regions where activity (contrast estimates) decreased with increasing animacy ratings (one meant least animate and four meant most animate) included the right anterior inferior parietal lobule (IPL) and the right inferior frontal gyrus (IFG; lateral view, occipital pole at the left).*

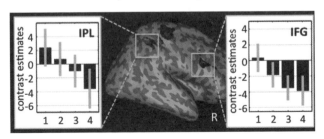

(Reprinted from NeuroImage, 53/1, Santos et al., Animated brain: A functional neuroimaging study on animacy experience, Copyright 2010, with permission from Elsevier.)

In contrast to the previous studies that employed simple geometric shapes, inherently animate stimuli have also been employed to investigate social processing. Mitchell, Heatherton, & Macrae (2002) presented participants with noun-adjective word pairs during fMRI. The nouns were either a name (such as "Emily") or an object (i.e., a type of clothing or fruit, such as "shirt" or "grape"), while the adjectives could only describe a person or a single category of object (e.g., "nervous" or "seedless"). Participants identified whether each word pair was appropriately paired or not appropriately paired. In comparison with the moving shapes engaged in social actions that were used in the previous studies, the person-adjective pairs used in this study did not constitute a social interaction. However, these stimuli were arguably of potential social relevance and the task did engage social knowledge, thus this experimental paradigm fits within the social/animacy processing framework. Person noun versus object noun comparisons produced activity within the social network including the right medial prefrontal cortex, the left superior temporal sulcus, and the right fusiform gyrus.

Morris, Pelphrey, & McCarthy (2005) also compared person and object processing during fMRI, but used a virtual reality environment. Participants either approached a person who was still, approached a person who moved (i.e., made a gesture such as scratching their face or touching their hair) or approached an object that moved (such as a clock with a swinging pendulum; Figure 8.5, top). Approaching a person without movement versus approaching an object (a social processing versus non-social processing contrast) produced activity in the left and right fusiform

Figure 8.5 (overleaf) *Stimulus protocol illustration and activity associated with approaching a person with or without gestures. Top left, virtual reality environment with a closed door at the end of a hallway. The door opened as the participant virtually walked down the hallway toward a person that moved (made a gesture) or did not move. An inanimate object was next to the person. The participant then turned left or right down a new hallway. Top right, a similar sequence with a moving object next to a portrait of a human face. Bottom, activity (in black) associated with approaching people with no gestures or approaching people with gestures (right hemisphere and left hemisphere lateral views are shown to the left and right, respectively, with occipital poles toward the sides of the figure).*

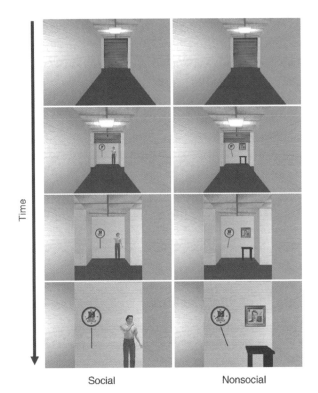

Social   Nonsocial

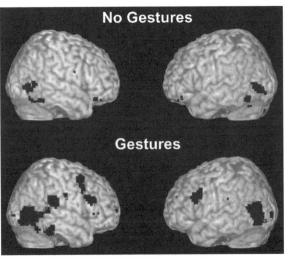

(Morris et al., Regional brain activation evoked when approaching a virtual human on a virtual walk, 2005, 17, 11, *Journal of Cognitive Neuroscience*, 1744–1752; Reprinted by permission of MIT Press Journals; Copyright 2005.)

gyrus (Figure 8.5, bottom, upper images). Approaching a person with movement versus approaching an object was also of relevance, as viewing a moving person would be expected to and did produce activity in the mirror network including the right inferior frontal gyrus and the right anterior inferior parietal lobule (Figure 8.5, bottom). This contrast also produced activity in social network regions including the right superior temporal sulcus and the left and right fusiform gyrus. Across both the person without movement condition and the person with movement condition, which both involved animate processing, activity was produced in the left and right fusiform gyrus within the social network, but only when the person moved did mirror network regions become active. This suggests that the mirror network was not activated by animacy per se, which was consistent across both conditions, but rather was activated by viewing a person making a gesture.

The use of person and object stimuli, as in the preceding two studies, is more realistic than employing simple shapes. However, it is difficult to equate such complex stimuli across conditions on other dimensions such as item familiarity or visual complexity, making it possible that these results were influenced by confounding factors. Even the previous moving shape studies used different movement patterns across conditions and thus did not eliminate low-level perceptual differences that might have modulated the effects to some degree. Wheatley et al. (2007) conducted an fMRI study that employed the identical target stimuli to avoid such low-level perceptual (non-social) confounds. Each of 12 moving shape movies was displayed on two different backgrounds that biased the interpretation of each shape as either animate or inanimate. On each trial, participants first viewed the background for 15 seconds, watched the moving shape on the background for 15 seconds (where, again, the background biased the interpretation of the object as either animate or inanimate), and then the background was displayed again for 15 seconds and participants were instructed to imagine (mentally replay) the motion of the object that had been seen during the preceding period (Figure 8.6, top). The contrast of moving shapes interpreted as animate versus moving shapes interpreted as inanimate, during both the watch condition and the imagine condition, produced activity in the entire social network including the right medial prefrontal cortex, the left and right cingulate cortex, the left amygdala, the right superior temporal sulcus,

Figure 8.6 *Social network regions are activated by animate processing and mirror network regions are activated regardless of animacy. Top, illustration of a trial where the context biased participants to interpret the moving shape as either animate (a figure skater) or inanimate (a spinning top). The background was displayed for 15 seconds (the look condition), the moving shape was added for 15 seconds (the watch condition), and then the background was shown again and participants were instructed to mentally replay the shape in motion (the imagine condition; the dashed arrows illustrate the motion trajectory and were not shown during the experiment). Middle, activity associated with animate versus inanimate*

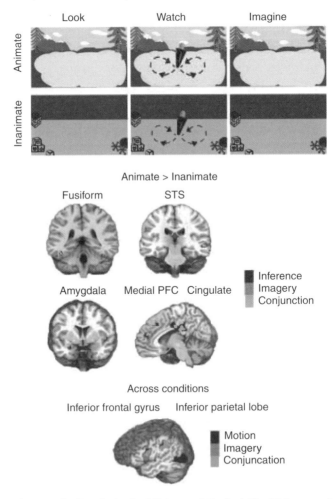

Figure 8.6   *(Continued) processing during the watch condition
(inference), the imagine condition (imagery), and the conjunction of these
conditions versus the baseline condition (regions are labeled above each
image; all coronal views, except for the sagittal view at the bottom right
with the occipital pole at the right; key to the right). Bottom, activity
during the watch condition (motion), the imagine condition (imagery),
and the conjunction of these conditions versus the baseline condition
(sagittal/lateral view, occipital pole at the right; key to the right.)*

and the left fusiform gyrus (Figure 8.6, middle). By comparison, the
anterior inferior parietal lobule and inferior frontal cortex, within
the mirror network, were not activated by this contrast (even at a
very lenient statistical threshold). However, these mirror network
regions were activated in the left and right hemisphere during
both the watch condition and the imagine condition regardless
of animacy (Figure 8.6, bottom), which may reflect participants
mirroring the perceived motion. These results provide compelling
evidence in support of the social network hypothesis, and directly
contradict the mirror network hypothesis.

Tavares, Lawrence, & Barnard (2008) also employed identical
stimuli and biased perception toward animate or inanimate movement. During fMRI, participants viewed 14 second movies of a blue
circle and a green circle in an environment with lines (Figure 8.7).
The circles had animated movement patterns that were affiliative
(such as coordinated approaching and touching), antagonsitic (such
as brief contact and then rapid retreating indicating aggression), or
indifferent (with no interaction). On each trial participants were
initially presented with a cue indicating that they should focus
on either behavioural characteristics or spatial characteristics of
the subsequent movie. To confirm participants were focusing on
the cued characteristics, a corresponding true/false probe statement followed each movie (e.g., the behavioural statement "soldiers
engaged in hand to hand combat" or the spatial statement "the blue
circle collided with one of the lines"). Attending to behavioural
characteristics versus attending to spatial characteristics produced
activity in the social network including the left and right dorsomedial prefrontal cortex, the left and right posterior cingulate cortex,
the left and right amygdala, the right superior temporal sulcus,
and the right fusiform gyrus. That this contrast activated the entire

Figure 8.7   *Frame of a movie where two circles had animated movement patterns that conveyed affiliative, antagonistic, or indifferent interaction.*

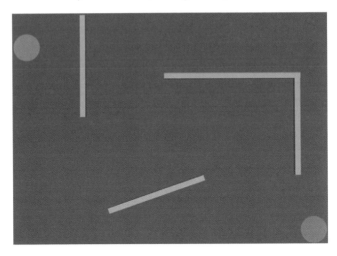

(Tavares et al., Paying attention to social meaning: An fMRI study, *Cerebral Cortex*, 2008, 18, 8, 1876–1885, by permission of Oxford University Press.)

social network is particularly striking considering that the stimulus materials were identical in both conditions and consisted of only two moving circles and a few stationary lines.

The two previous studies employed identical stimuli across animate and inanimate conditions to eliminate low-level perceptual confounds. However, it should be mentioned that viewing stimuli interpreted as animate might still engage additional processes such as emotion or attention that can be considered high-level confounds. Future studies in social cognitive neuroscience, like all areas of cognitive neuroscience, will make further progress by minimizing such confounds to better isolate the neural activity associated with the cognitive process of interest.

Lesion evidence

All the preceding results support the social network hypothesis of animacy processing. Patient lesion evidence has provided complementary evidence supporting this hypothesis. Heberlein & Adolphs (2004) reported a case study of a patient with relatively selective damage to the left and right amygdala due to Urbach–Wiethe disease (Figure 8.8, top; the patient also had also minor damage to the

Figure 8.8   *Amygdala lesions impair social processing. Top, MRI of a patient with selective left and right amygdala lesions demarcated by two symmetric black circles near the top (axial view, occipital pole at the bottom). Bottom, percentage of words in a description of the moving shape movie of Heider & Simmel (1944) as a function of word category (affect, social processes, or movement). Patient performance is shown by the x and the star, corresponding to the first test session and the second test session, respectively. Individual control participant performance is shown by the open circles and group (average) control participant performance is shown by the filled circles.*

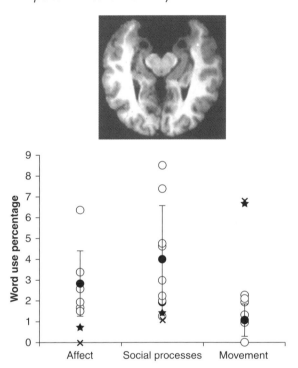

(Heberlein and Adolphs; Copyright (2004) National Academy of Sciences, U.S.A.; reprinted with permission of Ralph Adolphs.)

adjacent anterior entorhinal cortex). To assess whether the patient had impaired emotional processing or social processing, they were asked to describe the moving shape movie created by Heider & Simmel (1944; Figure 8.2). Unimpaired control participants were also asked to describe the movie, which served as a basis of comparison. To analyze these descriptions, the words that were emotional (such as "happy" or "nervous"), social (such as "he" and "share"), and movement (such as "move" and "go") in the movie descriptions were tallied and divided by the total number of words, to compute the percentage of words used from each category. The patient used relatively fewer emotional and social words to describe the movie, and used markedly more movement words as compared with control participants (Figure 8.8, bottom). This is illustrated by a few sentences in the patient's description: "OK, so, a rectangle, two triangles, and a small circle. Let's see, the triangle and the circle went inside the rectangle, and then the other triangle went in, and then the triangle and the circle went out and took off, left one triangle there. And then the two (pause) parts of the rectangle made like a [sic] upside-down V, and that was it." By comparison, the following is a control participant's description of the same segment: "The bigger triangle was in control, or trying to take control of the smaller triangle and the circle, the rectangular shaped place was similar to like a room with a closed door that um, if you went in there you were safe until that triangle came in. The small triangle and the circle were trying to escape from the large triangle and when they did, the large triangle became very furious and destroyed things." These patient lesion findings suggest that the amygdala, part of the social network, is necessary for social processing.

MINORITY VIEW

Evidence that social processing involves the mirror network, which supports the minority view, has also been reported. Iacoboni, Molnar-Szakacs, Gallese, Buccino, Mazziotta, & Rizzolatti (2005) presented participants with movies that each lasted 24 seconds during fMRI. Each movie consisted of a context condition (objects indicating tea time), an action condition (a hand grasping a cup), or an action within a context condition that conveyed the intention to drink or to clean up (Figure 8.9, top). The intention (action in context) condition can be assumed to involve a greater degree of social processing than the action condition, given the inferred intention can be assumed to be socially meaningful to the observer (e.g., it is time for tea). Of importance, both of these conditions contained the same animated stimulus (i.e., a grasping hand), in an effort to avoid a perceptual confound. The intention condition versus the action condition contrast produced activity in the right

Figure 8.9   *Intention versus action processing activated a mirror network region. Top, movie frames showing a context, an action (a hand grasping a cup), or an action in context. In the action in context condition, it appeared as if it was before tea (top row) or after tea (bottom row) to convey drinking or cleaning up, respectively. Bottom, activity (in dark grey) produced by the intention versus action contrast (left hemisphere and right hemisphere lateral views are shown to the left and right, respectively, with occipital poles toward the middle). Arrow indicates activity in the right inferior frontal gyrus.*

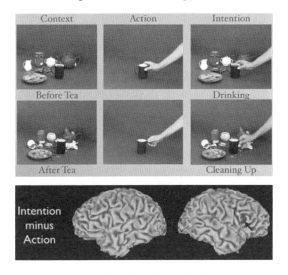

(Iacoboni et al., 2005.)

inferior prefrontal gyrus within the mirror network (Figure 8.9, bottom). These findings suggest that social processing involves the mirror network rather than the social network.

Oberman, Pineda, & Ramachandran (2007) conducted an ERP study in which participants viewed movies, each lasting 80 seconds, that consisted of three individuals tossing a ball to each other (the social action-spectator condition), tossing the ball to each other and occasionally tossing it toward the viewer (the social action-interactive condition), tossing a ball in the air to themselves (the non-interacting condition), or white noise (the baseline condition). Both social action conditions had a social processing component (with the greatest degree of social processing in the personally interactive condition) that was absent in the non-interacting condition. Of importance, all the conditions had similar actions to minimize

Figure 8.10 *Magnitude of activity at electrodes C3, Cz, and C4 within the 8 to 13 Hertz frequency range during the social action conditions and the non-interacting condition (key at the bottom).*

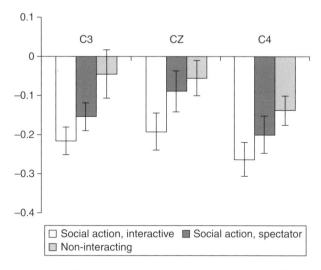

(Oberman et al., The human mirror neuron system: A link between action observation and social skills, *Social Cognitive and Affective Neuroscience*, 2007, 2, 1, 62–66, by permission of Oxford University Press.)

perceptual differences. Analysis was focused on ERP activity measured at electrodes C3, Cz, and C4 (at the top of the head) within the 8 to 13 Hertz frequency range. Activity was estimated by the log ratio of the power in this frequency range between each condition and the baseline condition. The specific electrode locations and frequency range analyzed were posited, based on evidence from previous studies, to reflect mirror network activity in the ventral premotor cortex (within the inferior frontral gyrus) that suppresses activity in the primary sensorimotor cortex. As such, it was assumed that an increase in mirror network activity would be manifested by a decrease in sensorimotor activity measured at these electrodes. Across conditions, the magnitude of activity tracked the degree of social processing, with the largest decrease in activity in the social action-interactive condition, an intermediate decrease in activity in the social action-spectator condition, and the smallest decrease in activity in the non-interacting condition (Figure 8.10). These results suggest that social processing is associated with activity in the mirror network.

COUNTERPOINTS

Although evidence has been taken to support the minority view, it is both sparse and of questionable validity. Iacoboni et al. (2005) reported fMRI activity in the inferior frontal cortex within the mirror network based on the comparison between the action with context condition and the action without context condition. It is possible that the intention condition as compared with the action condition might have been associated with a greater degree of social processing. However, the processing of additional stimuli in the intention condition (including many more objects) may have produced greater object processing effects in the inferior frontal cortex (corresponding to extension of the ventral object processing stream into the prefrontal cortex; Ungerleider, Courtney, & Haxby, 1998; Chapter 5), or may have biased participants to allocate a greater degree of attention to the grasping hand and thus amplified activity in motor processing regions (Handy, Grafton, Shroff, Ketay, & Gazzaniga, 2003). Due to these confounds, it is not possible to attribute the observed inferior frontal cortex activity reported by Iacoboni et al. to social processing with any degree of certainty. Oberman et el. (2007) showed that increasing social content was associated with a decrease in ERP activity at central scalp electrodes. However, the assumption that the ventral premotor cortex within the mirror network suppresses ERP activity measured at these electrodes is speculative, as acknowledged by the authors. Thus, only weak empirical evidence supports the mirror network hypothesis of social processing.

Fabbri-Destro & Rizzolatti (2008) have argued that the mirror network can be extended to include regions that are involved in more than motor processing. For example, they have proposed that the amygdala, the insula, and the anterior cingulate may be involved in a mirror system that processes emotion. Empirical evidence was considered to support this claim, including that reported in an fMRI study by Singer, Seymour, O'Doherty, Kaube, Dolan, & Frith (2004). In this study, activity in the anterior insula and anterior cingulate cortex was observed when participants received pain or when they observed a loved one receive pain. Of importance, such effects may have reflected activity in pain processing regions in response to viewing the pain of someone they loved via a mirror network explanation, where the brain regions associated with processing pain were activated such that the observer felt greater empathy. Alternatively, these effects may have reflected the observer's concern about the one they love, where it pained the observer when a loved one was in pain. That is, rather than the observer's pain being associated with mirror network processing, the observer's pain may have been driving the effects in both conditions. These interpretations may seem similar, but the first appeals to a mirror network explanation and the second does not. As the empirical evidence does not distinguish between these possibilities, there is no justification for extending the mirror network beyond the originally formulated regions.

Rather than expanding the mirror network to encompass other regions, a more productive strategy for proponents of the minority view might be to call for proponents of the majority view to evaluate activity in mirror network regions. Although activity in these regions may not have survived the statistical thresholds previously employed, a targeted analysis might reveal social processing activity in the mirror network regions. It could be the case that animacy processing activates the social network and, to a lesser degree, also activates the mirror network. Such weak activation could explain the current lack of evidence supporting the mirror network hypothesis. If such evidence was observed it would suggest that both hypotheses are correct, as the social network hypothesis and the mirror network hypothesis are not mutually exclusive. Proponents of the majority view should consider reanalyzing their data with a more lenient statistical threshold or by extracting activity from mirror network regions to more definitely distinguish between the social network hypothesis and the mirror network hypothesis.

Across all the studies evaluated, there is abundant evidence that processing animacy is mediated by the social network (Table 8.1). By comparison, the evidence that processing animacy involves the mirror network is weak at best. In fact, Morris et al. (2005; Figure 8.5) and Wheatley et al. (2007; Figure 8.6) found that the mirror network regions were not modulated as a function of animacy, but rather were modulated by motion (presumably due to participants mirroring the observed motion). Moreover, Santos et al. (2010) found that mirror network regions were most associated with inanimate motion and least associated with animate motion (Figure 8.4). The latter finding directly contradicts the

Table 8.1   *fMRI activity associated with processing animacy in the medial prefrontal cortex (mPFC), the cingulate cortex (CC), the amygdala (amyg.), the superior temporal sulcus (STS), and the fusiform gyrus (FG) within the social network in addition to the inferior frontal gyrus (IFG) and the anterior inferior parietal lobule (IPL) within the mirror network*

Study	Social					Mirror	
	mPFC	CC	Amyg.	STS	FG	IFG	IPL
Martin & Weisberg (2003)	X		X	X	X		
Castelli et al. (2000)	X		X	X	X		
Santos et al. (2010)	X	X		X	X		
Mitchell et al. (2002)	X			X	X		
Morris et al. (2005)					X		
Wheatley et al. (2007)	X	X	X	X	X		
Tavares et al. (2008)	X	X	X	X	X		
Iacoboni et al. (2005)						X	

mirror network hypothesis, and thus could be considered grounds for ruling out this hypothesis of processing animacy.

CONCLUSION

In support of the majority view, there is compelling evidence that animacy processing involves the social network and does not involve the mirror network. It is possible that evidence supporting the mirror network hypothesis of processing animacy, the minority view, might be uncovered if studies of animacy target mirror network regions for analysis. However, it is anticipated that additional evidence will contradict the mirror network hypothesis such that it will be ruled out as a viable model for processing animacy.

SUGGESTED READINGS

Majority view

Wheatley, T., Milleville, S. C., & Martin, A. (2007). Understanding animate agents: Distinct roles for the social network and mirror system. *Psychological Science, 18,* 469–474.

Heberlein, A. S., & Adolphs, R. (2004). Impaired spontaneous anthropomorphizing despite intact perception and social knowledge. *Proceedings of the National Academy of Sciences of the United States of America, 101*, 7487–7491. Open access.

Minority view

Iacoboni, M., Molnar-Szakacs, I., Gallese, V., Buccino, G., Mazziotta, J. C., & Rizzolatti, G. (2005). Grasping the intentions of others with one's own mirror neuron system. *PLoS Biology, 3*, e79. Open access.
Fabbri-Destro, M., & Rizzolatti, G. (2008). Mirror neurons and mirror systems in monkeys and humans. *Physiology, 23*, 171–179. Open access.

REFERENCES

Adolphs, R. (2001). The neurobiology of social cognition. *Current Opinion in Neurobiology, 11*, 231–239.
Castelli, F., Happé, F., Frith, U., & Frith, C. (2000). Movement and mind: A functional imaging study of perception and interpretation of complex intentional movement patterns. *NeuroImage, 12*, 314–325.
Fabbri-Destro, M., & Rizzolatti, G. (2008). Mirror neurons and mirror systems in monkeys and humans. *Physiology, 23*, 171–179.
Handy, T. C., Grafton, S. T., Shroff, N. M., Ketay, S., & Gazzaniga, M. S. (2003). Graspable objects grab attention when the potential for action is recognized. *Nature Neuroscience, 6*, 421–427.
Heberlein, A. S., & Adolphs, R. (2004). Impaired spontaneous anthropomorphizing despite intact perception and social knowledge. *Proceedings of the National Academy of Sciences of the United States of America, 101*, 7487–7491.
Heider, F., & Simmel, M. (1944). An experimental study of apparent behavior. *The American Journal of Psychology, 57*, 243–259.
Iacoboni, M., Molnar-Szakacs, I., Gallese, V., Buccino, G., Mazziotta, J. C., & Rizzolatti, G. (2005). Grasping the intentions of others with one's own mirror neuron system. *PLoS Biology, 3*, e79.
Martin, A., & Weisberg, J. (2003). Neural foundations for understanding social and mechanical concepts. *Cognitive Neuropsychology, 20*, 575–587.

Mitchell, J. P., Heatherton, T. F., & Macrae, C. N. (2002). Distinct neural systems subserve person and object knowledge. *Proceedings of the National Academy of Sciences of the United States of America, 99*, 15238–15243.

Morris, J. P., Pelphrey, K. A., & McCarthy, G. (2005). Regional brain activation evoked when approaching a virtual human on a virtual walk. *Journal of Cognitive Neuroscience, 17*, 1744–1752.

Oberman, L. M., Pineda, J. A., & Ramachandran, V. S. (2007). The human mirror neuron system: A link between action observation and social skills. *Social Cognitive and Affective Neuroscience, 2*, 62–66.

Rizzolatti, G., & Craighero, L. (2004). The mirror-neuron system. *Annual Review of Neuroscience, 27*, 169–192.

Rizzolatti, G., & Fabbri-Destro, M. (2008). The mirror system and its role in social cognition. *Current Opinion in Neurobiology, 18*, 179–184.

Santos, N. S., Kuzmanovic, B., David, N., Rotarska-Jagiela, A., Eickhoff, S. B., Shah, J. N., Fink, G. R., Bente, G., & Vogeley, K. (2010). Animated brain: A functional neuroimaging study on animacy experience. *NeuroImage, 53*, 291–302.

Singer, T., Seymour, B., O'Doherty, J., Kaube, H., Dolan, R. J., & Frith, C. D. (2004). Empathy for pain involves the affective but not sensory components of pain. *Science, 303*, 1157–1162.

Tavares, P., Lawrence, A. D., & Barnard, P. J. (2008). Paying attention to social meaning: An fMRI study. *Cerebral Cortex, 18*, 1876–1885.

Ungerleider, L. G., Courtney, S. M., & Haxby, J. V. (1998). A neural system for human visual working memory. *Proceedings of the National Academy of Sciences of the United States of America, 95*, 883–890.

Wheatley, T., Milleville, S. C., & Martin, A. (2007). Understanding animate agents: Distinct roles for the social network and mirror system. *Psychological Science, 18*, 469–474.

9 The Adequacy of fMRI

The large majority of evidence considered in this book was gathered using fMRI, with the notable exception of the ERP findings bearing on the V1 attention debate (Chapter 3). A major reason for this heavy reliance on fMRI is that this method has become the gold standard in the field of cognitive neuroscience. This is illustrated in Figure 9.1, where the number of fMRI papers published in *Nature Neuroscience, Neuron,* and *The Journal of Neuroscience* – the three journals with the highest-impact factors in the field – dwarfs the number of ERP papers (only human studies were considered; articles were identified using PubMed). Specifically, more than ten times as many fMRI papers as ERP papers have been published in these journals. If all journals are considered, regardless of impact factor, there have still been close to two times the number of fMRI papers published as ERP papers. These comparisons illustrate that the highest-impact research is nearly always conducted using fMRI and that this is the most widely used technique in cognitive neuroscience. Our reliance on fMRI is not surprising as this method alone is widely accessible and offers excellent spatial accuracy, which is necessary to identify the specific brain regions associated with a given cognitive process. It is notable that cortical surface and depth electrode recording in patients also offers excellent spatial resolution, but this technique can only rarely be used and whole-brain analysis is not possible due to restricted electrode placement.

The widespread use of fMRI is illustrated by seemingly countless cognitive neuroscience laboratories that offer readily available data acquisition procedures and analysis scripts in which the next wave of scientists can receive training. The majority view is that fMRI is sufficient to measure brain function.

Figure 9.1   *The number of fMRI and ERP articles published each year from 1990 to 2010 in the three highest-impact cognitive neuroscience journals (key at the bottom).*

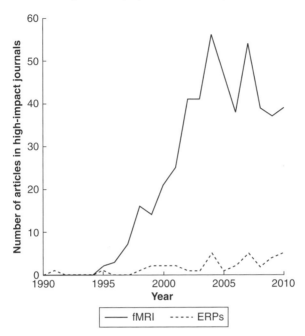

However, even though fMRI offers excellent spatial resolution, the temporal resolution of this method is poor. Essentially, this method takes a snapshot of brain activity that occurs in each two-second time period, while neural activity modulates in milliseconds. As such, fMRI is approximately 1000 times too slow to track neural activity. Some investigators, proponents of the minority view, have employed data acquisition methods such as ERPs that have sufficient temporal resolution to track brain function in real-time. It is important to underscore that proponents of the minority view do not oppose the use of fMRI, but rather employ alternative techniques or techniques in conjunction with fMRI to track the rapid spatial-temporal dynamics of brain function.

MAJORITY VIEW

Cognitive neuroscientists typically employ standard fMRI data acquisition protocols, illustrated by all of the fMRI studies considered in this book thus far, as the spatial accuracy of approximately four millimetres is adequate to answer the large majority of current research questions. More advanced fMRI protocols are only rarely used, but highlight the degree of spatial resolution that is possible with this technique. The advanced fMRI studies considered below either employed protocols with very high spatial resolution or tested for interactions between neural regions.

High-resolution fMRI

Suthana, Ekstrom, Moshirvaziri, Knowlton, & Bookheimer (2009) employed high-resolution anatomic and functional MRI to investigate memory effects in sub-regions of the hippocampus including CA fields 1, 2, and 3, the dentate gyrus, and the subiculum. These sub-regions of the hippocampus are localized at a much finer spatial scale than is commonly evaluated (as illustrated by the studies in Chapter 4 where the hippocampus was considered a single region). In this study, participants encoded building locations in a small virtual city from either the same starting point or multiple starting points and then recalled building locations. The CA1 field was predicted to be preferentially active in the multiple-starting-points condition, as this sub-region has been associated with memory integration. Anatomic MRI had a 0.391 millimetre spatial resolution, as compared with a standard resolution of one millimetre, while fMRI was acquired with a 1.6 millimetre spatial resolution, which was sufficient to isolate activity in individual sub-regions of the hippocampus. MRI images were used to identify the sub-regions of each participant's hippocampus in addition to the surrounding cortical regions (Figure 9.2, left). These structures were then flattened, using a software program, and warped onto an average anatomic template to allow for viewing the group fMRI results. The contrast of encoding locations from multiple starting points and encoding locations from a single starting point produced activity in the CA1 sub-region of the hippocampus (Figure 9.2, right). These findings illustrate that advanced fMRI techniques can be used to identify activity with greater spatial resolution than is typically achieved using standard fMRI protocols.

Cheng, Waggoner, & Tanaka (2001) used fMRI with even higher spatial resolution to map ocular dominance columns in V1 that are known to alternate between left eye and right eye representations across the cortex. Cortical columns are found in many regions

Figure 9.2   *Memory encoding fMRI activity in the CA1 sub-region of the hippocampus. Left, medial temporal lobe sub-regions CA2, CA3, and the dentate gyrus (in white), CA1 (in light grey), the subiculum (sub, in grey), and surrounding cortical regions including the parahippocampal cortex (PHC, in dark grey) and the fusiform gyrus (in black; partial coronal view). Right, activity (in white) on a flattened cortical representation of the same areas in addition to the perirhinal cortex (PRC) and the entorhinal cortex (ERC; distance in the anterior-posterior and lateral-medial directions is shown in millimetres).*

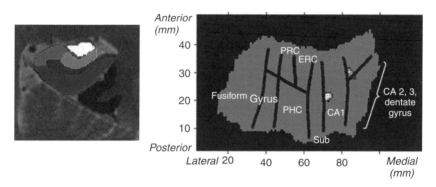

(Suthana et al., 2009; The journal of neuroscience: the official journal of the Society for Neuroscience by SOCIETY FOR NEUROSCIENCE Copyright 2009. Reproduced with permission.)

of the brain, with each column consisting of neurons that process a similar type of information (e.g., the cortical columns in the inferior temporal cortex that process complex object features described in Chapter 2). In this study, anatomic MRI and fMRI were acquired with a very high spatial resolution of 0.47 millimetres. fMRI activity associated with left eye stimulation versus right eye stimulation, and vice versa, revealed alternating left eye-right eye ocular dominance columns that were each approximately one millimetre in width (Figure 9.3). It should be noted that this study used fMRI to resolve individual columns, as compared with the previous study that primarily relied on anatomic MRI to achieve high spatial resolution. fMRI has also been used to identify orientation columns in V1, where neurons in each cortical column process stimuli at specific orientations such as bars rotated 0, 45, 90, or 135 degrees (Yacoub, Harel, & Uğurbil, 2008). These findings show that fMRI can identify neural activity at the level of the cortical column, which underscores the excellent spatial resolution of

Figure 9.3 *fMRI activity within ocular dominance columns. Activations in V1 within the right hemisphere were produced by stimulation of the left eye (in white) or the right eye (in dark grey) as demarcated by alternating white and grey arrows (partial coronal view; one centimetre scale bar to the bottom left). The calcarine sulcus (CS), intralingual sulcus (ILS), and inferior sagittal sulcus (ISS) are labeled.*

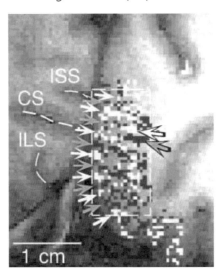

(Reprinted from Neuron, 32/2, Cheng et al., Human ocular dominance columns as revealed by high-field functional magnetic resonance imaging, Copyright 2001, with permission from Elsevier.)

this method as cortical columns are often considered to be the functional processing unit of the brain. That is, the spatial resolution of fMRI can be described as capable of matching the spatial resolution of information processing in the brain.

It could be argued that only high-resolution fMRI should be conducted, as its spatial resolution is superior to standard fMRI and it only requires altering the data acquisition parameters. However, the speed of fMRI data acquisition is currently limited such that high-resolution fMRI cannot be used for whole-brain analysis, which is of primary interest to almost all cognitive neuroscientists. The approximately two-second temporal resolution of fMRI is essentially set by balancing fMRI hardware limitations (which pushes to decrease temporal resolution) and the speed of cognitive processing (which pushes to increase temporal resolution).

Due to hardware limitations, whole-brain acquisition can currently be conducted with a resolution of only about four millimetres. Fortunately, fMRI acquisition time is periodically reduced with advances in hardware. As such, it is anticipated that whole-brain high-resolution fMRI will, at some point, become the new standard.

Tracking brain region interactions with fMRI

Although fMRI can identify the regions involved in a given cognitive process, as illustrated by both standard-resolution and high-resolution studies, such localization does not delineate how regions interact. Such interactions reflect the neural mechanisms mediating a particular cognitive process, and thus are of paramount importance to understanding brain function. With this in mind, a relatively small number of fMRI studies have assessed whether there might be interactions between different regions of activity. Leff, Schofield, Stephan, Crinion, Friston, & Price (2008) aimed to delineate the nature of language region interactions during speech processing. During fMRI, participants were presented with intelligible word pairs (such as "mint condition" or "cloud nine") or unintelligible reversed word pairs (such as "mint nine") spoken in a male or a female voice, and made a gender judgment for each word pair. The comparison of intelligible word pairs versus unintelligible word pairs produced language activity that included the left posterior superior temporal sulcus (Wernicke's area), the left inferior frontal gyrus (Broca's area), as expected (Chapter 6), in addition to the left anterior superior temporal sulcus (Figure 9.4, top). A procedure termed *dynamic causal modeling* was used to assess whether there were interactions between these regions. Two hundred and sixteen models were constructed that each included the regions of interest, the interactions between each pair of regions, and the ways in which auditory stimuli could enter the system. Figure 9.4 (bottom left) shows the basic model structure illustrating all possible configurations. The interaction and input values of each model were adjusted until that model produced the best fit to each region's timecourse of activation. For example, if region 1 and region 2 activation timecourses were correlated (i.e., modulated with similar peaks and valleys across time) and the region 1 timecourse was shifted earlier in time, this would indicate that there was an interaction between region 1 and region 2 and that region 1 was the

Figure 9.4 *Dynamic causal model of speech processing. Top, activity (in black/white) produced by the contrast of intelligible word pairs and unintelligible word pairs (lateral view, occipital pole at the right). Regions of interest included the left posterior superior temporal sulcus (P), the left anterior superior temporal sulcus (A), and the left inferior frontal gyrus (F). Bottom left, the basic model structure illustrating all possible between-region interactions (dotted arrows) with auditory input (black squares with protruding arrows). Bottom right, the best-fit model, with connections modulated by intelligibility shown by solid arrows.*

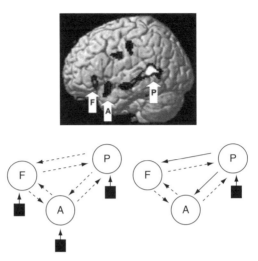

(Leff et al., 2008; The journal of neuroscience: the official journal of the Society for Neuroscience by SOCIETY FOR NEUROSCIENCE Copyright 2008. Reproduced with permission.)

information source and region 2 was the information target. After evaluating the goodness-of-fit for all the models, the best-fit model indicated that auditory stimuli entered the left posterior superior temporal sulcus and this information was transferred to the left anterior superior temporal sulcus and the left inferior frontal gyrus (Figure 9.4, bottom right).

Such findings suggest that fMRI can go beyond the identification of regions to also measure the interactions between regions that mediate a cognitive process. However, it should be highlighted that fMRI studies have only rarely conducted such interaction analyses and have rather focused on localizing the regions associated with a given cognitive process, the great strength of this method.

MINORITY VIEW

Although fMRI has excellent spatial resolution, this method has a poor temporal resolution of about two seconds. With regard to brain function, this is an eternity. To illustrate, within two seconds of trial onset during nearly all cognitive tasks, a stimulus is presented and processed, the associated processes are initiated and completed, and a behavioural response is made. Due to its poor temporal resolution, fMRI can only identify which regions were active during this entire process. That is, fMRI provides virtually no information with regard to how the brain functions over time.

By comparison, methods such as ERPs have a temporal resolution in the millisecond range, and thus can track brain operation in real-time. High temporal resolution is arguably of equal importance as spatial resolution, as it is known that the brain processes information at the millisecond time scale. As illustrated in Chapter 3, ERP attention effects occurred at a different rate in V1 and extrastriate cortex, while fMRI results only showed that attention effects occurred in both V1 and extrastriate cortex and thus provided no information about the timing of neural activity. Such ERP findings, where the relative timing of activations in different regions have been compared, will not be covered again, but illustrate the rapid temporal dynamics of neural activity and support the minority view that fMRI is not adequate to study brain function.

In addition to identifying the precise time at which a region is active, it is known that activity in neural regions can modulate at certain frequencies (measured in cycles per second, Hertz) with periods of only a fraction of a second. If two neural regions are activated with the same frequency of modulation, analyses can be conducted to determine whether and how these regions interact. Mircea Steriade has meticulously detailed such interactions by simultaneously recording from multiple neural regions in anesthetized cats. Figure 9.5 (left) illustrates activity that was simultaneously measured from electrodes in cortical area 5 and the centrolateral (CL) nucleus of the thalamus during brainstem stimulation (Steriade, Contreras, Amzica, & Timofeev, 1996). Visual inspection suggests that these regions were synchronously active, as indicated by the similar activation peaks and valleys over time. To more precisely measure the relationship in activity between these regions, a *cross-correlogram* was generated by computing the

Figure 9.5 *Cat depth electrode cortical-thalamic cross-correlation results. Left, high frequency (15 to 80 Hertz) activity (millivolts per second) simultaneously measured in cat cortical area 5 and the centrolateral (CL) nucleus of the thalamus (scale bars to the lower right). Right, cross-correlogram generated at each time point by computing the correlation between the two waveforms to the left after shifting the thalamic signal in time/phase between -0.2 to 0.2 seconds. The peak value near zero indicates these regions are synchronously active/in phase.*

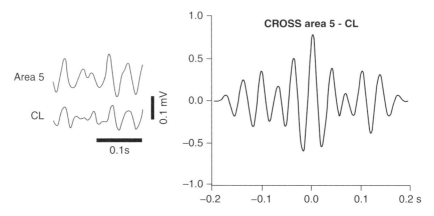

(Steriade et al., 1996; The journal of neuroscience: the official journal of the Society for Neuroscience by SOCIETY FOR NEUROSCIENCE Copyright 1996. Reproduced with permission.)

correlation between these two waveforms without any time shift (referred to as a *phase lag* of 0 seconds), computing the correlation between these two waveforms after the thalamic signal was shifted earlier or later in time/phase, and then plotting these correlations as a function of time shift/phase (Figure 9.5, right). The cross-correlogram quantifies the following between signal characteristics: 1) the maximum correlation between the waveforms, where a correlation of one indicates identical activation profiles and a correlation of 0 indicates no relationship between the activation profiles, 2) the dominant common frequency, which is illustrated by periodic peaks and valleys that occur because the peaks of the shifted waveform will periodically line up with the peaks of the non-shifted waveform, and 3) the phase lag, which refers to the shift in time (from time 0) corresponding to the maximum correlation. Phase lag is often of primary interest as a value of or near 0 indicates two regions are synchronously active – referred to as *phase-locked* – and thus operate together during a process, while a constant but non-zero phase lag may indicate information is transmitted between regions in a particular temporal direction. As illustrated by the examples below, different forms of analysis have been used to measure the frequency and phase relationships between neural regions during a given cognitive process.

Fell, Klaver, Lehnertz, Grunwald, Schaller, Elger, & Fernández (2001) recorded from rhinal (perirhinal and entorhinal) cortex and hippocampal electrodes in nine epilepsy patients to investigate the mechanisms of memory encoding (Figure 9.6, top). To avoid measuring from disrupted neural tissue data was only analyzed from the hemisphere opposite to the seizure focus. Participants were presented with sets of 12 nouns at study and then at test recalled as many of the words as possible. The frequency and phase of the response at each electrode was identified using a set of waveforms, called wavelets, each with a specific frequency of modulation and a limited number of cycles (each wavelet is similar to the waveforms shown in Figure 9.5, left, but is only modulated at a single frequency). Each wavelet was compared with the electrode activity at each time point, like the cross-correlation analysis above (Figure 9.5, right), which produced the magnitude and phase of the activity at the corresponding frequency. During the study phase, within the gamma frequency range (32 to 48 Hertz), subsequently recalled words versus unrecalled words produced greater rhinal-hippocampal synchronization, defined as a more constant phase difference between two electrodes as compared with activity before stimulus onset, a baseline measure of asynchonous activity (Figure 9.6, middle; the gamma frequency was selected for analysis as neural activity in this frequency range has been observed during many cognitive tasks). The subsequent memory synchronization started within approximately 100 milliseconds after stimulus onset and continued until approximately 300 milliseconds, a later period of synchronization occurred between approximately 500 to 600 milliseconds after stimulus onset, and there was a decrease in synchronization from approximately 1000 to 1100 milliseconds after stimulus onset. The rhinal cortex and hippocampus activity were also phase-locked, as shown by the peak phase lag distributions near zero, and there were also a greater number of gamma frequency synchronization occurrences during subsequently recalled words than subsequently unrecalled words (Figure 9.6, bottom). The

Figure 9.6 *Memory encoding rhinal-hippocampal depth electrode frequency and phase results. Top, MRI of a patient with implanted medial temporal lobe depth electrodes (the hippocampus, Hi, is illustrated to the left; axial view, occipital pole at the bottom, with the right hemisphere, R, shown on the left). Middle, rhinal-hippocampal gamma frequency synchronization over time (in seconds) for subsequently recalled and unrecalled words (key to the upper right). Bottom, rhinal-hippocampal phase difference distributions for subsequently recalled and unrecalled words.*

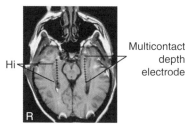

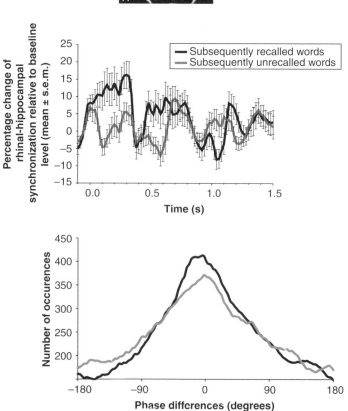

(Reprinted by permission from Macmillan Publishers Ltd: *Nature Neuroscience, 4,* Fell et al., copyright 2001.)

peak phase difference of approximately eight degrees corresponds to a phase lag of less than one millisecond (as the mean frequency of 40 Hertz dictates 360 degrees/1 cycle occurs every 25 milliseconds). These results show that the rhinal cortex and the hippocampus interact during memory encoding. Moreover, this process was initiated very rapidly and had multiple stages within the first second after stimulus onset, well before fMRI could have finished acquiring a single data point. That is, fMRI could have only shown that the rhinal cortex and hippocampus were both active during memory encoding, and could not have provided any temporal information such as the nature (increase or decrease in synchronization) or the phase relationship between these regions.

Slotnick (2010) investigated whether there were long-range cortical interactions during retrieval of visual-spatial information using ERP cross-correlation analysis. At study, participants were presented with abstract shapes in either the left visual field or the right visual field (similar to those illustrated in Figure 4.5, top). At test, old and new shapes were presented at fixation and participants classified each shape as old and previously on the "left," old and previously on the "right," or "new." Accurate memory for old items previously presented in the right visual field (referred to as *old-right-hits*) versus accurate memory for old items previously presented in the left visual field (referred to as *old-left-hits*, a baseline measure) produced greater activity in the left (contralateral) frontal, occipital, and temporal regions than the right (ipsilateral) frontal, occipital, and temporal regions (Figure 9.7, top). Furthermore, this contralateral activity occurred very rapidly, within the 50 to 250 millisecond (early) epoch after stimulus onset, and continued throughout the 400 to 800 millisecond (middle) and the 1000 to 1900 millisecond (late) epochs (Figure 9.7, upper middle). Previous ERP studies have associated these three time epochs with sensory, parietal, and frontal retrieval effects, respectively. The opposite comparison of old-left-hits versus old-right-hits also produced contralateral activity in frontal, occipital, and temporal regions in all three epochs (not shown). Note that these contralateral memory effects in occipital-temporal sensory regions are reminiscent of the contralateral attention effects reported in Chapter 3. Contralateral frontal, occipital, and temporal regions were sometimes concurrently active, which would be required for but does not necessarily imply between-region interaction. Between-region interactions

Figure 9.7 *Memory retrieval control-sensory ERP cross-correlation results. Top, ERP activity 1417 milliseconds after stimulus onset associated with accurate memory for shapes previously presented in*

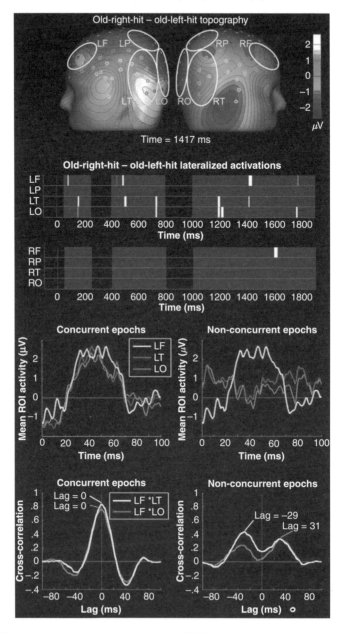

(Reprinted from Brain Research, 1330, Slotnick, Synchronous retinotopic frontal-temporal activity during long-term memory for spatial location, Copyright 2010, with permission from Elsevier.)

Figure 9.7   *(Continued) the right visual field (old-right-hits) versus baseline (old-left-hits; lateral views, occipital poles toward the middle; greyscale bar to the right, in microvolts). White ovals demarcate the left (L) and the right (R) frontal (F), parietal (P), occipital (O), and temporal (T) regions of interest (small grey disks show electrode locations). Upper middle, white bars illustrate time periods in which there was greater region of interest activity in one hemisphere than the other hemisphere (early, middle, and late retrieval epochs are shown in grey). Lower middle left, LF, LT, and LO activity (microvolts per millisecond) from 1377 to 1477 milliseconds after stimulus onset (concurrent epochs; key to the middle). Lower middle right, LF activity from 1377 to 1477 milliseconds after stimulus onset and LT and LO activity from 430 to 530 milliseconds after stimulus onset (non-concurrent epochs). Bottom, cross-correlograms corresponding to waveforms directly above with phase lags labeled at the maximum cross-correlation values (key to the middle).*

---

were suggested, however, by the contralateral frontal, occipital, and temporal activation waveforms that appeared to be synchronously active during some concurrent epochs (Figure 9.7, lower middle, left) but did not appear to be synchronously active during non-concurrent epochs (a baseline measure of asynchronous activity; Figure 9.7, lower middle, right). A cross-correlation analysis was conducted to determine the degree of synchronous activity between regions, as estimated by the phase lag at the maximum of the cross-correlogram. Specifically, the phase lag was computed from the activation waveforms in all pairs of contralateral frontal and occipital regions and all pairs of contralateral frontal and temporal regions during concurrent and non-concurrent epochs. All eight concurrent epoch frontal-temporal waveforms were synchronous, with phase lags ranging from zero to one milliseconds, while the eight concurrent frontal-occipital waveforms were sometimes synchronous, with five of eight phase lags ranging from zero to one milliseconds and the remaining phase lags ranging from four to nine milliseconds (Figure 9.7, bottom left; the cross-correlogram illustrates synchronous/phase-locked activity). As expected, non-concurrent epochs were not associated with synchronous activity, as indicated by the mean frontal-temporal phase lag of 20.6 milliseconds and the mean frontal-occipital phase lag of 19.8 milliseconds (Figure 9.7, bottom right; the cross-correlogram illustrates asynchronous activity). fMRI was also conducted during the same task and contralateral memory effects were localized to the frontal eye field, near the junction of the superior frontal sulcus and the precentral sulcus (Chapter 5). These fMRI results illustrate both the major strength and the major weakness of this method, when considered in light of the ERP findings. fMRI was able to provide the specific locus of the contralateral frontal memory effects, which is not possible with ERPs due to the limited spatial resolution of this technique. However, fMRI revealed nothing about whether the frontal regions interacted with occipital or temporal regions. Only when ERP cross-correlation analysis was employed was synchronous activity between frontal and temporal regions revealed, which provides compelling evidence that these regions interact during visual-spatial memory.

Gregoriou, Gotts, Zhou, & Desimone (2009) conducted a monkey study in which single-cell activity was simultaneously recorded in the frontal eye field and V4 to assess whether these regions interact during visual-spatial attention. Of relevance, previous monkey and human studies have consistently reported attention effects in these regions (such as the extrastriate attention effects detailed in Chapter 3). On each trial, monkeys either directed attention toward or away from a stimulus that fell within the overlapping receptive fields of a V4 cell and a frontal eye field cell (Figure 9.8, top). Attention increased the firing rate in both of these regions, and these attention effects occurred at an earlier time in the frontal eye field than in V4 (80 milliseconds versus 130 milliseconds after cue onset, respectively; Figure 9.8, middle). This timing difference suggests that the frontal eye field may have produced an early top-down signal that triggered attentional enhancement in V4, although this possibility could only be weakly supported without direct evidence that these regions interacted. To garner such evidence, between-region synchrony/coherence was estimated – where coherence varied from 0 when there was no phase relationship to 1 when there was a constant phase relationship – and attention was found to increase coherence within the gamma (40 to 60 Hertz) frequency range (Figure 9.8, bottom left). Moreover, within this frequency range, frontal eye field activity and V4 activity were phase shifted by 142 degrees (approximately half a gamma cycle; Figure 9.8, bottom right), which at this frequency translates into an eight millisecond

Figure 9.8 *Monkey spatial attention FEF-V4 depth electrode frequency and phase results. Top, during central fixation, stimuli in different colours (shown in different shades of grey) appeared, one of which was inside the overlapping V4 and frontal eye field (FEF) receptive fields (RFs) shown by dotted and solid rectangles, respectively. When the fixation point (cue) changed colour, attention was directed to the stimulus with the matching colour (inside the RFs in this example), and then made a response when that stimulus changed colour. Middle, FEF and V4 response (firing rate per millisecond after cue onset) when attention was directed toward or away from the stimulus inside the RFs (recorded from the specified number of cells, n; key to the upper right). The times of initial attention effects are shown by dotted vertical lines and*

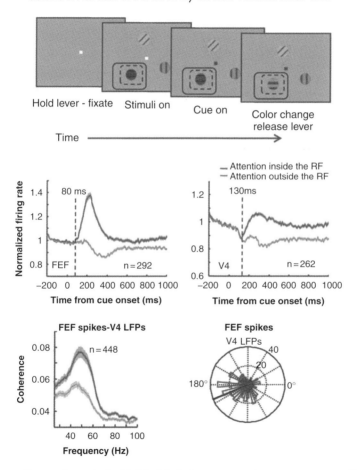

(From Gregoriou et al., 2009, High-frequency, long-range coupling between prefrontal and visual cortex during attention, *Science*, 324, 1207–1210. Reprinted with permission from AAAS.)

Figure 9.8 *(Continued) labeled. Bottom left, attentional enhancement of synchronization (coherence) between FEF spikes and V4 local field potentials (LFPs) as a function of frequency. Bottom right, attention related 40 to 60 Hertz phase differences (in degrees).*

time shift between activation in the frontal eye field and V4. The attention related synchrony of these two regions indicates that they interacted during this cognitive process. Furthermore, the earlier onset of attention effects in the frontal eye field coupled with the eight millisecond frontal eye field-to-V4 phase lag provides strong support for a mechanism where the frontal eye field initiates a top-down signal that results in the amplification of processing in V4. Note that this result should not be taken to suggest that these regions do not subsequently operate together in a non-hierarchical manner. If fMRI had been conducted with the same paradigm, attention effects would have likely been reported in the frontal eye field and V4. However, fMRI would not have been sensitive to the 50 millisecond earlier attention effects in the frontal eye field, the attention related boost in synchrony between the frontal eye field and V4, or the between-region phase difference of eight milliseconds that provide invaluable insight into the neural mechanisms underlying visual-spatial attention.

The preceding studies show that the brain processes information in milliseconds. Such rapid temporal dynamics would have been invisible to fMRI. This limited view of fMRI appears to be at odds with studies that have employed dynamic causal modeling, such as the Leff et al. (2008) study described above, to characterize between-region interactions. However, there are a number of serious issues with fMRI dynamic causal models including: 1) modeling the between-region direction of information flow is speculative given that the fMRI activation timecourses are so slow, 2) different regions of the brain are known to produce different fMRI activation time-course profiles, such as the relatively slow frontal cortex response, which will perturb between-region weights and directionality, 3) the models typically do not consider important brain regions that if included would change the connection weights and directions, and 4) although the best-fit model is selected, this model almost never adequately fits the data, which is unacceptable from a quantitative psychology (statistical) perspective. Some fMRI investigators are clearly interested in investigating between-region interactions, and with that in mind have employed dynamic causal modeling. However, there are so many potential issues with this technique it is questionable whether it should be used to study brain region interactions, particularly when other methods such as ERP cross-correlation analysis can definitely be used to accurately study such interactions.

Although fMRI alone cannot convincingly investigate between-region interactions, such interactions have been investigated by combining fMRI and TMS. This critically important line of research has been spearheaded by Jon Driver, whose recent and untimely death has dealt a major blow to the field of cognitive neuroscience. Ruff, Bestmann, Blankenburg, Bjoertomt, Josephs, Weiskopf, Deichmann, & Driver (2008) applied TMS to right hemisphere frontal or parietal control regions (Figure 9.9, top) and simultaneously measured the resultant visual sensory activity using fMRI while participants viewed coloured moving visual patterns. Of importance for interpretation, the TMS pulse sequence employed activated the targeted cortical region, rather than inhibited the targeted region (which was the case in all of the previously described TMS studies in this book). Although TMS to the right frontal eye field at high versus low intensity did not differentially modulate activity in motion processing region MT+, TMS to the intraparietal sulcus at high versus low intensity produced a lower magnitude of MT+ activity (Figure 9.9, middle). Assuming TMS activated the stimulation site, these results suggest that the right intraparietal sulcus may typically inhibit MT+ and that this inhibition was magnified by high versus low intensity TMS. By comparison, the intensity of TMS to the right frontal eye field was positively correlated with activity in V1, while the intensity of TMS to the right intraparietal sulcus was not correlated with activity in V1 (Figure 9.9, bottom). The positive correlation suggests that the right frontal eye field may typically facilitate processing in V1, which was magnified with increased TMS intensity. These findings show that parietal and frontal control regions interact with different sensory regions, and also provide insight into whether these interactions are inhibitory or facilitatory in nature. The use of fMRI alone could have only identified the regions associated with processing the complex visual stimulus, and could not have provided any information regarding which regions interacted or the nature of those interactions.

Figure 9.9 *Causal control-sensory TMS-fMRI results. Top, TMS sites in the right frontal eye field (FEF, black circle) and the right intraparietal sulcus (IPS, white circle) of one participant (top view, occipital pole at the bottom). Middle, fMRI activity (percent blood oxygen level dependent, BOLD, signal) in motion processing region MT+ following TMS to the FEF or the IPS at low intensity or high intensity (key to the right). Bottom, correlation between the intensity of TMS applied to the FEF or the IPS and the corresponding fMRI activity in V1.*

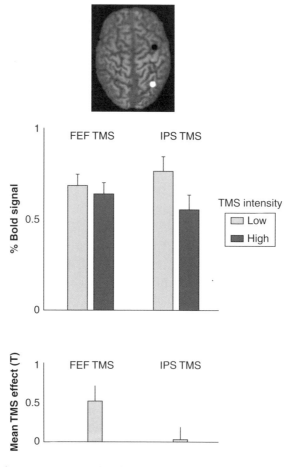

(Ruff et al., Distinct causal influences of parietal versus frontal areas on human visual cortex: Evidence from concurrent TMS-fMRI, *Cerebral Cortex*, 2008, 18, 4, 817–827, by permission of Oxford University Press.)

COUNTERPOINTS

The findings in the previous section show that brain activity changes rapidly across time and that brain regions rapidly interact (Cohen, 2011, provided additional examples that highlight temporal aspects of brain function), providing strong support for the minority view that the static picture of brain activity painted by fMRI alone is inadequate for tracking brain function. Despite the evidence to the contrary, proponents of the majority view believe that fMRI is adequate for investigating brain function. Before turning to the arguments in support of this position, a parallel will be drawn between the tenets of phrenology, developed by Franz Joseph Gall about two centuries ago, and those of fMRI research today. After studying hundreds of human skulls, Gall hypothesized that there were 27 skull protrusions that could be measured on the scalp, each of which was associated with a characteristic behaviour such as the sense of colour or the potential to commit murder. Gall's system of phrenology had the following premises (van Wyhe, 2004):

1 "Aptitudes and tendencies [that is, faculties] are inborn in humans and animals."

2 These have their "seat, their basis, in the brain."

3 & 4 "Not only are the aptitudes and tendencies varied and independent, but in addition they are essentially separate and independent of one other, therefore they must have their seat in various and independent parts of the brain."

5 "From the various divisions of the various organs, and the varying development of these, arises the varying shapes of the brain."

6 "From the composition and development of particular organs arises the particular shape of particular parts of the brain or regions of the same."

7 "From the genesis of the bones of the skull from infancy to the greatest age, the shape of the exterior surface of the skull is determined by the shape of the brain; therefore so far as the outer surface of the skull and the inner coincide, and no exception is made for the usual contours, particular aptitudes and tendencies can be concluded." This was to be determined by examining the shape and contours of a head with the hands. (pp. 16–17)

In the above premises, if *cognitive processes* are substituted for *aptitudes* and *fMRI activity* is substituted for *skull shape*, it is elementary to see that fMRI is identical in all substantive ways to phrenology (Uttal, 2003, also reasoned that fMRI is a form of phrenology). Of course, fMRI has higher spatial resolution than phrenology, but users of both techniques have assumed a one-to-one mapping between a specific attribute/cognitive process and a particular region of the skull/brain.

There is nothing inherently incorrect with the hypotheses that the skull (phrenology) or the brain (fMRI) or the mind (Fodor, 1983) consists of independent modules. The problem with the widespread belief in these hypotheses is that all of them have been falsified by empirical findings. The modular hypothesis of fMRI activity, in particular, has been proven false in a number of ways including: 1) there is no compelling evidence for the existence of independent processing modules, as illustrated in this book through careful examination of the fusiform face area (Chapter 2), the most widely accepted processing module in the brain, and the visual word form area (Chapter 6), 2) as shown throughout this book, there are always many regions involved during a given cognitive process (even if those activations are ignored), which directly contradicts the idea that each cognitive process is mediated by a single neural processing module, 3) it is known that multiple regions interact during any cognitive process, and such interactions are inconsistent with the notion that an individual module mediates a given process, and 4) the assumption that fMRI can identify the single module that mediates a cognitive process rests on the further assumption that temporal modulation is unimportant (because this method has virtually no temporal resolution), which is in conflict with the rapid temporal dynamics that are known to occur during all cognitive processes.

Although no one would admit to being a phrenologist, the modular view is still widely believed by fMRI investigators. The parallel between phrenology and fMRI modularity can also be illustrated by comparing a reproduction of a phrenology bust originally made by L. N. Fowler in the latter half of the nineteenth century and a brain with Kanwisher's (2010) areas (Figure 9.10). Another example of an fMRI-based modular map could be generated with word processing regions that would include the *visual word form area*, the *auditory word form area*, and the *lateral inferotemporal multimodal area* (Cohen,

Figure 9.10   *Phrenology bust and Kanwisher's regions. Left, phrenology bust head with each region outlined by black lines (lateral view, occipital pole toward the middle). Right, brain with a subset of Kanwisher's regions outlined by dashed ovals; each cognitive function is labeled in the same shade of grey at the bottom (lateral view, occipital pole toward the middle).*

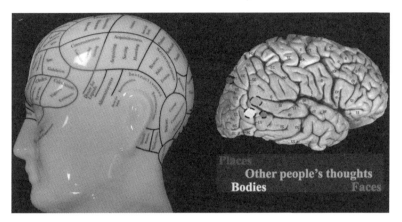

(Kanwisher; Copyright (2010) National Academy of Sciences, U.S.A.)

Jobert, Le Bihan, & Dehaene, 2004). The point is that although fMRI might produce results that appear as individual activations in the brain, this does not mean that the brain operates by performing independent computations within each activation (as Kanwisher's map strongly implies). fMRI can only be used to identify the location of the activations associated with a given cognitive process, but cannot be used to identify modules because there is no convincing evidence that brain modules exist. With that said, fMRI does offer the highest spatial resolution of any method that is widely accessible in cognitive neuroscience. For this reason, fMRI will remain invaluable for precise localization of brain activity.

Proponents of the majority view have offered arguments against the notion that fMRI research aims only to localize the region(s) associated with a particular cognitive function. Terrazas & McNaughton (2000) correctly pointed out that fMRI research is often hypothesis driven such as when activations are predicted or interpreted based on previous findings, as compared with phrenology which had no valid empirical basis and was ultimately debunked. Jonides, Nee, & Berman (2006) submitted that fMRI has value because the results can go beyond behavioural measures (such as reaction time) and can distinguish between cognitive hypotheses. Regarding both arguments, hypothesis-driven research is a hallmark of any respectable scientific investigation whether it is conducted with fMRI or not; thus, these are not compelling arguments in support of this method. Donaldson (2004) argued that by assessing whether fMRI activity is relatively more sustained or transient over time, insight can be gained into the functional role of a region. However, like dynamic causal modeling discussed above, this suggestion relies on the timing of fMRI activity that cannot be used to accurately track neural activity. That is, the reasoning is sound that it might be possible for fMRI to go beyond simple localization of activity, but this will never be realized due to the inherent temporal limitations of this method.

Beck (2010) has argued that the press are attracted to fMRI because it provides neural explanations for behaviour (e.g., the brain reward structures of chocolate lovers are particularly active when tasting chocolate, which can explain this trait), there is increased confidence in biological results, and fMRI provides a simple message. The same reasons can explain why fMRI is so attractive to cognitive neuroscientists, because this method identifies/explains which regions mediate a cognitive process, it provides those in psychology who have little training in neuroscience to conduct biological research, and the results are simple to interpret without the complicated dimension of time to worry about. Moreover, fMRI data acquisition and analysis techniques are readily available and can be used with relatively little understanding, while offering the appearance of expertise or even a fast track to scientific fame. The latter potential benefit illustrates another way that fMRI is reminiscent of the phrenology, where non-academics capitalized on the relatively quick mastery of this method to gain notoriety and wealth (van Wyhe, 2004).

In contrast to fMRI, ERP data acquisition and analysis techniques are not readily available and the interpretation of the results are not that straightforward, thus the employment of this technique can be described as intellectually challenging from both technical and theoretical perspectives. Many scientists thrive on such intellectual challenge, which offers excitement and the promise of true scientific discovery when it is overcome. It should also be highlighted that a high-resolution (128 channel) ERP system costs approximately 100,000 dollars to set up and has essentially no maintenance costs, while a standard (3 Tesla) fMRI system costs about 3 million dollars to set up and costs approximately 300,000 dollars per year in maintenance (6 million dollars in total if the life of an MRI system is assumed to be ten years). In terms of cost-benefit analysis, this leads to the following question: Is fMRI data worth 60 times as much as ERP data? Considering the points covered in this chapter, the answer to this question should be apparent. A related question: Will government agencies realize, at some point, that funding research that only employs fMRI is not a good use their limited resource pool? There is no scientific justification for these massive costs differences, as it is arguable that ERP data has equal scientific value as fMRI data. Furthermore, a combined fMRI-ERP study, that can actually investigate the spatial-temporal dynamics of brain function, costs approximately the same as an fMRI study alone. Perhaps the realization that funding agencies may figure out that the cost-benefit ratio of ERP research is far superior to fMRI research coupled with a desire to study actual neural mechanisms will motivate some in the next wave of cognitive neuroscientists to learn how to conduct ERP research.

There are many reasons for cognitive neuroscientists to employ fMRI; however, the large majority of these reasons have nothing to do with understanding how the brain actually functions. Our aim should not be "given the method I like the best, I will investigate my topic of interest" but rather needs to be "given my topic of interest, I will use the methods that are necessary to accurately investigate it." The first aim focuses on the method while the second aim focuses on the topic. Of course, a true scientist will always have the aim of investigating their research topic and learn the techniques required to do so (Platt, 1964). In cognitive neuroscience, all research topics deal with neural activity that is modulated in space and time (whether those investigating the brain like it or not); thus, methods need to be employed that have both high spatial resolution and high temporal resolution. Ultimately, if cognitive neuroscientists do shift to studying the spatial-temporal dynamics of brain function, it will become commonplace for studies to combine methods with high spatial resolution, such as fMRI, and high temporal resolution, such as ERPs.

As discussed in the subsequent chapter, if cognitive neuroscience maintains its dependence on fMRI, the field may have something else in common with phrenology – an end.

CONCLUSION

During any cognitive process it is known that many brain regions rapidly interact. fMRI has excellent spatial resolution and thus can be used identify the regions involved, but this method offers virtually no temporal information. Therefore, the widespread belief that fMRI alone can be used to investigate brain function is unequivocally false. If cognitive neuroscientists aim to study the mechanisms of brain function, we must break our addiction to fMRI and embrace techniques such as ERPs that can track the critically important temporal dimension of neural processing.

SUGGESTED READINGS

Majority view

Suthana, N. A., Ekstrom, A. D., Moshirvaziri, S., Knowlton, B., & Bookheimer, S. Y. (2009). Human hippocampal CA1 involvement during allocentric encoding of spatial information. *The Journal of Neuroscience, 29*, 10512–10519. Open access.

Leff, A. P., Schofield, T. M., Stephan, K. E., Crinion, J. T., Friston, K. J., & Price, C. J. (2008). The cortical dynamics of intelligible speech. *The Journal of Neuroscience, 28*, 13209–13215. Open access.

Minority view

Gregoriou, G. G., Gotts, S. J., Zhou, H., & Desimone, R. (2009). High-frequency, long-range coupling between prefrontal and visual cortex during attention. *Science, 324*, 1207–1210. Open access.

Slotnick, S. D. (2010). Synchronous retinotopic frontal-temporal activity during long-term memory for spatial location. *Brain Research, 1330*, 89–100.

REFERENCES

Beck, D. M. (2010). The appeal of the brain in the popular press. *Perspectives on Psychological Science, 5,* 762–766.

Cheng, K., Waggoner, R. A., & Tanaka, K. (2001). Human ocular dominance columns as revealed by high-field functional magnetic resonance imaging. *Neuron, 32,* 359–374.

Cohen, L., Jobert, A., Le Bihan, D., & Dehaene, S. (2004). Distinct unimodal and multimodal regions for word processing in the left temporal cortex. *NeuroImage, 23,* 1256–1270.

Cohen, M. X. (2011). It's about time. *Frontiers in Human Neuroscience, 5,* 1–16.

Donaldson, D. I. (2004). Parsing brain activity with fMRI and mixed designs: What kind of a state is neuroimaging in? *Trends in Neurosciences, 27,* 442–444.

Fell, J., Klaver, P., Lehnertz, K., Grunwald, T., Schaller, C., Elger, C. E., & Fernández, G. (2001). Human memory formation is accompanied by rhinal-hippocampal coupling and decoupling. *Nature Neuroscience, 4,* 1259–1264.

Fodor, J. A. (1983). *The modularity of mind.* Cambridge, MA: MIT Press.

Gregoriou, G. G., Gotts, S. J., Zhou, H., & Desimone, R. (2009). High-frequency, long-range coupling between prefrontal and visual cortex during attention. *Science, 324,* 1207–1210.

Jonides, J., Nee, D. E., & Berman, M.G. (2006). What has functional neuroimaging told us about the mind? So many examples, so little space. *Cortex, 42,* 414–417.

Kanwisher, N. (2010). Functional specificity in the human brain: A window into the functional architecture of the mind. *Proceedings of the National Academy of Sciences of the United States of America, 107,* 11163–11170.

Leff, A. P., Schofield, T. M., Stephan, K. E., Crinion, J. T., Friston, K. J., & Price, C. J. (2008). The cortical dynamics of intelligible speech. *The Journal of Neuroscience, 28,* 13209–13215.

Platt, J. R. (1964). Strong inference. *Science, 146,* 347–353.

Ruff, C. C., Bestmann, S., Blankenburg, F., Bjoertomt, O., Josephs, O., Weiskopf, N., Deichmann, R., & Driver, J. (2008). Distinct causal influences of parietal versus frontal areas on human visual cortex: Evidence from concurrent TMS-fMRI. *Cerebral Cortex, 18,* 817–827.

Slotnick, S. D. (2010). Synchronous retinotopic frontal-temporal activity during long-term memory for spatial location. *Brain Research, 1330,* 89–100.

Steriade, M., Contreras, D., Amzica, F., & Timofeev, I. (1996). Synchronization of fast (30–40 Hz) spontaneous oscillations in intrathalamic and thalamocortical networks. *The Journal of Neuroscience, 16,* 2788–2808.

Suthana, N. A., Ekstrom, A. D., Moshirvaziri, S., Knowlton, B., & Bookheimer, S. Y. (2009). Human hippocampal CA1 involvement during allocentric encoding of spatial information. *The Journal of Neuroscience, 29,* 10512–10519.

Terrazas, A., & McNaughton, B. L. (2000). Brain growth and the cognitive map. *Proceedings of the National Academy of Sciences of the United States of America, 97,* 4414–4416.

Uttal, W. R. (2003). *The new phrenology.* Cambridge, MA: MIT Press.

van Wyhe, J. (2004). *Phrenology and the origins of victorian scientific naturalism.* Aldershot: Ashgate.

Yacoub, E., Harel, N., & Uğurbil, K. (2008). High-field fMRI unveils orientation columns in humans. *Proceedings of the National Academy of Sciences of the United States of America, 105,* 10607–10612.

10 Cognitive Neuroscience at a Crossroads

This book has detailed many of the most contentious controversies in the field of cognitive neuroscience. It is telling that nearly all the controversies focused on the region(s) associated with a particular cognitive process, while the timing of neural activity was largely ignored (with the exception of the attention debate, Chapter 3). This illustrates that cognitive neuroscientists do not typically investigate how cognitive processing is mediated by real-time interactions between multiple brain regions, which can be attributed to our over-reliance on fMRI. Cognitive neuroscientists are addicted to fMRI primarily because this technique offers a simple view of brain function (Chapter 9). However, temporal dynamics cannot be investigated with fMRI, thus cognitive neuroscientists have not focused on the mechanisms of actual brain function.

The current non-mechanistic approach of cognitive neuroscience is entirely compatible with the field of psychology (the study of the mind). One major aim of cognitive psychology is to separate mental functions into distinct processes, typically by identifying dissociations between behavioural measures such as reaction time and accuracy. Cognitive neuroscience results have offered cognitive psychologists another way to dissect mental functions, as distinct mental processes should be evidenced by distinct neural activations. As such, largely since the early 2000s, psychologists have increasingly embraced cognitive neuroscience findings, in conjunction with behavioural measures, to investigate mental processing. This is illustrated by the rapid increase in the number of fMRI articles published in the ten highest-impact psychology journals since 2002 (Figure 10.1; journal titles: *Annual Review of*

Figure 10.1 *The number of fMRI articles published from 2002 to 2010 in the ten highest-impact psychology journals.*

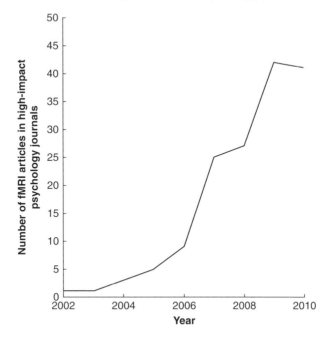

Psychology, Psychological Bulletin, Annual Review of Clinical Psychology, Psychological Review, Psychotherapy and Psychosomatics, Psychological Medicine, Biological Psychology, Psychosomatic Medicine, Social Cognitive and Affective Neuroscience, and *Cognitive Psychology*; articles were identified using PubMed).

Neuroscience (the study of the brain), in contrast to psychology, is centrally concerned with the mechanisms of brain function. Systems neuroscientists, who are the most closely aligned with cognitive neuroscientists, investigate exactly which brain regions interact, how they interact, and when they interact (which includes the identification of the precise neural circuits and neurotransmitters that mediate a given behaviour). This mechanistic approach of neuroscience is at odds with the current focus of cognitive neuroscience on simple process-to-region mapping, and may explain why the number of fMRI publications in top-tier neuroscience journals has leveled out or dropped since 2002 (Figure 9.1).

The relationships between cognitive neuroscience, cognitive psychology, and neuroscience have been changing over time and will continue to change. The reasons for these changes almost certainly stem from the nature of research in cognitive neuroscience, given that the other fields have been well established for over a century. When cognitive neuroscience emerged in the early 1990s, the field had the potential to be well balanced between cognitive psychology and neuroscience (Figure 10.2, top). Since the early 2000s, however, the use of fMRI has become more widespread in both cognitive neuroscience and cognitive psychology, and it appears that neuroscientists have started to realize that fMRI cannot be used to study neural mechanisms. These factors have likely caused the

Figure 10.2 *Relationships between the fields of cognitive psychology, cognitive neuroscience, and neuroscience in the past, the present, and the future.*

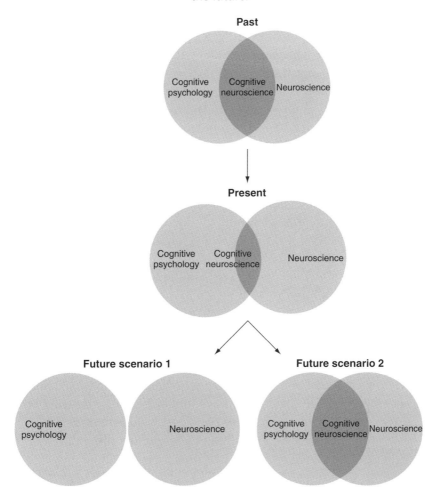

shift in the previously balanced position of cognitive neuroscience between cognitive psychology and neuroscience toward the current standing of cognitive neuroscience that largely overlaps cognitive psychology (Figure 10.2, middle).

Where will cognitive neuroscience fit in the future? The most likely scenario is that cognitive neuroscientists will continue to do what they have been doing, employing fMRI to study a static picture of the brain rather than investigating the spatial-temporal dynamics of brain function. If this happens, it is reasonable to assume that the field of cognitive neuroscience will ultimately be rejected by the field of neuroscience, will be folded into the field of cognitive psychology (which has a big tent), and cease to exist (Figure 10.2, bottom left). At the other extreme, cognitive neuroscientists might shift to studying brain mechanisms, such as by combining fMRI and ERPs to investigate both spatial and temporal aspects of brain function (Chapter 9). This would bring cognitive neuroscience back into its proper balance between cognitive psychology and neuroscience (Figure 10.2, bottom right). An alternative scenario is that cognitive neuroscience will be almost completely absorbed by cognitive psychology, but a small group of mechanism-based cognitive neuroscientists will splinter off and join the field of neuroscience (perhaps establishing a new branch of systems neuroscience).

The current status of cognitive neuroscience can be described within the framework proposed by Thomas Kuhn (1996). Kuhn proposed that scientific inquiry is guided by a paradigm that guides the direction and interpretation of research (fostering otherwise unimaginable focus and productivity), an anomaly appears that is inconsistent with that paradigm and produces a crisis, and then following a *scientific revolution* a new paradigm is established that can account for the anomaly. With regard to methodology, Kuhn states:

> Led by a new paradigm, scientists adopt new instruments and look in new places. Even more important, during revolutions scientists see new and different things when looking with familiar instruments in places they have looked before. It is rather as if the professional community had been suddenly transported to another planet where familiar objects are seen in a different light and are joined by unfamiliar ones as well.
>
> (p. 111)

It could be said that the current paradigm in cognitive neuroscience focuses on the localization of regions associated with a mental process (due to our over-reliance on fMRI), the anomaly may be the realization that neural activity is modulated rapidly in time (at a temporal resolution invisible to fMRI), and a new paradigm might lead investigators to study both spatial and temporal aspects of neural function. This new paradigm might promote a revised standard, where more advanced techniques are employed such as combining fMRI with ERPs. However, fMRI is still the most widely used technique in cognitive neuroscience and there are no signs of an impending crisis; therefore, a revolution does not appear to be on the horizon. Moreover, followers of the old paradigm are known to resist the new paradigm, which will even further delay any potential transformation of the field (Kuhn, 1996). As such, a new generation of cognitive neuroscientists, not yet been ensnared by fMRI, will likely be needed to lead a revolution and bring about a new paradigm in cognitive neuroscience. Perhaps someone reading these words will take part in or even lead this revolution.

Cognitive neuroscience is at a crossroads. If we continue to focus on neural localization rather than neural mechanisms, we will in all likelihood be choosing the path toward oblivion. If we correct our course and begin to investigate the brain mechanisms that mediate cognitive function, the field of cognitive neuroscience will finally live up to its name – the science of the mind and brain.

REFERENCE

Kuhn, T. S. (1996). *The structure of scientific revolutions* (3rd ed). Chicago: University of Chicago Press.

Index